THE FLAVOUR PRINCIPLE

LUCY WAVERMAN & BEPPI CROSARIOL

PHOTOGRAPHY BY RYAN SZULC

THE FLAVOUR PRINCIPLE

Enticing Your Senses
with
Food and Drink

HarperCollinsPublishersLtd

The Flavour Principle

Published by HarperCollins Publishers Ltd

First edition

Food styling by Eshun Mott • Prop styling by Madeleine Johari

HarperCollins books may be purchased for educational, business, or sales promotional use through our Special Markets Department.

HarperCollins Publishers Ltd
2 Bloor Street East, 20th Floor
Toronto, Ontario, Canada, M4W 1A8

www.harpercollins.ca

Library and Archives Canada Cataloguing in Publication
information is available upon request

ISBN 978-1-44341-343-5

Printed and bound in Canada
TC 9 8 7 6 5 4 3 2 1

To David Geneen,
with love and respect.
—L.W.

To Tony Crosariol, and John Crosariol.
—B.C.

CONTENTS

1 *Introduction*

19 BITTER

55 HERBAL

93 SMOKY

125 CREAMY

161 NUTTY

195 EARTHY

239 SALTY

285 SWEET

325 TART

363 SPICY

397 UMAMI

433 *Acknowledgements*

437 *Index*

INTRODUCTION

THIS BOOK WAS BORN WHERE MANY JOURNEYS BEGIN, IN A CAR . . .

Palates sated and bottles emptied after a sumptuous meal at Lucy's house, the host had kindly offered to drive her guest home. (Good thing one of us was sober.) We got to talking, as many food enthusiasts do, about our favourite subject—about hot new restaurants, talented chefs, exotic ingredients, memorable meals. Then things turned philosophical. What makes a great recipe tick? we wondered aloud.

The answer, in retrospect, seems simple to us now, though it took the better part of the drive to nail it down. Every great dish has a centre of gravity, an overarching flavour or essence that pulls together other ingredients into a compelling whole. It's not necessarily the main ingredient, but it's fundamentally what the dish is "about." The aromatic spices in an Indian curry, for example, the earthy bass note of a porcini-crusted veal chop, the fiery chilies in a Thai soup, the smoky rub on barbecued ribs or the zesty grapefruit in a Saigon-style salad.

"Flavours" seemed to us like a fine working principle for a book that would showcase Lucy's latest globe-trotting kitchen explorations, a culinary passport, if you will. On one level, that's what you're holding in your hand. It's an eclectic flavour-based journey of menus that embrace fresh trends in gastronomy emerging from such regions as Spain, Vietnam, Korea, Scandinavia, southern Italy, the Pacific Northwest and the American South.

But we're here to satisfy your thirst too, because in our world it would be unthinkable to dine and entertain with casual flair without having something transcendent to sip between bites. That's another reason for the theme. Key flavours serve as critical cues for selecting blissfully perfect wines, beers, cocktails and spirits. Feel like fragrant curry? An oily-textured, aromatic white such as viognier has the necessary power to stay the course. Creamy soup? Match its texture with a full-bodied buttery chardonnay. Smoky barbecue? Jammy zinfandel or a cool mint julep delivers a slightly sweet, fruity complement to keep up with the sugar in the barbecue sauce (sweet food always calls for sweetness in the beverage). Beppi's suggestions, sometimes very personal and unconventional, are there to make things easy—or at least to inspire debate. (We'll be monitoring Twitter for your feedback.)

If you already know a lot about the world of drink, we hope our approach will make it easier for you to play matchmaker should you care to take on the rewarding challenge. Lean on the chapter headings as a rough guide to pair a spicy dish with peppery syrah or gingery gewürztraminer. Or take the opposite approach and serve a piquant dish with a boldly fruity wine to cool the palate with rounded sweetness—underscore or contrast, they both can work. Feel free to use these pages as a sort of reverse phone book too. When you've got a wine begging for a dish to help it shine, consult the index for a suitable match.

We pay due respect, of course, to classic regional pairings where relevant. It's tough to beat raw oysters with crisp, ice-cold muscadet. But many of the fresh menus here open up the field to a vast array of affordable and tantalizing wines that have cropped up around the world. Argentine malbec, New Zealand sauvignon blanc, Chilean carmenère, Oregon pinot noir and Niagara riesling, among other styles, enjoy a welcome place at our table. So do robust West Coast pale ales, refreshingly bitter Czech-style pilsners and old and new cocktails based on bourbon, gin, rum, tequila and sake.

This is much more than a recipe book. We've included a liberal sprinkling of tips on cooking techniques and descriptive passages about some of our favourite ingredients and beverage styles. Be prepared for the occasional rant, as well, because—like most of you—we hold strong opinions about food and drink. You're welcome to disagree, as you inevitably will. We, too, have had our share of friendly food fights in Lucy's kitchen while compiling this book. Lucy still can't believe she let Beppi get away with his contention that most cheeses are a catastrophe with red wine, and Beppi continues to harbour a grudge over Lucy's refusal to include his experimental bacon Jell-O recipe, which he thought would be a bold showcase for California pinot noir. To quote the cook: "Beppi, some flavours are best left alone."

We're honoured to be
partners in your kitchen.
We're just sorry we can't be
there to help with the dishes.

Senape
Muskat
Ginger.

Nutmeg.

GLOBAL STORE CUPBOARD

Here are the basic ingredients for a global pantry. If you have them on hand, there's probably no cuisine that you can't make an attempt at cooking. —Lucy

SPICES

Although many recipes call for ground spices—and they're fine if that's all you have on hand—for the freshest flavour it's best to buy them whole and grind as needed.

allspice
ancho chili
cardamom
cayenne pepper
chili flakes
Chinese 5 spice powder
cinnamon
cumin
curry powder
dry mustard
fennel seeds
garam masala
ginger
mace
paprika
saffron
shichimi togarashi
(Japanese chili peppers)
star anise
sumac
turmeric
za'atar

BOTTLES AND PASTES

Asian chili sauce
capers
dark soy sauce
fish sauce
harissa
hoisin sauce
Indian curry pastes
(mild, medium and hot)
Korean chili paste
(gochujang)
mirin
miso
rice wine
sambal oelek
soy sauce
sriracha sauce
Thai curry pastes
(green, yellow and red)
wasabi

FRESH HERBS AND PEPPERS AS NEEDED

cilantro
garlic
ginger
jalapeño peppers
lemongrass
lime leaves
shiso (perilla) leaves
Thai basil
Thai chili peppers

DRIED GOODS

bonito flakes
dashi granules
nori sheets

SALTS

fleur de sel
kosher salt
Maldon salt

VINEGARS

balsamic vinegar
red and white wine vinegar
rice vinegar
seasoned rice vinegar
Sherry vinegar

OILS

olive oil
extra-virgin olive oil
vegetable oil
hazelnut oil
sesame oil
walnut oil

CANS

anchovies
various beans
chickpeas
coconut milk
San Marzano tomatoes

HOME BAR

I suspect my home bar is more comprehensive than most. It goes with the territory. I write about drinks. So I'm forever testing new products, and I keep many classic ingredients around for cocktail experimentation (and personal pleasure). Let's just say thirst is not a major peril in my house. But if I had to close down the cocktail lab and keep just a sane, compact liquor cabinet, here are the choices I couldn't live without.

—Beppi

A BARE-BONES BAR PANTRY

Single malt Scotch: Not for mixing, for sipping. Glenmorangie is a superb standby, fruity-floral, with a serious pedigree yet delicate enough not to intimidate the blended-whisky habitué.

Rye: Spicy sibling to sweet bourbon. I love genuine rye, which is based chiefly on the grain of the same name. It's not synonymous with Canadian whisky, which (though colloquially called rye) in most cases is distilled mainly from corn. Rittenhouse and Sazerac from the United States are exemplary brands. Lot No. 40 and Wiser's Legacy from Canada are superb.

Gin: The white spirit with class and oodles of bracing flavour, and the only acceptable base for a proper martini. Plymouth from England is a standard-bearer for quality at a not outrageous price. Hendrick's, a premium Scottish brand with the cool essence of cucumber, is another excellent product, as is No. 3 London Dry from England.

Vermouth: White goes with gin, red with rye (as in a Manhattan). Noilly Prat for the former, Martini for the latter.

Vodka: Not my thing, truth be told, but guests will call for it, and a frozen shot is nice with caviar, pickled herring or oysters on New Year's Eve. I like Tito's from, of all places, Texas.

Pilsner: My preferred all-round beer if I had to stick to one style through the seasons. It's lager-light but with enough bitter backbone to appeal to hard-core suds-ophiles. Pilsner Urquell is the Czech classic, though various craft breweries in North America, such as Creemore in Ontario, make fine examples.

Angostura bitters: Many cocktails benefit from a dash or two of this aromatic elixir.

Peychaud's Bitters: A crimson-hued, slightly sweet, anise-scented flavouring that adds verve to brown-spirit cocktails such as New Orleans' famed Sazerac.

Lemons, limes, club soda and tonic: Need I explain?

Ice: This—not last year's pesto—is what your freezer is for.

EQUIPMENT

Shot glass: This is the bartender's analogue to a kitchen measuring cup, essential for mixing. Prefer to pour straight into the glass while counting to three? That way danger lies.

Bar spoon: One of those long-handled doohickeys for probing past the ice cubes and soda to gently stir up precious booze at the bottom of the glass.

Cocktail shaker: What?! You put it out in the last garage sale? Get another—at a garage sale.

Paring knife: All you really need to peel off citrus rind for garnish duty.

Juicer: In a pinch, the business end of a fork, stabbed into the pulp of a half-section of citrus and twisted as you squeeze with the other hand, is an acceptable alternative, and it will score points for resourcefulness.

Toothpicks: For martini olives and fancy skewer garnishes.

A BARE-BONES WINE PANTRY

Chianti: No guest can turn a nose up at decent Chianti, the safest red bet when the doorbell rings unexpectedly. Nipozzano Riserva Chianti Rufina from Frescobaldi wins for consistency and wide availability.

Chablis: As a wine geek, I should say riesling, the sommelier's favourite white grape. But this is my death row wine style, crisp chardonnay in all its glory. Crowd-pleaser: William Fèvre Champs Royaux.

Cava: Bargain style of Spanish bubbly made with the Champagne technique. Store it in the fridge so there's never an excuse not to celebrate. Segura Viudas is a steal.

GLASSWARE 101

Cardinal rule: Don't sweat it.

If space, budget and a healthy minimalist aesthetic dictate just one glass, make it the well-priced Riedel Ouverture Red Wine model. Despite the name, it's good for anything, even bubbly, and features a dishwasher-manageable short stem and generous tulip-shaped bowl to focus and concentrate aromas. But, as with romantic partners, six is better than one. (Kidding!) Here they are:

Full-bodied reds: A honking-big, oval bowl tapering gently toward the rim. Think cabernet, merlot, shiraz and malbec. Some glassmakers call this their Bordeaux or cabernet glass.

Flute: Nice for framing the bubble streams in sparkling wine because it's tall and thin, but the "most whites" glass does the aroma more justice.

Plain old tumbler: What can I say? It won't particularly flatter the wine's finer nuances, but a simple, cozy meal at a crowded kitchen table sometimes calls for casual. Even wine needs a day off to relax in jeans.

WHISKY WONDERS

{in no particular order}

Ardbeg 10-Year-Old: The peat monster from Scotland's island of Islay. But beyond the smoke there's riveting complexity (a lovely note of bacon fat, for one thing) and gorgeous balance.

Glenfiddich 21-Year-Old Gran Reserva: A familiar brand name but a special bottling from a distiller with vast storehouses of old stock maturing in barrels. A brief "finishing" period in casks that once held rum adds a layer of depth.

Johnnie Walker Red: I know, it's the world's most popular Scotch, but the world is on to something here. Perfect balance of malty smoothness with earthy peat. It rocks on ice. Try it again for the first time.

Pappy Van Winkle's Family Reserve: Bourbon gets no better than this pricy, long-aged nectar. Mesmerizing—if very hard to find.

Forty Creek Double Barrel Reserve: A blend of rye, barley and corn from the father of Canada's modern craft whisky movement, John Hall. Spicy, nutty and creamy, and good to the last drop.

Wiser's Legacy: Big on spicy rye, it's a glorious dip into Canadian whisky's past, based on an old recipe.

Rittenhouse Straight Rye: Oily, round, spicy and very dry, American whisky in the old-school style.

Jameson 12-Year-Old Special Reserve: Oloroso Sherry casks lend a delectable nutty quality to the underlying fruit and grain. An Irish charmer.

Ardbeg
TEN

BARGAIN BOTTLES

Wouldn't life be grand if we could all gulp Montrachet with mac and cheese and keep a cellar stacked with Pétrus to plunder for Sunday night meat loaf? Consolation: thanks to technology, hygiene and modern vineyard practices, inexpensive wines have closed the quality gap with the vaunted nectars, just as Honda Civics put a sweet ride within the reach of the masses. Humbly, I offer a few bargain destinations:

Australia: shiraz

Argentina: malbec

Austria: grüner veltliner

Chile: cabernet sauvignon, merlot, sauvignon blanc and carmenère

Languedoc-Roussillon: especially reds labelled Minervois, Saint-Chinian and Corbières, stars of France's much-improved vast southern crescent

New Zealand: sauvignon blanc

Southern Italy: montepulciano d'Abruzzo, arguably the world's best dirt-cheap reds; negroamaro and primitivo from Puglia; nero d'Avola from Sicily

Spain: reds from Cariñena, Montsant, Navarra and Toro; whites from Rueda; sparkling wines labelled Cava

South Africa: sauvignon blanc and chenin blanc

MENUS BY SEASON

SPRING

A Trouble-Free Spring Dinner 23
European Unity 129
Spring Has Sprung 147
A Sushi-Free Japanese Meal 243
An Edgy Franco-American Menu 341
Vietnamese Flavours 349
Multicultural Senegalese Dinner 385

SUMMER

Casual Chic 59
C Is for Chile 69
Cruising the Mediterranean 77
A Family Menu Right Off the Grill 105
Bones 113
An End of Summer Dinner 181
Italian Simplicity 253
An Eclectic Asian Menu 377
Truck-Stop Treats 277

FALL

Bitter British 33
Salmon with a Cup of Tea 97
Sophisticated Vegetarian Dinner 137
A First Nations Dinner 215
A Rosh Hashanah Dinner 291
Lovely Lemons 331
A Modern Indian Menu 367
The Pleasure of Porcini 401
Essence of Soul 417

WINTER

From Tapas to Table 41
Modern Korean 165
A Tapas Menu 173
An Argentinian Odyssey 201
A Vegetarian Holiday Dinner 223
Brining: A Celebratory Menu 263
Icewine Extravaganza 301
Easy-Peasy Brunch 309
A Beppi-Influenced Menu 407

Award
TRADITIONAL

BITTER

dark leafy greens • wild chicory • chard
endive • artichokes • watercress • broccoli • thistles
cabbage • Brussels sprouts • cauliflower • chayotes
pak choi • asparagus • lettuce • tomatoes
dandelion greens • milk thistle leaves • uncured olives
onion • cucumbers • citrus peel • pumpkins • zucchini
collard greens • extra-virgin olive oil
Seville oranges • bitter gourd • fenugreek seeds
coffee • dark chocolate • cocoa powder
Angostura bitters • mustard greens • arugula
kale • rapini • escarole • mizuna • sorrel
radicchio • eggplant • hops

BITTERNESS NEEDS A BETTER PR AGENT.

The mere word leaves a bad taste in some people's mouths. Bitter enemies, the bitter end, bitter pills to swallow—how did a flavour we cherish come to be a poster child for distress? In a word: biology. We're hard-wired to recoil from the sensation, the tongue's siren that poison might be lurking in that benign-looking leaf or root. Plants lack legs to flee, so evolution gave them chemical arsenals to repel predators. Through trial and error, humans learned to distinguish the truly harmful threats from the false alarms. With the advent of cooking, curing and inventive cocktail mixology, we made peace with, even learned to crave, bitterness. Life without it would be life without lettuce, olives, garlic, coffee, Campari, beer and chocolate. Wouldn't that be a bitter pill to swallow?

Evolution played a trick too. It turns out that bitterness is a hallmark of those great-for-you vegetables—broccoli, Brussels sprouts, cabbage, cauliflower and the like—all rich in phytochemicals that curb the risk of some cancers and other diseases. Acrid roots and herbs can even cure the sick. Quinine, the invigorating jolt in tonic water derived from cinchona tree bark, was the first reliable treatment for malaria. (It's still the most reliable treatment for gin, next to vermouth and an olive.) In some cultures, bitter herbs are believed to stimulate appetite and settle the stomach, paving the way for what's really important—more eating. That's how such restorative "bitters," or amari, as Campari and vermouth were born, emerging from the early European pharmacist's playbook.

We're drawn to something else in those amari besides bitterness. They're sweet at the same time. As with some happy marriages (and cookbook-writing teams), opposites attract. Sugar brings bitterness into balance. Think of Lucy as sweet and Beppi as, well, never mind. This is why you'll also often encounter fruit in salads.

Guess what else helps the balance? Salt. Cooks long ago intuited something that sensory scientists have only recently come to confirm: sodium suppresses bitterness. Romans were hip to the phenomenon two thousand years ago, bequeathing the term *salad* by way of *salata* (Latin for "salted"), based on the ancient practice of salting leafy greens.

There's another trick we like to employ to mellow bitterness: heat. Slow cooking transforms the chemical structure of sugars found in many vegetables, like onions and fennel, yielding sweeter flavour.

One need not look far in the beverage aisles to encounter appealing bitterness. Besides amari, there's beer. Most is flavoured with hops, the bitter seed cones of a plant, which add backbone to malted barley's sweetness. Tannins, astringent compounds found in the skins, seeds and stems of grapes as well as in wooden barrels, are responsible for much of the flavour in wine. And alcohol itself has a bitter edge, one reason de-alcoholized wines, in our opinion, tend to lack verve.

Bear this in mind when choosing a beverage: bitterness in food exacerbates the same quality in a drink. So don't throw an especially tannic red, such as cabernet sauvignon or Barolo, at our menus here. Unless, of course, you want to follow through to the bitter end.

Menu 1

A TROUBLE-FREE SPRING DINNER

Sorrel Soup with Chive Oil
Dandelion Pesto on Naan
Grilled Pork Skewers
Rhubarb Sponge Pudding

Step into spring with this seasonal menu. Many of our first greens have a bitter profile—think sorrel, dandelions and rhubarb—and these are successfully combined in this menu for a trouble-free dinner. The soup may be made ahead, as can the dandelion pesto. This pesto is helpful to have around, as you can dollop it on eggs or serve it as a condiment with chicken or fish. Mixed with mayonnaise, it makes an unusual but tasty dip.

SORREL SOUP WITH CHIVE OIL

French sorrel has a slightly different flavour from the more common garden variety. It tastes like a bite of tart green apple with a lemony edge. While the common variety works in this soup, I prefer the more approachable flavour of French sorrel. Plant it, because sorrel will spread like wildfire in your garden. And it's a perennial, giving you years of pleasure. This soup is excellent either hot or chilled. **Serves 4**

- 2 tbsp butter
- 1 cup diced onion (about 1 medium onion)
- 1 cup diced peeled Yukon Gold potato (about 1 medium potato)
- ½ cup diced cored peeled tart green apple, such as Granny Smith or Crispin
- 4 cups chicken stock
- 2 bunches sorrel (French or otherwise), stems removed (enough to make 2 cups packed)
- ¼ cup whipping cream
- 2 tsp lemon juice
- Salt and freshly ground pepper

Melt butter in a soup pot over medium heat. Add onion, potato and apple and sauté for 3 minutes or until slightly softened. Pour in stock and bring to a boil. Reduce heat and simmer for 10 minutes or until potatoes are tender.

Stir in sorrel and simmer for about 2 minutes or until sorrel has wilted.

Blend soup with a hand blender or in a food processor until smooth. Return to pot and stir in cream. Bring back to a boil, stir in lemon juice, then simmer for 5 minutes. Season to taste. Drizzle chive oil (page 25) on top.

PAIRING: **Unoaked chardonnay**

The soup pulls in two directions. On the one hand it's like a herbaceous, tart apple, which suggests a super-crisp white. On the other, the texture leans on potatoes and cream, demanding the silkier fullness of, say, a buttery oaked chardonnay. Solution: unoaked or lightly oaked chardonnay—two wines in one!

Sorrel cooks very quickly. A brief boil suffices. Although its colour changes to a kind of faded green when cooked, the taste stays the same. Use sliced spinach with lots of extra lemon juice if sorrel is unavailable.

CHIVE OIL

This is a useful oil to keep on hand. It will add a dot of colour and flavour around a plate. **Makes ½ cup**

1 cup coarsely chopped chives
½ cup olive oil
Pinch kosher salt

Place chives in a blender or food processor. Turn machine on and add oil slowly until incorporated. Add salt. Place in jar and leave to macerate at room temperature overnight. Strain through a fine sieve. The oil will keep refrigerated for 4 weeks. Use to garnish plates, soups, fish and poultry dishes.

HAND BLENDERS, A.K.A. IMMERSION OR STICK BLENDERS

Hand blenders are efficient and easy to clean, and they take up far less space than food processors or blenders. They have myriad uses, from blending soups, cocktails, mayonnaise and salad dressings to whipping cream and even chopping nuts. They froth milk and thicken it to look like whipping cream. I love mine and think no kitchen is complete without one. It should be the loft dweller's main machine. Look for good quality, and it will last for years. Two ways to avoid spatters: bring your pot to the sink before blending, or blend in a tall, narrow container, which comes with some machines.

DANDELION PESTO ON NAAN

This dish is inspired by one I had in Rome, where salty cheeses such as Pecorino Romano are very popular. It was served on flatbread, but naan is widely available and works just as well. If dandelion greens are unavailable, replace them with arugula, although it will not have quite the same punch. I serve this with the pork (page 29), but it could easily be a first course on its own. **Serves 4**

4 cups packed dandelion greens, stems removed
¼ cup packed flat-leaf parsley
1 tsp chopped garlic
¾ cup shaved Pecorino Romano
⅓ cup olive oil
Salt and freshly ground pepper
2 naan breads

Combine dandelion greens, parsley, garlic and ½ cup Pecorino in a food processor and process until still slightly chunky. Stir in olive oil and season with salt and pepper to taste.
Grill naan for 2 minutes. Flip, then spoon pesto over naan, sprinkle with remaining ¼ cup Pecorino and grill 2 minutes more. Cut in half.

PAIRING: **Verdicchio**

I grow dandelion greens in my garden, chop them up and eat them like potato chips (whenever I'm too lazy to walk to the store for potato chips). Lucy thinks I need to raise my dandelion game, which I suspect is one reason she came up with this fine dish. Now all I have to do is walk to the liquor store for a bottle of verdicchio, the zippy northern Italian white with a hint of herbs.

GRILLED PORK SKEWERS

This dish is easy to make and succulent to eat. Serve on top of the naan (page 27) and include a salad tossed with sliced red onions and roasted whole cherry tomatoes.

Serves 4

1½ lb (675 g) pork tenderloin
2 tbsp olive oil
¼ cup chopped fresh parsley
1 tbsp chopped fresh rosemary
1 tsp chopped garlic
1 tsp grated lemon zest
Salt and freshly ground pepper

Cut pork into 1-inch cubes. Combine olive oil, parsley, rosemary, garlic and lemon zest in a bowl. Toss with pork cubes. Marinate for 30 minutes at room temperature. At the same time, soak 4 wooden skewers in water.

Preheat grill to high.

Season pork with salt and pepper and thread on to skewers, leaving a little space between each cube. Each skewer will have 4 or 5 pieces on it. Grill for about 2 minutes per side (8 minutes in total) or until pork is just cooked. Increase cooking time if you like it better done.

Serve with Dandelion Pesto on Naan.

PAIRING: **Chilean merlot**

There are Mediterranean flavourings here, but I think the most suitable option comes from the other side of the world. Chilean merlot, smooth and fruity but with a dusting of minty character, would make a fine lubricant for these fun and simple pig spears. Alternative: a white greco di Tufo from southern Italy.

RHUBARB SPONGE PUDDING

This was one of the most popular recipes in my Globe and Mail *columns. Sometimes I serve it with custard, British style, but you could also top it with whipped cream. Lyle's golden syrup, a thick and caramel-like syrup made from sugarcane, is available in supermarkets. You can substitute maple syrup, although it is not quite so rich.*

Serves 4 (with leftovers for breakfast)

1 lb (450 g) rhubarb, cut in 1-inch pieces
⅓ cup golden syrup
½ cup butter, diced, at room temperature
½ cup granulated sugar
2 large eggs, lightly beaten
¾ cup self-rising flour (see note)

Preheat oven to 375°F.
Spoon rhubarb into a well-buttered deep-dish 9-inch pie plate or gratin dish. Drizzle syrup on top.
Beat butter and sugar together in a large bowl with an electric mixer until light and fluffy. Beat in eggs. Gently but thoroughly fold in flour. Spread batter over rhubarb.
Bake for 30 to 35 minutes or until a toothpick comes out clean.
Serve warm with custard, whipped cream or ice cream.

PAIRING: **Marsala**

Nobody drinks Marsala any more. Or that's what one producer told me when I visited the city of the same name on Sicily's west coast. It's a shame. The sweet, fortified version is a little like cream Sherry, only not as nutty or tangy. It's a dream with fruity pastries, and the texture will welcome custard or whipped cream as warmly as a Sicilian homeowner would a stranger into his or her home.

Self-rising (American spelling) or self-raising (British spelling) flour is originally from Great Britain. It is available at the supermarket, or you can make your own by combining 1 cup all-purpose flour, 1 tsp baking powder and ½ tsp kosher salt. British self-raising flour does not contain salt, but the North American version does. If you are using British recipes, then salt will be added in the recipe. North American recipes assume the salt is in the flour.

SUPERTASTERS

Does the mention of radicchio prompt you to dash for the exit sign? Do you surreptitiously feed broccoli to Fido under the dinner table? Are Brussels sprouts a recurring theme in your nightmares? You may just be a supertaster.

Roughly one-quarter of the population finds bitterness strongly off-putting, the result of a genetic trait associated with a higher number of taste buds. Scientific grounds for the phenomenon were mapped out in the 1990s thanks largely to the work of Linda Bartoshuk, then of Yale University. Based on taste-bud density, she divided the world into supertasters, normal tasters and non-tasters.

Her work caused such a stir (who wouldn't want to be a supertaster?) that it soon entered the realm of pop culture. In a 2009 episode of *The Simpsons*, Homer becomes a supertaster after bratty son Bart dupes him into extinguishing a fire in his mouth with lighter fluid.

If you want to know where you stand, you'll need a prescription chemical called propylthiouracil, or PROP. A filter-paper disc impregnated with the substance is placed on the tongue. If you sense strong bitterness, you're part of the well-endowed 25 per cent. Mild bitterness means you're "normal." If you sense nothing, you can console yourself by tucking into a plate of Brussels sprouts.

Bitterness is just one sensation that elicits grimaces in supertasters, a population that, odds are, likely includes George H. W. Bush, who famously banished broccoli from the White House. PROP sensitivity is linked to keener discernment across the board—heightening perception of sweetness, the fatty texture in dairy products and even the fruit–acid balance in wine. Perhaps not surprisingly, wine professionals are more likely to be supertasters. Maybe that's why they find that broccoli goes down easier with a glass of crisp sauvignon blanc.

Menu 2

BITTER BRITISH

Shaved Root Vegetable Salad

Irish Cheddar, Bacon and Chard Tart

Stout Cake

This is a casual dinner with an edge of bitterness, and it reflects my own heritage. My Irish grandmother adored Irish ale and cheese tarts. On special occasions my parents often served Black Velvets, a creamy combination of Guinness and champagne. And of course my Scottish heritage meant plenty of bittersweet root vegetables. Cheers!

SHAVED ROOT VEGETABLE SALAD

Young, fresh vegetables give a whole different look and taste to salads. Use whatever root vegetables you can find for this one, such as baby turnips and baby carrots. Bunches of baby beets also work beautifully, but don't mix red ones into the salad until the very end or you'll turn everything red. The squash I call for is not a root vegetable, but it adds another texture to the salad. If you go with larger vegetables, use a mandoline for shaving them. With the smaller ones, a vegetable peeler works well. **Serves 4**

Vegetables:
1 bunch baby white turnips, peeled
2 bunches baby carrots, peeled
1 bunch yellow or red beets, peeled
4 baby pattypan squash
Salt and freshly ground pepper

To finish:
3 thin slices pancetta
2 cups peppery greens
½ cup shaved Pecorino Romano or Parmesan

Shallot Vinaigrette:
1 tbsp chopped shallots
1 tsp Dijon mustard
2 tbsp lemon juice
⅓ cup extra-virgin olive oil
Salt and freshly ground pepper
2 tbsp chopped fresh parsley

Shave turnips, carrots, yellow beets and pattypans using a vegetable peeler or mandoline into a bowl. Shave red beets (if using) into a separate bowl. Season with salt and pepper.

Stir shallots, mustard and lemon juice in a bowl. Whisk in olive oil until emulsified. Season with salt and pepper. Stir in parsley.

Fry pancetta in a skillet until crisp. Drain on paper towels and finely chop.

Place peppery greens on a platter. Drizzle over a little vinaigrette. Toss root vegetables, including red beets, with enough vinaigrette to moisten. Place on top of greens. Sprinkle pancetta over salad and finish with shaved cheese.

PAIRING: **Sancerre**

I'm accustomed to eating radishes and carrots straight from the ground after giving them a quick splash with my garden hose. But raw beets and turnips were unknown to me until I tasted this salad. I love the bitter earthiness. And if, like me, you need a little liquid courage to give it a first shot, make the wine a crisp, lean, citrusy Sancerre from France, based on sauvignon blanc.

IRISH CHEDDAR, BACON AND CHARD TART

I have packed a celebration of Irish culture and cuisine into this unusual, flaky, tasty tart with its beer pastry, Irish cheddar cheese and thick Irish bacon. If Irish cheddar is unavailable, use aged Canadian cheddar. Use double-smoked Canadian bacon as a substitute for Irish. **Serves 4 hungry eaters or 6 normal ones**

Crust:
1½ cups all-purpose flour
½ tsp kosher salt
½ cup unsalted butter, cubed
4 to 5 tbsp cold Irish ale

Filling:
1 tbsp unsalted butter
4 oz (115 g) Irish bacon, diced
1 bunch Swiss chard, stems and thick ribs removed
1 tbsp Dijon mustard
4 oz (115 g) Irish cheddar, shredded
3 eggs
1 cup whipping cream
Salt and freshly ground pepper

Combine flour and salt. Cut in butter by hand or using a food processor. Stir in just enough beer to bring pastry together into a ball.

Roll out pastry to fit a 10-inch tart pan with removable bottom or a 9-inch pie plate. Fit it into the pan and trim edges. Prick bottom with a fork. Freeze for 30 minutes or until firm.

Preheat oven to 425°F.

Place tart pan on a baking sheet and bake for 10 minutes or until pastry looks dry and puffed. Prick pastry base with a fork to deflate. Bake 5 to 10 minutes longer or until pale gold and cooked through.

Reduce heat to 375°F.

Melt butter in a skillet over medium heat. Sauté bacon for 4 minutes or until edges are golden and fat is rendered. Drain bacon on paper towels and reserve.

Bring a pot of salted water to a boil over high heat. Add Swiss chard and blanch for 1 minute or until tender. Drain and squeeze out any liquid. Chop coarsely.

Brush base of pastry with mustard. Sprinkle in bacon, Swiss chard and shredded cheese. Beat together eggs and cream. Season well with salt and pepper. Pour into pastry shell.

Bake tart for 25 to 30 minutes or until filling is lightly golden and just set.

PAIRING: **Irish ale**

Pretty obvious, I know, but at least I didn't say Guinness, the dark stout that's as emblematic of Ireland as green meadows and Bono's sunglasses. Time to explore the lighter side of Irish beer, such as Kilkenny, Smithwick's or Murphy's Irish Red, all with a creamy caramel maltiness that rounds out the tangy cheddar.

STOUT CAKE

This easy cake is part of the British baking lexicon. It tastes rich and extra chocolaty because of the slight bitterness of the Guinness stout. You can make this with a heavy ale too. Elizabeth Fryer, daughter of Alison Fryer, doyenne of Toronto's Cookbook Store, gave me this recipe. Store leftovers in an airtight container.

Serves 4 (with leftovers)

1 cup stout, such as Guinness
1 cup unsalted butter
2 cups granulated sugar
¾ cup unsweetened cocoa powder
2 large eggs
⅔ cup sour cream
1 tbsp vanilla
2 cups all-purpose flour
2½ tsp baking soda

Garnish:
Icing sugar or whipped cream

Preheat oven to 350°F. Butter a 9-inch springform pan and line bottom with parchment paper.

Pour stout into a large pot over medium heat. Add butter and heat until melted. Remove from heat and whisk in sugar and cocoa powder. Reserve.

Combine eggs, sour cream and vanilla in a bowl and beat until smooth. Whisk sour cream mixture into stout mixture. Whisk in flour and baking soda.

Pour batter into prepared pan and bake for 50 minutes to 1 hour or until a cake tester comes out with crumbs clinging to it. Place pan on a rack and cool completely. Before serving, dust with icing sugar or serve with lightly sweetened whipped cream.

PAIRING: **Stout beer**

I love a recipe that contains the "wine" match in its title, in this case stout beer, a dark, creamy brew made with roasted malt or roasted barley. The best-known brand is Guinness, from Ireland, though Beamish and Murphy's, also both from Ireland, make suitable alternatives, as would a host of excellent examples now made by microbreweries in North America and beyond. The same creamy, chocolaty character that stout brings to this recipe makes it a perfect beverage partner for the wholesome cake. Alternative: tawny Port.

CAMPARI KIR

I've survived countless Italian weddings—other people's, not my own. What I mean is, I survived the food, which is always a marathon. As you might imagine, the wine in suburban Italian banquet halls can leave something to be desired, unless you're fond of bargain-basement trebbiano. My debt goes to a sweet young barkeep at one such union for a drink that has since seen me through more nuptials than those of Mickey Rooney and Liz Taylor combined. Spike the bland white with a splash of bittersweet Campari, Italy's famous aperitivo with the crimson phosphorescence of a bridesmaid's dress. At home, it's a great way to rehabilitate a stale half-bottle of pinot grigio. Campari and sparkling prosecco make a Campari Royale.

To me, these are more refreshing than the original Kir, a classic aperitif named after a Catholic priest and postwar mayor of Dijon, France. Father Félix made his with undistinguished aligoté and the local blackcurrant liqueur, cassis, which I find too sweet for this application. Try the Campari Royale for brunch, or serve it at your wedding. Just don't spill it on your gown.

Menu 3

FROM TAPAS TO TABLE

Anchovy and Tomato Tapas

Speedy Spanish Halibut

Saffron Rice

Braised Escarole

Caffè Latte Panna Cotta with Decadent Chocolate Cookies

Spanish food was on top of the world recently with its star chefs such as the inimitable Ferran Adrià. It is the home of molecular gastronomy, or modernist cuisine, a method of cooking that, through science, specifically chemistry, and equipment, strives to produce the essence of flavour. It's not really an approachable style for home cooks, though, which is partly why I believe the trend is useful only for restaurants. This menu has only one modernist technique in it—making the froth for the caffè latte panna cotta. The rest of the recipes use traditional Spanish ingredients with simpler methods that you can play with in your kitchen.

ANCHOVY AND TOMATO TAPAS

At night, tapas bars are hopping in Spain. Social life takes place in restaurants around good food and wine, tapas first, followed by dinner at about 10 or even later. This is one of my favourite tapas because anchovies are just so full of flavour. It can be made in two different ways: you can rub the grilled bread with the cut side of a tomato, or you can top the toast with a whole tomato slice. I like the taste of the rubbed toast better, but the look of the tomato slices is more appealing. Take your pick. Serve as a nibbly or a first course.

Serves 4

4 slices country-style bread
12 anchovy fillets
1 garlic clove, cut in half
4 slices tomato
2 tbsp extra-virgin olive oil
Freshly ground pepper

Brush bread on both sides with oil from anchovy can. Grill for 1 minute per side or until toasted.
Rub one side of each toast slice with garlic.
Top with a tomato slice and drape over anchovies. Dot with olive oil and sprinkle with pepper. Cut each toast in half before serving.

PAIRING: **Rueda**

Tony Crosariol, my father, became enamoured with this rubbed-tomato toast as we grazed our way through Spain together many years ago. After we returned home, there was no stopping him. Tomatoes on toast started every meal at Tony's for months. Try these anchovy-adorned snacks with white Rueda, a crisp, invigorating wine from northern Spain based mainly on the verdejo grape. It's as simple and satisfying as the dish. Alternative: albariño, a similarly lean, electric-crisp Spanish white finding popularity in California and Australia.

SPEEDY SPANISH HALIBUT

Halibut has the strength and texture to stand up to the hot, spicy and bitter flavours in this dish. You can also make this with chicken or shrimp, but most other fish will fall apart in the cooking. **Serves 4**

- 1¼ lb (565 g) skinless halibut fillets, cubed
- Salt and freshly ground pepper
- 2 tbsp olive oil
- 1 cup diced onions
- 1 red pepper, cut in 1-inch dice
- 2 chorizo sausages, diced (about 7 oz/ 200 g total)
- 2 zucchini, cut in 1-inch dice
- 1 tsp chopped fresh rosemary
- 1 tsp hot Spanish paprika
- 2 cups diced seeded tomatoes
- 1 cup chicken stock
- 2 tbsp chopped fresh flat-leaf parsley

Season halibut with salt and pepper. Reserve.

Heat oil in a large skillet over medium-high heat. Add onions, red pepper and chorizo and sauté for 1 minute. Add zucchini, rosemary and paprika and continue to sauté for 5 minutes or until vegetables are softened and tinged with gold.

Stir in tomatoes and stock. Cook for 5 minutes or until tomatoes are softened. Nestle halibut into sauce, cover and cook for 5 minutes or until halibut is cooked through and white juices are just beginning to appear.

Sprinkle with parsley.

PAIRING: **Mencía**

It may be hard to find, but mencía is worth the footwork if you're keen to run with the fashionable wine crowd and don't mind a wake-up jolt of acidity. Bierzo in northwest Spain excels with this local variety, which some people liken to pinot noir for its bright fruit and lean body. It puts up a more bracing fight than pinot, though, and that stands it in good stead for the chorizo and hot paprika. Alternatives: dry rosé or the Smoked Caesar cocktail, page 122 in our "Smoky" chapter.

SAFFRON RICE

The pungent flavour of saffron makes this rice the perfect foil for the spicy halibut. Buy saffron threads, not the powder, which has very little flavour and is often adulterated. Saffron is one of those spices that should be bought from a reputable company. Spanish rice is usually short-grain, so I substitute arborio if necessary.

Serves 4

2 tbsp butter
½ cup chopped onion
1 tsp chopped garlic
1 tsp Spanish paprika
1½ cups short-grain Spanish or arborio rice
1 tsp saffron threads
4 cups hot chicken stock
Salt and freshly ground pepper
2 tbsp chopped fresh parsley

Melt butter in a heavy pot over medium heat. Add onion, garlic and paprika and sauté for 2 to 3 minutes or until onion is soft. Add rice and turn in butter until coated.

Stir saffron into hot stock and pour over rice. Bring to a boil, reduce heat to medium-low and cook rice, uncovered and stirring occasionally, until stock is absorbed and rice is tender, 15 to 20 minutes. Season well with salt and pepper and sprinkle with parsley.

Combatting Bitter: When a dish is too bitter, don't reach for the sugar, reach for the salt. Salt is the yin to the bitter's yang, and will make the dish zing.

BRAISED ESCAROLE

Use escarole, frisée, Belgian endive, Swiss chard, beet tops, collard greens or a mixture of these, removing any tough stems. Eaten raw, these greens are slightly bitter, but the flavour mellows when they are cooked. You can substitute bacon for the pancetta.

Serves 4

- 1 large or 2 small heads escarole (18 oz/500 g total)
- 1 tbsp olive oil
- 1 oz (28 g) pancetta, diced
- ½ cup sliced red onion
- ½ cup vegetable or chicken stock
- Salt and freshly ground pepper

Bring a pot of salted water to a boil. Separate escarole into leaves, add to pot and boil for 2 minutes or until just tender. Drain, rinse in cold water and squeeze out excess water. Reserve.

Heat olive oil in a large skillet over medium-high heat. Add pancetta and sauté for 1 to 2 minutes or until crispy. Add onion and sauté for 1 minute.

Stir in escarole and cook for 1 minute. Add stock and season with salt and pepper. Reduce heat to low, cover and cook for 5 minutes. Uncover and continue to cook for 3 to 5 minutes or until any remaining liquid disappears. Season if needed.

CAFFÈ LATTE PANNA COTTA WITH DECADENT CHOCOLATE COOKIES

If you don't have a hand blender or frother to make the froth, you could easily just whip some cream for the topping. The number of servings will depend on the size of your coffee cups. Have any leftovers for breakfast the next morning and the caffeine will perk you right up.

Serves 4 to 8

Panna Cotta:
1 cup cold strong coffee
1 cup granulated sugar
1 tbsp gelatine
½ tsp kosher salt
1 cup whole milk
1 cup whipping cream
1 tsp vanilla

Froth:
¼ cup whole milk
½ tsp gelatine
½ tsp granulated sugar

Decadent Chocolate Cookies (p. 48)

Combine coffee, sugar, gelatine and salt in a medium pot. Bring to a simmer, stirring constantly. Add milk, cream and vanilla and continue to stir until mixture is warm. Cool slightly, stirring occasionally to make sure gelatine is well distributed.

Pour into espresso or coffee cups. Cover with plastic wrap and chill until set.

Heat milk for froth with gelatine and sugar in a small pot over low heat until gelatine has dissolved. Pour into a small bowl, cover and refrigerate until it just begins to set. Froth mixture with a hand blender until frothy.

Spoon froth on top of panna cottas. Sprinkle with shaved chocolate if desired.

Chill until needed, and serve with Decadent Chocolate Cookies.

PAIRING: **Recioto**

I love the name recioto. It comes from *recie*, Venetian dialect for "ears," a reference to the tendency of certain grape clusters to form two little lobes that dangle from the main bunch. The exposed lobes receive the most sunlight, yielding super-ripe grapes that for centuries have been used to produce a sweet wine in the Veneto region of Italy, the precursor to a now more famous dry red called Amarone. Recioto today is more typically made using the whole cluster, left on mats after harvest to dry and concentrate sugars. If left to ferment to complete dryness, the wine becomes Amarone, but when fermentation is halted part way, it becomes recioto. Alternatives: California black muscat or espresso coffee.

DECADENT CHOCOLATE COOKIES

These soft, ultra-chocolaty bites complement the taste of the panna cotta. Use very dark chocolate (70% cocoa) for the biggest flavour hit. These can also be made as larger cookies using a heaped tablespoon of dough, which will yield 20 cookies. Bake them for 12 minutes. Large or small, they keep well.

Makes 70 small cookies

½ cup butter
4 oz (115 g) dark chocolate (70% cocoa)
2 eggs
1 cup granulated sugar
2 tsp vanilla
1 cup all-purpose flour
¼ cup unsweetened cocoa powder
½ tsp baking powder
½ tsp kosher salt
70 small (or 12 medium) squares chocolate
Icing sugar for dusting

Preheat oven to 375°F. Line 2 cookie sheets with parchment paper.

Melt butter and dark chocolate in a medium, heavy pot over low heat. Stir until smooth. Remove from heat and cool slightly.

Stir together eggs, sugar and vanilla. Blend into melted chocolate mixture. In a separate bowl, sift together flour, cocoa powder, baking powder and salt. Fold into chocolate mixture.

Place heaped teaspoons of dough on prepared cookie sheets about 1 inch apart. Press into rounds with the back of a spoon. Cookies should be about ½ inch thick. Top each one with a square of chocolate.

Bake for 7 minutes or until the inside is still soft. Cool on racks. The cookies harden a little as they cool. Sprinkle with icing sugar.

MARMALADE OF GREENS

This spread for grilled bread contains contrasting flavours and textures. Leafy greens are one of the healthiest vegetables to eat. They are low in fat and high in dietary fibre, folic acid, vitamin C, potassium and magnesium. Studies show that they may provide protection against cancer and heart disease. Use a combination of greens for the best results. I like chard, rapini, spinach and the dinosaur (or black) kale also known as cavolo nero. Use any or all.

Serves 6

2 lb (900 g) fresh leafy greens, stems and thick ribs removed
2 tbsp olive oil
1 tsp chopped garlic
6 anchovy fillets, chopped
2 tsp capers
¼ tsp chili flakes
½ cup chopped pitted Kalamata olives
2 tbsp raisins
Salt and freshly ground pepper
3 slices grilled Italian bread, rubbed with cut side of garlic clove
½ cup shredded provolone or fontina

Boil greens in salted water for 10 minutes. Drain, refresh in cold water and squeeze out excess liquid.

Heat oil in a skillet over medium heat. Add garlic and sauté for 30 seconds or until fragrant. Add greens and sauté (using tongs to separate greens) for 2 minutes or until well flavoured with garlic. Add anchovies, capers and chili flakes and sauté for another minute or until anchovies have softened. Stir in olives and raisins and remove from heat. Season with salt and pepper to taste. Cool.

Preheat broiler.

Pile marmalade on grilled bread, sprinkle with cheese and broil for 1 to 2 minutes or until cheese is melted. Cut in half.

HOP MONSTERS

I used to believe beer's sole mission was to deliver pleasure. So naive. Some brews are branded for the fear factor. A few examples: Hop Mess Monster, Agitator, Palate Wrecker, Hopocalypse, Alimony Ale, Hopsecutioner, Ruination. With names like that, it's hard to know whether to drink or run—from the puns, at least.

These heavily hopped members of a style called India Pale Ale are strongly bitter and increasingly popular, especially among hipster craft-brew devotees looking to put as much social distance as possible between themselves and the Bud Light crowd.

Like everything in beerdom, IPAs are not new. They date to the early nineteenth century, when ales shipped from England to the empire's outpost of India tended to spoil en route. Enter hops, a bitter flavouring that also acts as a preservative. More hops, more freshness.

Refrigerated lager eventually took the wind out of India Pale Ale's sales, but the style returned with a vengeance on these shores, particularly the West Coast, where microbreweries have been engaging in a hops arms race, bringing new meaning to the term *bitter rivals*.

BEER TOASTS

This is a truly great toast. With a lighter texture than regular toasts, it complements any kind of cheese topping. Because they are on the softer side, pop them into the oven for a few minutes to re-crisp before using. Store in a plastic bag, refrigerated.

1 baguette
1 cup lager
Salt and freshly ground pepper

Preheat oven to 350°F. Oil a baking sheet with olive oil.
Slice bread ½ inch thick on the diagonal.
Place lager in a bowl and dip in bread slices, removing bread immediately. The bread should be moistened but not soaked. Drain excess liquid.
Arrange bread on the baking sheet. Season with salt and pepper. Bake for 20 minutes, turning over once, or until golden and firm to the touch.

CHEDDAR ALE BREAD

This crusty quick bread takes just 5 minutes to put together. Serve this with soups or salads. It is a good bread for a melted cheese sandwich too.

Makes 1 loaf

- 3½ cups all-purpose flour
- 2½ tbsp granulated sugar
- 1½ tsp baking powder
- 1½ tsp kosher salt
- 1 tsp caraway seeds (optional)
- 1½ cups shredded cheddar
- ¼ cup shredded Asiago
- 1 bottle (12 oz/355 mL) ale
- ¼ cup butter, melted

Preheat oven to 375°F.

Stir together flour, sugar, baking powder, salt, caraway seeds (if using), cheddar and Asiago in a large bowl. Stir in beer with a wooden spoon just until moistened. Using hands, gently knead dough in bowl until it comes together. Be careful not to over-mix, as this will result in a tough loaf.

Lift dough into a well-oiled loaf pan. Pour melted butter over top. Sprinkle with kosher salt.

Bake for 1 hour to 1 hour 10 minutes or until loaf is golden and crusty and the top springs back when lightly depressed. Cool in pan for 10 minutes, then turn out onto a rack.

KALE AND BEAN SOUP

Cavolo nero, also known as Tuscan, dinosaur or black kale, is a sweeter and more flavourful version of the regular green curly kale. If you can find it, use it, but regular kale will work too. **Serves 6**

- 2 tbsp olive oil
- 1 large onion, chopped
- 1 tsp chopped garlic
- 1 tsp fresh or dried thyme leaves
- 1 bunch kale, stems removed up to the leaf
- 5 cups chicken stock or water
- 1 can (14 oz/398 mL) white beans, drained and rinsed
- 1 dried red chili
- Salt and freshly ground pepper

Garnish:

- ¼ cup extra-virgin olive oil
- Hot sauce
- 1 cup grated Parmesan

Heat oil in a soup pot over medium heat. Add onion, garlic and thyme and sauté for 5 minutes or until onion is softened.

Slice kale into ½-inch shreds. Add to pot and sauté until coated with oil. Pour in stock, bring to a boil, reduce heat and simmer for 20 to 25 minutes or until kale is tender. Add beans and dried chili. Simmer for 10 minutes to unite flavours. Season with salt and pepper and remove chili.

Ladle soup into 6 soup bowls. Sprinkle with olive oil, hot sauce to taste and cheese.

angelica • anise • arugula • basil • bay leaves • bee balm
borage • bouquet garni • caraway • chervil • chicory • chives
cilantro • dill • epazote • fennel • fenugreek • garlic chives
garden cress • hyssop • hops • juniper • lavender • lemon balm
lemongrass • lemon verbena • thyme • rosemary • sage • tarragon
lemon thyme • oregano • savory • parsley • green onions
mint • spearmint • English mint • shiso leaves

REMEMBER THE PARSLEY GARNISH?

It rested on mashed potatoes like a lonely, fallen tree on a snowy peak. It floated on cream soups. Sometimes, when Mom felt the artist's impulse, she'd surround the perimeter of a poached fish with scads of the curly variety like a pre-Martha wreath. The venerable green sprig was the definition of herbal flavour on North American tables, a proxy for freshness and a jolt of colour on an otherwise anemic plate. Ironically, it might as well have been made of plastic, because few people actually ingested it.

Eventually, overworked parsley began to welcome little green friends into its bunk in the vegetable crisper. Cilantro leaves popped up in guacamoles, salsas and Asian curries. Fresh thyme, oregano and rosemary joined their dried counterparts to create zippier sauces and pot roasts. Tarragon brought licorice-like verve to French-style vinaigrettes. Fragrant basil gave us pizza margherita and pesto. And humble parsley graduated from ornamental-sprig status to star by the fistful in tabbouleh, gremolata and linguine *alle vongole*.

Bartenders, too, have been going green. The julep and mojito, summery classics that elevate mint to its highest calling, are winning new respect thanks to another trend, the rise of quality bourbons and rums. And that's just the tip of the ice cube. How about sage margaritas, thyme Bellinis, gin and tonics with rosemary, and vodkas infused with cilantro or dill? Talk about garden cocktails.

Keep in mind that herbs, like spices, vary in potency. You've got to know when to go easy or go crazy. We think a little tarragon and sage go a long way, for instance, but the subtle, grassy flavour of fresh parsley tends to be like designer stilettos in the closet of one of this book's authors: the more the merrier. Fresh basil and mint, though bolder, can be equally forgiving, particularly in Mediterranean and Middle Eastern dishes.

If herbs take centre stage on the plate, companion beverages need special zip. This can come in the form of complementary herbal overtones, like those exhibited most classically in southern French reds based on grenache, syrah and mourvèdre grapes. Connoisseurs call the flavour *garrigue*, an essence of wild thyme, lavender, juniper and rosemary, all found in abundance along the Mediterranean coast. Chilean cabernet sauvignon often comes across with an uncanny note of mint or eucalyptus. And riesling, gewürztraminer and muscat, high in compounds called terpenes that are present also in basil, mint and evergreen plants, are especially good matches for dishes strong in, yes, basil, mint and rosemary.

But the options are broader than that. All you really need in the glass is lively acidity. No matter how full bodied, the wine should possess a lively step. Herbs give lift to a dish; a crisp beverage carries it to victory.

Menu 1

CASUAL CHIC

Vegetarian Charcuterie

Slow-Baked Arctic Char with Crisp Potatoes

Green Beans with Red Onions

Peach and Blackberry Compote

Lemon Balm Shortbread

This casual dinner has a main course of Arctic char, a beautiful fish with a gentle flavour. I slow bake it to keep all the herbal tastes and juices mingled together. Served with a counterpoint of slightly crispy potatoes, it is one of the loveliest of summer fish dishes. One of my favourite first-course ideas is to invite guests to make their own salad. It works best in the summer or fall, when lettuce, tomatoes and other produce are at their peak. Herbs add an intriguing note to the fruit compote, and using a lemony herb in the shortbread cookies keeps them chic.

VEGETARIAN CHARCUTERIE

Essentially, this is a make-your-own salad. My guests use dinner plates so the ingredients aren't crowded, and they all help themselves. It encourages conversation, and everyone gets to choose what they like. I make a herbal tarragon dressing and toss it with a variety of summery lettuces. On the table I place a bowl of lightly salted chopped red onion, a plate of wonderful juicy tomatoes dressed with a little olive oil and salt and pepper and sprinkled with basil leaves (no acid—tomatoes are acidic enough), a bowl of thinly sliced cucumber lightly salted and sprinkled with chives, and some sliced buffalo mozzarella, or burrata if it's available. I put out a grater with excellent Parmigiano-Reggiano and, for the final touch, Maldon salt and a pepper mill.

Tarragon Dressing

This is my favourite dressing, because I love tarragon. Creamy and herbal, it will improve any salad. It keeps for 2 weeks in the refrigerator.

Makes 1½ cups

- ⅓ cup mayonnaise
- ⅓ cup white wine vinegar
- 1 tbsp chopped fresh tarragon
- 2 tsp chopped garlic
- 1 cup olive oil
- Salt and freshly ground pepper

Combine mayonnaise, vinegar, tarragon and garlic. Slowly whisk in olive oil. Season with salt and pepper to taste.

PAIRING: **Sauvignon blanc**

This fun Bac-Os-free take on the family-restaurant salad bar might seem to warrant a selection of wines. If guests get to build custom plates, why not a smorgasbord of drink options? No need. Zesty, herbal sauvignon blanc is the potable analogue to a salad bar. Some guests will inquire about red (yes, even with fresh salad—the horror!), so be prepared with a high-acid variety, such as barbera from Italy or Beaujolais from France. Better—and almost as good as sauvignon blanc—would be an ice-cold pilsner.

SLOW-BAKED ARCTIC CHAR WITH CRISP POTATOES

Slow baking fish is not time-consuming. I like slow baking fish because you get a very even colour and a slightly softer texture than when you use high temperatures. The vegetable accompaniment cooks on top of the stove. The herb butter, with its refreshing lemony saltiness, makes the char even better. Leftover herb butter will keep refrigerated for a week or frozen indefinitely.

Serves 4

Crisp Potatoes:
1 tbsp olive oil
2 oz (55 g) bacon or pancetta, diced
4 cups diced unpeeled red potatoes
4 oz (115 g) shiitake mushrooms, stemmed and diced
Salt and freshly ground pepper
2 tbsp chopped fresh parsley

Herb Butter:
¼ cup chopped shallots
3 tbsp chopped fresh parsley
2 tbsp chopped chives
2 tbsp capers
2 tsp chopped fresh lemon thyme
1 tsp grated lemon zest
¾ cup butter, softened

4 skin-on Arctic char fillets (8 oz/225 g each)

Preheat oven to 250°F.

Heat oil in a large skillet over medium-high heat. Add pancetta and sauté for 1 minute. Add potatoes and sauté, stirring occasionally, until a few potatoes start to brown, about 2 minutes more. Cover, reduce heat to medium and cook for 8 to 10 minutes or until potatoes are tender. Uncover skillet, add mushrooms, season with salt and pepper and stir everything together. Cover again and cook for another 5 to 6 minutes or until mushrooms are tender and potatoes are golden. Sprinkle with parsley. Reserve.

Combine shallots, parsley, chives, capers, lemon thyme and lemon zest while potatoes are cooking. Mix into butter.

Place char fillets skin side down in an oiled baking dish. Sprinkle with salt and pepper. Brush each fillet with about 1 tsp herb butter.

Bake for 25 to 28 minutes or until white juices are just beginning to appear. Place fish on serving plates and dot with remaining herb butter.

Reheat potato mixture and serve with the fish.

For Beppi's pairing, see page 63.

PAIRING: **Pinot gris**

This is the alter ego of pinot grigio. With the popularity explosion of easy-sipping Italian pinot grigio, a naming convention arose. Crisp, simple quaffs tend to get slapped with the grigio moniker, while more substantial "serious" wines are called pinot gris (though there are exceptions). The "serious" version is a specialty of Alsace in France as well as Oregon and British Columbia. The medium weight and subtle fruitiness find their mark with this delicate fish and earthy potato-based side.

Colloquially, herbs are leafy greens, in contrast to spices, which are the dried seeds, roots, bark or flesh of many plants. But the line is sometimes crossed. The herb cilantro (a.k.a. coriander) yields citrusy, nutty-tasting seeds generally classified as a spice. Ditto for dill.

GREEN BEANS WITH RED ONIONS

I've been called the green bean queen because I love to eat green beans as a side dish with anything. Their crunch, colour and taste are so appealing. You could also serve these cold with a sprinkle of lemon juice.

Serves 4

8 oz (225 g) green beans, topped and tailed
3 tbsp butter
1 medium red onion, thinly sliced
Salt and freshly ground pepper
1 tsp grated lemon zest

Bring a large pot of salted water to a boil. Add beans and boil for 3 to 4 minutes or until crisp-tender. Drain and run under cold water until cold. Reserve until needed.

Melt butter in a medium skillet over medium heat. Add onion and sauté for 5 minutes or until very soft. Add green beans and continue to sauté until beans are hot. Season with salt and pepper and sprinkle with lemon zest.

PEACH AND BLACKBERRY COMPOTE

The lemon balm adds a refreshing element to this simple dessert. Change the fruit here to whatever is in season. I use some late-harvest riesling in the syrup and then serve the rest with the dessert. **Serves 4**

Peach Syrup:
1½ lb (675 g) ripe peaches (about 4)
¼ cup granulated sugar
¼ cup sweet wine
¼ cup water

Whipped Cream Mixture:
1 cup whipping cream
½ cup mascarpone
1 tsp granulated sugar

To finish:
2 cups blackberries
4 sprigs fresh lemon balm

Bring a pot of water to a boil. Drop in peaches. Leave 30 seconds to 1 minute, then remove. When cool enough to handle, slip off skins and reserve. Cut peaches in half and remove pits. Reserve peeled peaches.

Place peels and pits in a small pot with sugar, sweet wine and water. Bring to a boil over high heat. Reduce heat to medium-low and simmer gently for 10 minutes or until syrup is flavourful and reduced to about ⅓ cup. Cool, then strain.

Beat together cream, mascarpone and sugar until mixture holds soft peaks.

Combine reserved peaches and blackberries with ¼ cup peach syrup. Taste and add more sugar if you like. Divide among 4 serving dishes. Top with whipped cream mixture and drizzle each serving with a little of the remaining peach syrup. Garnish with lemon balm and serve with Lemon Balm Shortbread (page 66).

PAIRING: **Late-harvest riesling**

Left on the vine until very late in autumn, late-harvested grapes become partially dried and intensify in sweetness. Think of them as precursors to icewine—at half the price. There's a delectable tinned-peach and apricot quality to most late-harvest rieslings, one reason Lucy favours the style in this recipe. The rest of the bottle, as she suggests, would indeed be perfect as an accompaniment. Waste not, want not.

LEMON BALM SHORTBREAD

These slightly crunchy herbal cookies make a delightful foil for the creamy compote. If lemon balm is not available, use rosemary, mint or lavender. The cookies will keep in an airtight container for up to 2 weeks.

Makes 36 cookies

1 cup unsalted butter, softened
½ cup granulated sugar
½ tsp kosher salt
⅛ tsp vanilla
2 cups all-purpose flour
2 tbsp minced fresh lemon balm

Cream butter, sugar and salt together with an electric mixer. Add vanilla and beat until combined. Add flour and lemon balm and beat until just incorporated. Place dough on the counter and knead lightly to bring dough into a ball. Flatten into a disc and wrap in plastic wrap. Chill until firm enough to work with, 20 to 30 minutes.

Roll out dough on a lightly floured surface to about ¼-inch thickness. Using a ruler and the point of a knife, cut dough into 1½-inch squares. Place on a parchment-lined baking sheet; prick each cookie once with a fork. Chill again until cookies are firm.

Preheat oven to 300°F.

Bake cookies for 20 minutes or until lightly golden at the edges. Cool completely on racks.

LEMON HERBS

Lemon Balm: A lemony Middle Eastern herb, fresh lemon balm leaves are an aromatic addition to salads and make a good stuffing for lamb and pork. Cover a roasting chicken with balm leaves and it will be moist and fragrant. Lemon balm is a refreshing addition to fruit drinks, ice creams and fruit salads. Dried leaves enliven any tea. Harvest from the beginning of May to the end of August. Cut often to prevent the plant from flowering and going to seed.

Lemon Verbena: South American in origin, lemon verbena is a tangy addition to any food or drink that calls for lemon. Use the sweet, strongly lemon-flavoured leaves fresh in fish, chicken or fruit dishes. Add to baked custard or homemade ice cream for a lemony lift. Dried leaves blend well with most tea herbs. Harvest from late July to August.

Menu 2

C IS FOR CHILE

Apple and Avocado Soup

Chilean Pulmay

Pebre

Sopaipillas

ABC is one of the major cooking trends today: Argentina, Brazil and Chile are the big three cuisines attracting chefs' interest. Chile is a long, narrow country with the ocean on one side, the Andes on the other and many valleys in between where most wine grapes are grown. Chilean cuisine is fascinating because the products they grow and harvest are so diverse, with fish and seafood from the ocean and fruit and vegetables from the centre. The mountains produce excellent beef, pork and lamb.

APPLE AND AVOCADO SOUP

This is a wonderful, mysterious summery soup. Avocados are grown all over Chile and are especially tasty. I like to serve this soup very cold, but it can be eaten warm if you prefer. The herbal elements in the salsa enhance the flavour of the avocado. If the soup is too thick, thin it with some extra stock. **Serves 6**

2 tbsp butter
1 small onion, chopped
1 tbsp chopped jalapeño pepper
1 tsp grated fresh ginger
1 green apple, peeled, cored and chopped
3 cups chicken stock
1 avocado, peeled and chopped
¼ cup whipping cream
Salt and freshly ground pepper

Mango Cilantro Salsa:
1 ripe mango, peeled and diced
½ cup chopped red onion
¼ cup chopped fresh cilantro
1 tsp chopped jalapeño pepper
1 tbsp lime juice
Salt

Melt butter in a pot over medium heat. Add onion and sauté until soft but not brown, about 2 minutes. Stir in jalapeño, ginger and apple and cook for 1 minute. Add stock. Simmer for 10 minutes or until apple is tender.
Purée mixture until smooth in a food processor. Add avocado and purée again.
Pour soup into a bowl. Stir in cream, then season with salt and pepper. Refrigerate until cold.
Combine mango, red onion, cilantro, jalapeño and lime juice. Season to taste with salt. Serve a spoonful of salsa on top of each serving of soup.

PAIRING: **Chilean sauvignon blanc**

Chile's flagship white is a bargain hunter's treasure. Under the country's sunny skies, the grape yields ample fruitiness while retaining its characteristic herbal essence and crisp verve. Those qualities bridge the rich texture and lively flavours in this refreshing green bowl.

CHILEAN PULMAY

In Latin cuisines, pork and seafood is a popular combination. Pulmay is a gutsy traditional dish from the islands off Chile's coast. It is traditionally cooked in a firepit lined with hot stones, but you can cook it in a pot either on the stove or on the barbecue. Serve with pebre and hot sauce as well as a lettuce, tomato and cucumber salad with a peppery vinaigrette.

Serves 8

2 tbsp olive oil
1½ lb (675 g) pork stewing meat
4 smoked Spanish chorizo sausages (about 14 oz/400 g total), cut in thirds
1½ lb (675 g) Yukon Gold potatoes, peeled and cut in 2-inch pieces
1 red pepper, sliced
1 medium Spanish onion, sliced
1 banana pepper or several small jalapeño peppers, thickly sliced in rings
2 tbsp chopped garlic
Salt and freshly ground pepper
1 cup white wine
1 savoy cabbage, outer leaves separated
2 lb (900 g) clams
2 lb (900 g) mussels
Pebre (page 74)
Hot sauce

Heat oil in a large, wide pot over high heat. Add pork and cook for 2 minutes per side or until lightly browned. Add sausages, potatoes, red pepper, onion, banana pepper and half the garlic. Season with salt and pepper. Cook for 4 minutes or until onion and peppers have softened. Add ½ cup wine and bring to a boil. Cover mixture completely with cabbage leaves. Reduce heat to medium-low and cover pot with a lid. Cook for 30 minutes or until pork is nearly tender.

Add clams, mussels and remaining garlic. Pour remaining ½ cup wine over top and cover with another layer of cabbage leaves. Cover pot tightly with a lid. Steam seafood for 10 to 15 minutes or until shells open. Discard any that don't open.

Shred the cooked cabbage and scatter over a platter. Arrange clams, mussels, sausage and pork on the platter, surrounded by potatoes. Serve the juice separately. Have everyone help themselves to pebre and hot sauce.

PAIRING: **Carmenère**

It's a safe guess there was no carmenère around when aboriginal Chileans were huddling around firepits lined with hot stones to make the original version of this dish. But the gutsy red, a Chilean signature, coincidentally would make a fine accompaniment. The carmenère vine, imported more than a century ago from Bordeaux, excels in Chile's dry heat. Newly fashionable, it's a fine foil for hearty dishes such as this, with ample body and nuances of red berries, spice, smoke and leather.

PEBRE

Pebre is a fresh-tasting Chilean herbal hot sauce. Heat it up with more chilies, if you like. It is excellent with simple roasted or grilled meats, chicken or fish. Combining it with some sour cream makes a lively dip for vegetable chips.

Makes about 1 cup

1 cup chopped green onions
1 cup loosely packed cilantro leaves
1 cup loosely packed flat-leaf parsley leaves
2 tbsp chopped seeded jalapeño pepper
¼ cup olive oil
1 tbsp red wine vinegar
1 tbsp lime juice
1 tsp chopped garlic
Salt

Place all ingredients except salt in a food processor or mini chopper and process until mixture is combined but still has a bit of texture. Season with salt.

SOPAIPILLAS

Sopaipillas are a kind of doughnut. In Chile they are usually served sprinkled with sugar and cinnamon, but I soak mine in a flavourful syrup. This recipe is adapted from one by Chilean chef Cristián Correa, who is an expert on his country's cuisine, travelling abroad to champion it. Serve warm or at room temperature.

Serves 6 (with leftovers)

2 cups self-rising flour (see note, page 30)
¼ tsp kosher salt
1 cup mashed cooked or canned pumpkin
¼ cup unsalted butter, melted
Vegetable oil for frying
1 cup whipping cream
¼ cup pomegranate seeds
Icing sugar for dusting

Syrup:
1 cup brown sugar
1 cup water
1 cinnamon stick
½ orange, cut into 8 pieces

Combine flour and salt in a large bowl. In a separate bowl, combine pumpkin and butter and stir until smooth. Make a well in the flour mixture, add pumpkin mixture and stir and then knead until well combined. Add a little water if dough is too dry.

Roll out dough on a floured surface to about ¼-inch thickness. Cut out 3-inch rounds with a cookie cutter.

Combine brown sugar, water, cinnamon and orange in a pot and bring to a boil over medium heat. Boil for 4 minutes or until slightly thickened. Strain into a gratin dish.

Heat 3 inches of oil in a wok or large pot to 350°F or until a cube of bread turns brown in 15 seconds. Add dough rounds a few at a time and fry until puffed and golden, turning halfway through, about 1 to 2 minutes. Drain on paper towels.

Working in batches, add fried sopaipillas to syrup and soak for about 3 minutes, turning once, or until they have absorbed some liquid. Transfer sopaipillas to a plate, reserving syrup.

Whip cream until thickened, then fold in pomegranate seeds.

Garnish sopaipilla with a dollop of cream. Top with another sopaipilla and dust with icing sugar. Drizzle plate with a little reserved syrup.

PAIRING: **Late-harvest gewürztraminer**

You won't find doughnuts like this at your local coffee shop. The luscious, fruity-gingery quality of late-harvest gewürztraminer, made by many Chilean producers, makes a splendid match, like jammy doughnut filling—served on the side.

Menu 3

CRUISING THE MEDITERRANEAN

Watermelon Gazpacho

Herbalicious Rack of Lamb

Quinoa Spinach Risotto

Lime Basil Éclairs

A Mediterranean menu with flavours from Spain to Provence is perfect for a late-summer dinner. Using watermelon instead of tomato in the gazpacho, the reigning soup of Spain, makes it lighter, fruitier and much more exciting. Lamb is always a perfect main course, especially when scattered with Provençal herbs. When I was last in Paris, I was happy to see that desserts that had been overlooked during the macaron craze, such as éclairs, were making a comeback. Instead of being filled with plain pastry cream, their flavours are modern. My lime and basil filling is unusual and mouth-watering.

WATERMELON GAZPACHO

Using watermelon instead of tomato makes this an unusual soup. The lime adds a kick to the otherwise bland but juicy watermelon. Using sriracha instead of the usual jalapeño gives it a slightly Asian flavour. Serve well chilled.

Makes 6 cups

1 seedless watermelon (5 lb/2.25 kg), cubed (about 8 cups)
2 tbsp lime juice
1 tbsp Sherry vinegar
1 tbsp olive oil
1 tsp sriracha sauce
Salt
1 cup finely diced cucumber
1 cup finely diced red onion
1 cup finely diced yellow pepper

Garnish:
⅓ cup plain yogurt
¼ tsp grated lime zest
1 tbsp lime juice
2 tbsp chopped fresh mint or basil

Purée 6 cups watermelon in a food processor or blender. Transfer to a bowl.
Stir in lime juice, Sherry vinegar, olive oil and sriracha. Season with salt to bring out the flavours. Stir in remaining watermelon, cucumber, onion and yellow pepper. Chill well.
Combine yogurt with lime zest and lime juice in a small bowl. Garnish each serving of soup with a swirl of yogurt and chopped mint.

PAIRING: **New Zealand sauvignon blanc**

It's hard to imagine a more refreshing soup than this, which adds an exclamation mark to the expression "cool as a cucumber" by marrying the vegetable with watermelon. You'll need a crisp, fruity white, and there's no better choice than New Zealand sauvignon blanc. Think of it as the Kiwi gazpacho of wine.

HERBALICIOUS RACK OF LAMB

Lamb is a perfect canvas for herbal flavours. I sear the lamb and start roasting it before I add the herb mixture to ensure that the herbs retain their fresh taste.

Serves 4 (with seconds)

- 1½ cups fresh bread crumbs
- ¼ cup finely diced seeded tomato
- ½ cup chopped fresh thyme
- ¼ cup chopped fresh flat-leaf parsley
- 2 tbsp chopped fresh rosemary
- 1 tsp finely chopped garlic
- Salt and freshly ground pepper
- ¼ cup butter, melted
- 1 tbsp vegetable oil
- 3 lamb racks (8 chops each), frenched
- 2 tbsp Dijon mustard

Combine bread crumbs, tomato, thyme, parsley, rosemary, garlic, salt, pepper and melted butter. Mix well and transfer to a shallow dish. Reserve.

Preheat oven to 400°F.

Heat a large ovenproof skillet over high heat and add oil. Season lamb with salt and pepper. Sear lamb, fat side down, for 2 minutes. Turn over and sear for 2 more minutes. Upend racks and sear meaty ends. Turn racks bone side down and place skillet in oven. Roast racks for 7 minutes.

Remove from oven and brush mustard over meat. Roll racks in bread crumb mixture and return to pan, bone side down. Roast for another 10 to 15 minutes or until just pink. Let lamb rest for 5 minutes before carving.

PAIRING: **Bandol red**

Near the Mediterranean coast, not far from Marseilles, lies Bandol, one of Provence's best wine districts. The reds, based mainly on tannic mourvèdre, are big and rugged, with dark-fruit flavours accented by nuances of herbs, spices and leather. Sip red Bandol in its youth and the tannic backbone can be jarring, but in the company of gamy, fatty lamb, the tannins soften while helping cleanse the palate. A blissful match. Alternative: Chilean cabernet sauvignon.

QUINOA SPINACH RISOTTO

Quinoa, a staple in Chile, is a healthful grain. Easy to cook and nutty in flavour, it takes well to all kinds of seasonings. Always wash it before using to get rid of its slightly bitter coating. This side dish is made just like a rice risotto but is much lighter. It's enjoyable as a main course on its own, but paired with the lamb it is outstanding.

Serves 4

2 tbsp olive oil
1 tbsp butter
1 cup chopped onions
2 tsp chopped garlic
1 cup quinoa, washed and drained
½ cup white wine
2 to 3 cups hot vegetable stock or water
3 cups packed baby spinach
½ cup edamame
¼ cup whipping cream
¼ cup grated Parmesan
1 tbsp chopped fresh mint
Salt and freshly ground pepper

Heat olive oil and butter in a medium or large pot over medium heat. Add onions and garlic and sauté until softened, about 2 minutes. Add quinoa and continue to sauté, stirring constantly, for 5 minutes or until nutty-smelling.

Deglaze pan with wine and cook, stirring, until wine has evaporated. Add stock as needed, 1 cup at a time, stirring often until liquid is absorbed before adding more, until quinoa is cooked but still a bit firm, 12 to 15 minutes.

Add spinach and edamame with another splash of stock. Stir until incorporated and spinach is wilted, about 2 minutes. Stir in cream, Parmesan and mint. Season with salt and pepper.

CUSTOM GIN AND TONIC

Born in India, raised everywhere, the gin and tonic found glory in Spain. Yes, Spain, land of Rioja, Cava, rosado and Sherry—and of hordes of sexy youth who frequent *gin tonic* bars, where mixologists have been taking the venerable highball to new heights.

Order a G and T and the show begins. Here's one scenario: A waiter ignites a thyme sprig under an overturned wine glass, seasoning the bowl with fragrant smoke. Into the upright bowl go ice and your choice from as many as two dozen gins and 10 tonic brands, the latter drizzled like a waterfall down the shaft of a long cocktail spoon, supposedly to preserve bubbles. If you try the smoke trick at home, use a fancy big-bowl Burgundy glass and make sure the thyme sprig has been allowed to dry for a day or two so that it smoulders properly. Three or four parts tonic to one part gin is sufficient.

The standard lime wedge is yours if you want it, but many devotees opt for garnishes that resonate with their gin of choice, such as a cucumber spear with Scottish brand Hendrick's, lemon peel with Bombay Sapphire, and rosemary, basil or a couple of tiny Arbequina olives with Spanish Gin Mare.

Granted, there is nothing wrong with the simple classic, improvised in nineteenth-century India by British officers seeking to mask the taste of anti-malarial quinine in their daily tonic water rations. Gin, you might say, was their tonic.

HERBS

Mint: This Mediterranean herb has over 2,000 known varieties. Use spearmint in cooking. It is excellent with carrots, peas and potatoes and in mint sauce for roast lamb. It stars in Asian dishes. English mint is another favourite for cooking, used in sauces and mint jelly and sprinkled over hot new potatoes with plenty of butter. It is also good with cooked peas, all young vegetables and minced beef, as well as in mint juleps. Mint pesto is a flavourful addition to pasta and a condiment for barbecued lamb. Peppermint is used for flavouring desserts and teas. Add a finely chopped leaf to hot chocolate to perk it up. Use fruit mints, such as banana, apple or lemon mint, anywhere some fruit flavour is called for. Dried mint doesn't have much flavour, so use only fresh leaves. Harvest from early April until the end of September.

Parsley: Parsley is one of the best-known herbs, and its aromatic taste is used extensively in many sauces, fish dishes and salads and with cooked vegetables. Unsurpassed for its versatility in the kitchen, it underlines the flavour of foods without ever dominating. High in vitamins A and C, parsley is also known as a natural breath freshener. Curly parsley is an attractive garnish, but for cooking nothing is better than the much tastier flat-leaved Italian variety. Always use fresh parsley; dried lacks flavour. It grows well in the garden and can be harvested from the end of May through September.

Rosemary: One of the most fragrant of herbs, with its pungent, pine-like woody scent, rosemary is the herb of remembrance, and as a culinary herb it creates memorable matchings with lamb, pork and chicken. Use it to flavour biscuits, egg dishes, jams and jellies. A little freshly chopped rosemary complements sweet orange sections. Fresh leaves lose their aroma in a few hours, dried leaves within a few months. A tender perennial, rosemary does not overwinter well in a northern climate, but grows well in pots indoors.

Basil: This favourite annual plant has a peppery, strong, pungent taste that increases with cooking. Sweet broad-leaf basil is the typical grocery store variety; Genovese basil is the best for pesto. Thai basil has a spicy anise-licorice aroma and flavour, excellent in green curries and Vietnamese noodle soups. Always use fresh—dried basil is tasteless. Add fresh basil to pasta sauces and to butter sauces for fish dishes, and use it to garnish a fresh tomato salad. Harvest leaves from the top of the plant from the end of July through August.

Sage: Garden sage has a warm, pungent taste that pairs well with almost all meat dishes, especially fatty meats like pork, goose, duck and sausage. It also complements carrot or pumpkin soups and is a stuffing mainstay. Chop finely and add to tomato dishes or fry whole leaves in oil as a garnish. The most commonly grown culinary variety has grey-green pebbly leaves. Purple or gold sages are lovely, but have milder flavours. Use fruit sages, like pineapple sage, in baking. Harvest from late June until the first heavy frost of fall. Leaves can be used fresh or dried. Sometimes sage continues to grow under the snow, and it always returns the next year.

***Garrigue*:** Yup, another one of those French wine terms with no straight translation. "Herbs" comes close but doesn't quite capture it. *Garrigue* is the low-growing vegetation—specifically lavender, thyme, rosemary and juniper—that grows wild along the Mediterranean coast. You'll know you're in the presence of a certified wine bore (or maybe just a French person) when you hear the word. You can be pretty certain of something else: the wine in question is a red from southern France. Most new wine drinkers have trouble discerning much beyond fruitiness. But when *garrigue* enters the mix—most notably in wines from the Rhone Valley and the Languedoc districts of Saint-Chinian, Minervois and Corbières—it's uncanny, and wonderful. Few flavour signatures are more strongly associated with a place. The French have a word for that too: *terroir*.

LIME BASIL ÉCLAIRS

Choux pastry—the basis for these irresistible éclairs—is surprisingly easy to make. This lime basil custard filling is delectable, but let your imagination be your guide. Think orange cardamom or fennel ginger. Lime leaves give the custard a delicately exotic fragrance. Look for them in Asian groceries. **Makes 20 éclairs**

Lime Basil Pastry Cream:
1½ cups milk
10 fresh basil leaves
3 lime leaves
1 tbsp grated lime zest
5 egg yolks
¼ cup granulated sugar
¼ cup all-purpose flour

Choux Pastry:
¾ cup water
3 tbsp butter
2 tbsp granulated sugar
Pinch kosher salt
¾ cup all-purpose flour
3 eggs
Lime Basil Icing (page 86)

Combine milk, basil leaves, lime leaves and lime zest in a heavy pot. Bring just to a boil over medium heat. Remove from heat and steep for 1 hour. Remove basil and lime leaves.
Whisk together egg yolks and sugar in a separate pot until well combined. Stir in flour. Whisk milk into yolk mixture.
Cook over medium heat, whisking constantly, for 3 minutes or until mixture thickens. Scrape into a bowl and press plastic wrap onto the surface to prevent a skin forming. Refrigerate.
Preheat oven to 400°F. Line a baking sheet with parchment paper.
Combine water, butter, sugar and salt in a medium pot. Bring to a rolling boil over medium-high heat. Reduce heat to medium and add flour all at once. Beat with a wooden spoon until flour is all incorporated. Continue to beat until dough leaves sides of pot, about 2 minutes. Remove from heat.
Beat in eggs, one at a time, with a wooden spoon until fully incorporated and dough is very shiny and soft.
Transfer dough to a piping bag fitted with a large plain tip. Pipe lines of dough onto baking sheet about 3 inches long, 1 inch wide and 1 inch apart. Bake for 20 to 22 minutes or until pastry is brown and crisp. Cool on racks.
Slice éclairs horizontally and fill with about 1 tbsp pastry cream. Glaze with Lime Basil Icing.

PAIRING: **Riesling icewine**

This dessert is like American Key lime pie by way of a French patisserie. Zippy riesling not only pairs well with lime but also contains herbal aromatic compounds called terpenes that are found in many plants, among them basil. Chemistry class was never this tasty. Alternative: sweet, sparkling Asti from Italy, made from the terpene-rich moscato grape.

LIME BASIL ICING

Bring a small pot of water to a boil. Drop in ½ cup basil leaves and cook for 30 seconds. Drain, rinse with cold water and pat dry with paper towels. Combine blanched basil, ¾ cup icing sugar, 1 tbsp butter, 1 tbsp lime juice and 1 tsp grated lime zest in a mini chopper or a small food processor. Whirl until fully puréed and bright green. If icing is too firm, add a few more drops lime juice. Spoon icing over éclairs. Let stand until icing is firm.

CLASSIC POACHED SALMON WITH SPICY GREEN HERB MAYONNAISE

This is one of the most delightful ways to eat salmon. It feeds a large group of people and is perfect for festive lunches or buffet dinners. It doubles beautifully. I prefer to poach whole salmon on the bone, because that way it retains its moisture, but since most people prefer not to deal with the bones, I developed this recipe using boneless fillets. It gives the same results without the inconvenience of bones. In this recipe you put one piece of salmon on top of the other to approximate the thickness of a bone-in piece of salmon.

Serves 12 generously

2 centre-cut salmon fillets (2 lb/900 g each)
Salt and freshly ground pepper
6 cups court bouillon (page 88)

Preheat oven to 450°F.

Season each piece of salmon with salt and pepper and place one on top of the other, thinner edge to thicker, skin side out. Wrap salmon in cheesecloth and place in a deep baking dish. Place dish on a baking sheet. Measure salmon vertically at its thickest part to determine how long to cook it.

Bring court bouillon to a simmer. Pour over fish until it comes three-quarters of the way up the side of the fish (to ensure even poaching).

Cover baking dish tightly with foil, transfer to oven and cook for 6 minutes per inch of thickness. Remove from oven, uncover, carefully turn fish over and cool in broth.

Place fish on a serving platter, using the cheesecloth to help with the transfer. Unfold cheesecloth and remove top layer of skin. Using cheesecloth again, turn salmon over and place skinned side down on serving platter. Remove cheesecloth and top layer of skin. Keep fillets together, mimicking the look of bone-in salmon.

Slice down through the centre of salmon to divide in half, then cut into portions and serve with Spicy Green Herb Mayonnaise (page 88).

PAIRING: **Unoaked chardonnay**

The herbal mayo demands something crisp. The rich salmon flesh begs for a wine with weight. That challenge is met beautifully by unoaked chardonnay. Most Chablis fall into that category, but there are now many fine examples from the New World, where producers helpfully include the word *unoaked* on the label. Red option: crisp Beaujolais.

COURT BOUILLON

Use this for poaching salmon or other large fish or for making fish soups. Court bouillon can be strained after poaching and refrigerated for a week or frozen for up to 6 months. Add water to top it up, if needed.

Makes about 6 cups

- 1 onion, sliced
- 1 carrot, sliced
- 1 bay leaf
- 3 sprigs fresh parsley
- 6 cups water
- ½ cup dry white wine
- ¼ cup white wine vinegar
- 4 star anise
- 2 tsp peppercorns
- ½ tsp dried thyme

Bring all ingredients to a boil in a large pot over high heat. Reduce heat and simmer for 15 minutes.

SPICY GREEN HERB MAYONNAISE

This also makes a tasty dip for vegetables.

Makes about 1½ cups

- 2 cups arugula
- ¼ cup chopped green onions
- 2 tbsp chopped fresh basil
- 2 tbsp chopped fresh mint
- 2 tbsp chopped fresh flat-leaf parsley
- 1 cup mayonnaise
- 1 tbsp lemon juice
- 1 tsp Thai green curry paste
- Salt and freshly ground pepper

Place all ingredients in a food processor and process until mixture is combined but still has a little texture. Season with salt and pepper.

MINT SALSA VERDE

This fine sauce is amazing with grilled lamb or chicken, asparagus or broccoli. It is also excellent as a marinade for lamb racks. Turn it into a dip by adding about ½ cup mayonnaise. **Makes about ¾ cup**

3 green onions, finely chopped
1 cup packed fresh mint leaves
½ cup packed fresh parsley leaves
1 tbsp white wine vinegar
1 tsp granulated sugar
1 tsp chopped jalapeño pepper
½ tsp coarsely chopped garlic
2 anchovy fillets, chopped
1 tbsp chopped capers
⅓ cup olive oil
Salt to taste

Combine green onions, mint, parsley, vinegar, sugar, jalapeño and garlic in a food processor. Pulse to mix.
Add anchovies and capers. Pulse until chunky.
Stir in oil. Add salt to taste.

SAVOURY APPLE AND THYME TART

A superb tart that is served as a savoury first course. Make individual tarts if desired or bake in a 9-inch round tart pan with a removable base.

Serves 6

Shortcrust Pastry:
1½ cups all-purpose flour
½ tsp salt
½ cup unsalted butter, cubed
4 to 5 tbsp cold water
1 tbsp white vinegar or lemon juice

Garnish:
3 cups baby arugula
1 tbsp olive oil
2 tsp lemon juice
Salt and freshly ground pepper

Filling:
2 large Pink Lady apples, cored and sliced ¼-inch thick (about 3 cups)
1 cup apple cider
1 egg, lightly beaten with 1 tbsp cream
2 tbsp Dijon mustard
2 cups grated aged cheddar
2 tsp fresh thyme leaves

Sift together flour and salt in a large bowl. Cut in butter until mixture resembles coarse bread crumbs. Alternatively, use a food processor.

Combine water and vinegar in a separate bowl. Sprinkle 4 tbsp of the liquid over flour mixture, gathering mixture together with your fingertips until a dough forms and adding additional liquid if mixture is too dry. Knead together for 1 minute. Press into a disc and wrap with plastic wrap. Refrigerate for 1 hour.

Preheat oven to 375°F.

Bring apples and cider to a boil in a medium skillet. Reduce heat to medium and simmer for 10 minutes or until apples are tender. With a slotted spoon, remove apples to a bowl. Continue simmering cider until it is thick and syrupy and reduced to 2 tbsp, about 5 more minutes.

Roll out pastry on a lightly floured surface into a 10-inch square, ¼ inch thick. Brush the outside inch with egg wash. Brush remaining pastry with mustard. Sprinkle with half the cheddar. Top with apples, thyme and remaining cheddar. Drizzle with cider syrup. Fold up edges of pastry over the apples.

Bake until crust is golden and cooked through, about 30 minutes. Cool for 5 minutes before serving.

Toss arugula with olive oil and lemon juice in a large bowl. Season with salt and pepper. Top tart with arugula salad and slice into 6 portions.

Thyme: Thyme has a pungent, tangy taste that highlights the flavour of poultry and red meats, fish, stuffing and stews. Because it has a strong flavour, use with caution. Often associated with strength and happiness, in the Middle Ages it was a symbol of courage, and sprigs of it were embroidered into the clothes of Crusaders. French thyme has narrow leaves and is distinctly greyer and sweeter than English, which is the most common variety, with broad dark green leaves. Citrusy lemon thyme is perfect with chicken and pork. Harvest just before it flowers in late June until the end of September. If conditions are not too harsh, thyme will return year after year.

SMOKY

smoked paprika • smoked fish • smoked meats
smoked cheeses • smoked salts • Lapsang Souchong
Earl Grey • smoked oysters • barbecue • smoked ham
honey • smoky water • spareribs • poblanos
chipotles • bacon

IT PROBABLY STARTED IN A CAVE.

Butchered flesh that was hung on twine to thwart pesky scavengers inevitably absorbed fumes from a warming fire. (Chimneys and carbon-monoxide sensors were still a few epochs away.) Our sooty-pelted ancestors surely noticed that the day's catch spoiled not nearly as quickly. It probably tasted better too. Smoked meat was born.

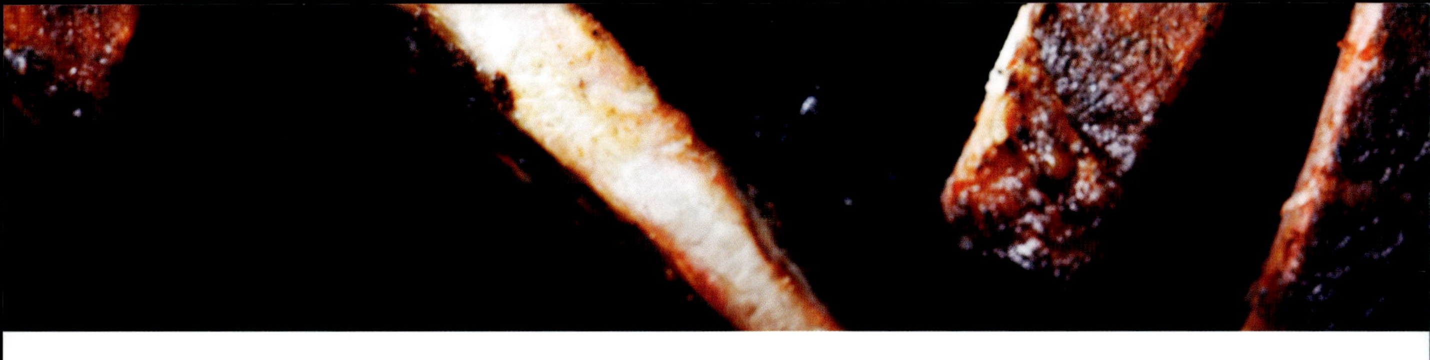

Along with drying, salt-curing, freezing, pickling and fermenting, smoking is a fundamental technique for extending shelf life. Bacteria are the great vandals of tomorrow's dinner, and phenols in smoke impede their insidious growth. Smoking is found in virtually all cultures and is used with countless foods, from salmon, kippers, oysters and eels to tea-smoked Szechuan duck, bib-staining southern barbecue and the smoked meat sandwiches of Montreal. Although still used chiefly as a preservative in less developed societies, smoking today is more commonly practised for pure pleasure, to impart outdoorsy flavour and tenderize tough cuts of meat.

You don't need a fancy smoker or poorly ventilated cave to work smoke into your culinary repertoire. We often add a pinch of smoked paprika or smoked sea salt to meat or fish. We also like to cook with blazing heat on our back patios. The fats and oils that drip to the bottom of the barbecue ignite and smoulder, releasing fumes that rise up to infuse the food. Chinese chefs harness the flavour through such ingredients as toasted sesame oil and pan-roasted Szechuan peppers or simply by cranking up their oil-seasoned woks to volcanic temperatures. Where there's fire, there's smoke.

The beverage world has come late to the bonfire, but it's been making up for lost time, nowhere more conspicuously than with whisky. If one could melt charcoal into a tumbler, it might taste a lot like the astonishingly sooty spirits of the island of Islay, where the centuries-old custom of drying barley malt over peat-fuelled fires remains alive and well.

Barrels provide another conduit, both in whisky and wine. During construction, coopers typically char the interior of oak staves over an open flame. American bourbon, aged for at least two years in new, heavily charred oak, owes its smoky overtones to wood, the ideal complement to the whisky's sweet, corn-based mellowness. Barrel-aged chardonnay also sees toasty action.

In our homes, both of us love to set the stage with cocktails based around peated whiskies and bourbon. But for the smoky main course, boldly fruity wines, such as California red zinfandel or Australian shiraz, are often better bets. They add a sweet counterpoint to the aromatic char. Like jam on toast.

Menu 1

SALMON WITH A CUP OF TEA

Asian Shrimp Cocktail

Tea-Smoked Salmon

Bok Choy Stir-Fry

Smoky Dark Chocolate Bars

Not all smoking is done on the barbecue. In Asia the wok is used for smoking on the stovetop, and this is good way to smoke in your own kitchen. Shrimp cocktail is always a winner as an appetizer; our recipe has a spiced but fresh flavour that highlights the smokiness of the salmon. The smoky, spicy bittersweet dessert mixes elements of these flavours to give an all-over punch to the palate.

ASIAN SHRIMP COCKTAIL

Grilled shrimp with a spicy green curry dip will make you forget overcooked shrimp with the ketchup-based cocktail sauce of old. Serve this as a first course with a salad of Asian greens or as an hors d'oeuvre with some little forks for dipping.

Serves 4 to 6

1 can (400 mL) coconut milk
4 lime leaves (or 1 tbsp grated lime zest)
2 tbsp lime juice
2 tbsp fish sauce
1 tbsp granulated sugar
1 tbsp chopped fresh ginger
2 tsp Thai green curry paste
2 tbsp chopped fresh mint
2 tbsp chopped fresh cilantro
1 lb (450 g) large shrimp, peeled
Salt
¼ cup unsweetened shredded coconut

Combine coconut milk, lime leaves, lime juice, fish sauce, sugar, ginger and curry paste in a large skillet over high heat and bring to a boil. Reduce heat to low and simmer for 20 minutes or until reduced by about three-quarters—the sauce should be the consistency of whipping cream. Stir in 1 tbsp each of mint and cilantro. Cool.

Divide sauce in half in 2 bowls; reserve 1 bowl of sauce for dipping sauce. Season shrimp with salt and stir into remaining half of sauce. Marinate shrimp for 30 minutes.

Preheat grill to high. Remove shrimp from marinade and discard marinade. Grill shrimp for 1 to 2 minutes per side or until pink and slightly curled. Cool.

Stir coconut and remaining mint and cilantro into dipping sauce. Serve with shrimp.

PAIRING: **Reverse Saketini**

One good cocktail deserves another. In this case, I'd suggest a "reverse" Saketini, the Asian-inspired twist on the classic gin martini, which swaps sake for dry vermouth. By leading with a Japanese rice beverage (and using only a splash of gin), you'll reduce the alcohol while retaining enough botanicals from the gin to echo the fragrant dipping sauce. Mix 2 oz good-quality cold sake with 1 oz gin in a cocktail shaker with ice. Shake and strain into a V-shaped martini glass. Or, if you want to use a martini glass for serving the shrimp, try the drink in a tumbler for aesthetic contrast. Garnish with a slice of cucumber or a lime wheel. Prefer wine? Opt for a fruity, aromatic white, such as grassy New Zealand sauvignon blanc or grapey, dry muscat.

TURNING YOUR BARBECUE INTO A SMOKER

Small charcoal smokers with automatic lighters are a good option for would-be smokers, as are large smokers. But if you are a very occasional dabbler like me, you can get your gas barbecue to do the job for you.

The first step is to make smoking pouches. They make all the difference in gas barbecue smoking. Cedar, applewood, mesquite, hickory and cherrywood chips all work well. Soak the wood chips for 30 minutes. Lay a large square of foil on the counter and loosely pack it with 2 cups chips. Fold all sides over to seal the pouch. Punch holes with a fork in both sides of the pouch. One pouch smokes for about 45 minutes to 1 hour, so make a few at a time so you have them on hand to replace the used ones.

Start your barbecue on high and place the smoking pouch on the back burner. Immediately turn off two front burners and keep the third one at medium-low. Close the lid and heat for 10 minutes. You should see smoke rising. The barbecue temperature should hover between 210 and 230°F after you add the meat. Use the same method with 2-burner or 4-burner barbecues. It is all about maintaining the right temperature.

Heavily sprinkle the meat with rub and place it on the turned-off side of the grill. Pork and brisket take 12 to 14 hours to smoke on the grill, ribs 7 to 10.

Alternatively, smoke meat for 4 hours in the barbecue, then wrap in foil and move to a 225°F oven for the remaining time. This method works just as well, with the meat juicy and tender but not quite as smoky.

All the recipes in this chapter can be made without smoking the meat. Instead of smoke, you will have a nice charred barbecue flavour, which is fabulous in itself.

TEA-SMOKED SALMON

In Asia, tea leaves are often used as a smoking agent. Tea provides a light, not overwhelming, smoke which gives pizzazz to this salmon—everybody loves its slightly smoky, gingery flavour. Smoking the fish on the barbecue keeps the smoke out of the house. If you do use the stovetop to smoke, take the pan outside before taking the lid off. Serve with rice. This salmon is also good cold. **Serves 4**

2 tbsp soy sauce
2 tbsp Sherry
1 tbsp vegetable oil
2 tsp grated fresh ginger
1 tsp cracked peppercorns
½ tsp kosher salt
1 skin-on salmon fillet (2 lb/900 g)

Smoking Mixture:
½ cup tea leaves, preferably Lapsang Souchong or Earl Grey
2 tbsp packed brown sugar
¼ cup rice

Combine soy sauce, Sherry, oil, ginger, peppercorns and salt in a small bowl. Rub marinade over salmon flesh. Marinate for 30 minutes at room temperature.

Line a wok with heavy-duty foil. Place tea and sugar in wok and top with rice. Place wok on barbecue on high heat until wok is smoking. Spray a round rack with nonstick cooking spray and place in wok. Place salmon on rack skin side down. Cover wok and close barbecue lid.

Smoke salmon for 15 minutes for a light smoke. Remove wok from heat and leave covered for 5 minutes before serving.

PAIRING: **Alsatian riesling**

I don't know why it works chemically, but smoked fish adores riesling, whether the wine is dry, like most Alsatian and North American examples, or off-dry, as in many German varieties. Maybe it's because the bold fruit sings through the smoke while the lively acidity dances with the delicate texture. As a cocktail alternative, you may want to try the Red and Green, page 198 in our "Earthy" chapter, a mix of delicately smoky Johnnie Walker Scotch with green tea—smoke and tea in your glass to match what's on the plate.

BOK CHOY STIR-FRY

I serve this simple, tasty side with all sorts of dishes when I want a green vegetable. If you can't find baby bok choy, use several larger ones and separate into leaves.

Serves 4

2 tbsp vegetable oil
1 tsp grated fresh ginger
1 tsp chopped garlic
4 cups baby bok choy
¼ cup chicken stock
1 tbsp soy sauce
Salt and freshly ground pepper

Heat oil in a wok or skillet over medium-high heat. Add ginger, garlic and bok choy. Stir-fry until bok choy is slightly wilted. Add chicken stock, cover and steam for 2 minutes or until bok choy is crisp-tender. Uncover and reduce liquid until a spoonful remains. Add soy sauce and season with salt and pepper.

SMOKY DARK CHOCOLATE BARS

Dark, dark chocolate, craggy and rocky, a bit like the moon's surface. The espelette pepper in this brownie-like bar highlights the chocolateness and gives a background of heat and a little smoke. These are one of the best bars I have made. If you can't find espelette, use ground chili flakes. **Makes 16 to 20 bars**

- 8 oz (225 g) dark chocolate (64 to 70% cocoa), chopped
- 1 cup unsalted butter, at room temperature
- 1½ cups granulated sugar
- 4 eggs
- 1 cup all-purpose flour
- ½ tsp salt
- ½ tsp ground espelette pepper
- 2 tsp vanilla
- ½ cup plum jam

Preheat oven to 350°F. Grease an 8-inch square cake pan and line bottom with parchment paper.

Melt chocolate in a heavy pot over low heat, stirring occasionally. Set aside to cool.

Cream butter with sugar until fluffy and pale, about 2 minutes. Beat in eggs, one at a time, until incorporated. Beat in flour, salt and espelette. Stir in vanilla and melted chocolate.

Pour into prepared pan and smooth top. Place 16 dollops of jam on top of batter. Run a sharp knife through batter to swirl in the jam.

Bake for 28 to 30 minutes or until a cake tester comes out with a few crumbs attached. You want the centre to be slightly wobbly. Transfer to a rack and cool in pan.

PAIRING: **Botrytized semillon**

The white semillon grape is particularly susceptible to invasion by a beneficial fungus known as *Botrytis cinerea*, or "noble rot." The grey mould extracts water from the pulp, intensifying the fruit and acidity, and yielding a rich, honeyed dessert elixir with a delectable, balanced opulence that would round out these bars. Sauternes from Bordeaux is the most famous example, especially the expensive glory made by Château d'Yquem, but there are many fine versions from Australia (such as De Bortoli Noble One) and California (Beringer Nightingale is excellent).

Menu 2

A FAMILY MENU RIGHT OFF THE GRILL

Grilled Bread and Vegetable Salad
Grilled Hanger Steak with Smoky Corn and Tomato Salsa
Grilled Peanut Butter and Banana Bread Sandwiches

Grilling the whole meal on the barbecue—salad, main, side and dessert—certainly saves cleanup time but also gives that special smoky taste to all the courses. Kids and adults alike love the peanut butter and banana bread sandwiches. Grilling them is a whole new way of enjoying them.

GRILLED BREAD AND VEGETABLE SALAD

Tomato and bread salads pop up everywhere these days. In this new take, I grill lots of summery vegetables and then toss them with the bread. You'll still need some tomatoes to give enough moisture. **Serves 6**

1 ciabatta loaf
2 garlic cloves, crushed (about 2 tsp)
2 tbsp finely chopped fresh basil
1 tbsp finely chopped fresh oregano
½ cup olive oil
1 red onion, thickly sliced
2 Asian eggplants, cut in half lengthwise
1 summer squash, cut in half lengthwise
2 zucchini, cut in half lengthwise
1 yellow pepper, cut in half and ribs removed
12 cherry tomatoes, halved, or quartered if they are very large (about 1½ cups)
Salt and freshly ground pepper

Lemon Dijon Vinaigrette:
3 tbsp lemon juice
1 tbsp fresh thyme leaves
1 tbsp Dijon mustard
Pinch sugar
½ cup olive oil

Slice the ciabatta loaf horizontally. Stir together garlic, basil, oregano and olive oil in a small bowl. Brush both sides of bread and all vegetables with oil.

Preheat grill to high. Place bread on grill and cook with the lid closed, turning twice, for about 4 minutes or until good grill marks have appeared. You may need to brush with more oil. Reserve.

Add onion, eggplants, squash, zucchini and yellow pepper to grill. Grill onion and squash for 9 to 10 minutes or until softened, turning once. Grill eggplants, zucchini and pepper halves, turning once, for 5 to 6 minutes or until tender and grill-marked. Transfer to a chopping board and cut vegetables into 1-inch chunks. Tear or cut grilled ciabatta into 2-inch pieces. Toss 4 cups torn bread with grilled vegetables and cherry tomatoes in a large bowl, keeping the remaining bread for snacking. Season with salt and pepper.

Combine lemon juice, thyme, mustard and sugar in a small bowl. Whisk in olive oil until emulsified. Season with salt and pepper.

Toss dressing with vegetables and bread. You may have dressing left over depending on how well you coat the salad.

PAIRING: **Vernaccia di San Gimignano**

Grilled bread and tomato salad is popular in Tuscany, where it goes by the name panzanella. The star white wine of the region, vernaccia di San Gimignano, is based on the crisp, citrusy white grape vernaccia. The virtues that make this simple and popular variety attractive on a sunny patio work in its favour here. The salad is zesty and fragrant, demanding little of a wine besides clean refreshment, vernaccia's virtue. Alternative: zippy, low-alcohol vinho verde from Portugal.

ALTERNATIVE STEAKS

The quality of the meat you buy makes all the difference. Good-quality naturally raised or organic meat has flavour, texture and juiciness. There's no need to go heavy on the seasonings, since most of the flavour is already built in. Many steak cuts are available today that don't carry the hefty price tag of New York or rib-eyes but have just as much flavour. These steaks include hanger, tri-tip, flatiron and bavette. They are all cut from muscles that work a little harder than the filet or rib-eye. This workout gives them more flavour but not quite the tenderness. They are usually found at butcher shops rather than supermarkets. These steaks are more chewy if they aren't sliced correctly. They must be cut against the grain for tender, juicy eating.

The hanger is my favourite. It's juicy, with loads of flavour and texture.

The tri-tip, shaped like a triangle and thickest in the middle, is soft and juicy, making it popular with people who look for tenderness first. It also delivers both medium and rare meat because of its shape. Another benefit to the shape: it's easy to slice.

The flatiron, or top blade, has a slightly gamier taste and is really flavourful, like grass-fed beef.

Bavette is tender but the least flavourful of the group.

GRILLED HANGER STEAK WITH SMOKY CORN AND TOMATO SALSA

Grilling steaks like hanger offer great flavour at a price that is easy on the wallet. It must be carved against the grain for tenderness. The easy marinade works for all types of steak, and pork and lamb too. **Serves 6**

2 tbsp Dijon mustard
2 tbsp red wine vinegar
1 tbsp chopped fresh thyme
1 tsp chopped garlic
1 tsp chili powder
1 tsp honey
¼ cup olive oil
1 hanger steak (2 lb/900 g)
Salt and freshly ground pepper

Combine mustard, vinegar, thyme, garlic, chili powder and honey in a small bowl. Whisk in olive oil. Pour marinade over steak and marinate in the refrigerator for 4 hours or overnight. Remove steak from refrigerator 1 hour before grilling to bring it to room temperature.

Preheat grill to high.

Season steak with salt and pepper and grill for 4 to 6 minutes per side for medium-rare (depending on thickness) or until desired degree of doneness. Remove from grill and let rest for 5 minutes.

Slice steak against grain and serve with Smoky Corn and Tomato Salsa (page 110).

PAIRING: **Monastrell**

Here's an incentive to get to know one of the world's greatest bargain reds. More commonly known by the French name mourvèdre, monastrell from Spain is a tannic grape typically used to give backbone to blends with spicy syrah and supple grenache, as in France's vaunted Châteauneuf-du-Pape district. Spanish wines based on monastrell are compelling solo players, particularly when crafted from the concentrated berries of precious old vines in the regions of Jumilla and Valencia. They offer both rich fruit to complement the salsa's smoky paprika and dry tannins to contrast with the meat's juices.

SMOKY CORN AND TOMATO SALSA

The smoked paprika in this salsa gives a real punch to the steak.

Serves 4

3 ears corn, shucked
3 plum tomatoes, cut in half lengthwise
1 red pepper, cut in quarters
3 tbsp olive oil
Salt and freshly ground pepper
¾ cup chopped red onion

Dressing:
3 tbsp olive oil
1 tbsp lemon juice
1 tsp coriander seeds
¾ tsp smoked paprika
2 tbsp chopped fresh cilantro

Preheat grill to high. Brush corn, tomatoes and red pepper with oil. Season with salt and pepper. Grill corn for about 3 minutes per side or until kernels are golden. Grill tomatoes until skin is shrivelled and flesh is soft, 2 minutes per side. Grill peppers for about 4 minutes per side or until skin is blackened. Cool.

Peel skin from pepper and discard. Dice pepper and transfer to a medium bowl. Slice corn from cobs and add to pepper with red onion.

Peel charred skin from tomatoes and discard. Place tomatoes in food processor with oil, lemon juice, coriander seeds and paprika. Process until smooth. Stir in cilantro. Toss vegetables with dressing.

Smoked Spanish paprika gives a smoky, spicy taste to everything it flavours. It is produced in Spain from pimento chilies that are smoked over wood and then ground. It is indispensable in Spanish cooking, flavouring everything from chorizo to paella. It comes in three strengths: mild, medium (also called bittersweet) and hot. Take your pick in strengths. Both Beppi and I love the hot.

GRILLED PEANUT BUTTER AND BANANA BREAD SANDWICHES

This is a kid favourite, but I've never known an adult to resist it either. These dessert treats can also be made in a skillet, although you lose that smoky taste. If peanut butter is not your thing, then use Nutella, or for a nut-free option try cream cheese and jam or a non-nut butter. You can make the banana bread batter in the food processor.

Makes 4 whole or 8 half sandwiches

Banana Bread:

2 cups all-purpose flour
1 tsp baking soda
½ tsp kosher salt
½ cup butter, softened
1 cup granulated sugar
2 eggs
2 cups mashed very ripe bananas

Filling:

½ cup peanut butter
¼ cup mascarpone
¼ cup butter, softened

Preheat oven to 350°F. Grease a 9- × 5-inch loaf pan.

Combine flour, baking soda and salt in a bowl.

Cream together butter and sugar in another bowl with an electric mixer until light and fluffy. Beat in eggs, one at a time. Beat in half of the flour mixture. Beat in bananas, and then beat in remaining flour mixture until just combined.

Pour batter into loaf pan and bake for 60 to 70 minutes or until a toothpick inserted in the centre of the bread comes out clean. Cool in pan for 5 minutes and then turn out onto a rack. Cool completely. Cut 8 slices about ½ inch thick.

Combine peanut butter and mascarpone until well blended. Spread 4 slices of banana bread with peanut butter mixture. Top with remaining slices and press down to compress slightly.

Preheat grill to medium-high. Brush both sides of sandwiches with butter. Grill sandwiches for about 2 minutes per side or until grill-marked and slightly toasted. Cut in half and serve with ice cream.

PAIRING: **Stout**

What's a sandwich without a cold beer? The roasted-malt character of creamy dark stout sometimes carries notes of coffee and dark chocolate, which would make for a harmonious, offbeat pairing. Alternatively, there's always real coffee, a natural foil for this dessert, especially when it's served with ice cream. For added decadence, spike it with a splash of Irish cream liqueur, such as Baileys.

Menu 3

BONES

The Definitive Stockyards Spareribs

Miami Ribs Miami Style

Kickass Chicken Wings

Bistecca Fiorentina

Meat on the bone is always tastier and juicier than boneless cuts. Bones add a certain lip-smacking flavour to meat. Think rib steak compared with a rib-eye. Chewing on bones is an art unto itself. Strong teeth help, and a desire to get all the flavour out of the bones. For anyone who has grown up in Asia, Europe or Africa, bones make the meal. Instead of a full menu, in this section I've given you a variety of different bones with meat on them to grill. Serve any of these with a salad and potatoes or grilled bread for a simple, smoky meal.

THE DEFINITIVE STOCKYARDS SPARERIBS

Perfect smoked ribs. In this recipe, from Chef Tom Davis at the excellent Stockyards restaurant in Toronto, the meat is juicy and smoky with a slight sweetness that balances the heat. This looks like a long recipe, but the ribs need virtually no attention except for spraying every hour. Serve with baked beans and pickles.

Serves 6 to 8

Rub:
2 tbsp paprika
2 tbsp chili powder
1 tbsp jerk seasoning
1 tbsp celery seeds
1 tbsp kosher salt
1 tsp cayenne
1 tsp ground cumin
1 tsp ground sage
Pepper to taste

Mop Sauce:
½ cup cider vinegar
¼ cup apple juice
1 tbsp hot sauce
½ tsp kosher salt

Barbecue Sauce:
½ cup cider vinegar
⅓ cup ketchup
1 tbsp brown sugar
1 tbsp prepared mustard
1 tsp hot sauce
¼ tsp hot smoked paprika

2 large racks side spareribs

Combine all ingredients in a bowl to make the rub.

Combine cider vinegar, apple juice, hot sauce and salt to make the mop sauce. Stir until uniform. Transfer to a spray bottle.

Combine cider vinegar, ketchup, brown sugar, mustard, hot sauce and paprika in a pot to make the barbecue sauce. Whisk. Cook over medium-low heat for 2 minutes or until flavours meld. Reserve.

Preheat grill to high and prepare smoking pouches (see page 99).

Coat ribs with rub. Turn off all but one burner (the one at the back) and reduce heat to about 225°F. Place ribs on barbecue bone side down, close lid and smoke for 1 hour. Replace smoking pouch and spray ribs with mop sauce. Continue to smoke, replacing smoking pouches and spraying every hour, for 7 to 9 hours or until ribs are tender and practically falling off the bone.

Brush barbecue sauce over ribs 15 minutes before the end of cooking time. Continue smoking until sauce is glazed. Cut into ribs and serve with remaining barbecue sauce.

PAIRING: **Southern French red**

Embrace your inner caveman. Resist the urge, should you have one, to squander elite Bordeaux on these delectably messy bones. You'll want a red with a figurative bib around its collar, such as gutsy Minervois, Corbières or Côtes du Rhône. The wines' herbal essence adds verve to the succulent meat, while acidity and tannins help cleanse the palate. Just as compelling: a bitter India Pale Ale. For the full caveman experience, drink it straight from the bottle.

MIAMI RIBS MIAMI STYLE

These are a family favourite. Miami ribs are thinly sliced cross-cut short ribs. They are available from butchers and many supermarkets. They need to be marinated for tenderness, but they only take a couple of minutes on a very hot grill. Smoking is an option here because the ribs do not grill for very long. Set the smoking pouches over the hot grill and wait until the smoke is swirling before starting the ribs. Serve with a corn and rice salad.

Serves 4

Mustard Barbecue Sauce:
¼ cup Dijon mustard
¼ cup olive oil
3 tbsp lemon juice
2 tbsp chopped fresh rosemary
1 tbsp Worcestershire sauce
2 tsp chopped garlic
½ tsp smoked Spanish paprika
½ tsp Asian chili sauce

12 racks Miami ribs
2 tbsp vegetable oil

Combine mustard, olive oil, lemon juice, rosemary, Worcestershire sauce, garlic, paprika and chili sauce in a small bowl and whisk together. Brush sauce over both sides of ribs and marinate in the refrigerator for 12 hours. Remove from refrigerator 1 hour before grilling.

Preheat grill to high.

Remove ribs from sauce (reserving sauce) and brush with vegetable oil. Place ribs on grill and grill for 2 minutes, brushing on extra sauce. Flip over and grill for another 1 or 2 minutes, depending on thickness, or until nicely grill-marked but still a little pink inside.

PAIRING: **Red zinfandel**

It's not far from Miami to California, is it? At least not where these ribs and a suitable wine are concerned. Zinfandel, the Golden State's heritage grape, will wrap its big, cuddly, jammy arms around the spicy slices of beefy glory while adding its own kick of cracked pepper. Just make sure it's red zin, not the light and too-sweet pink juice known as "white" zinfandel.

The Smoking Gun: A tool of modernist cuisine that works wonderfully in a home kitchen. Easy to set up, it uses ground charcoal. You turn it on and smoke—cheese, tomatoes, anything your heart desires.

PEATED WHISKIES

I became a Scotch man in 1978, the year I no longer had to use fake ID. My seducer was Lagavulin, a splurge shared with my older brother, John. Big bro and I had been dabbling with Jack Daniel's, but we were precocious in our thirst, keen to trade up to then-novel single malt, just as we were abandoning three-chord pop for jazzy Steely Dan. It was a baptism not by fire but by smoke. "Whoa, tastes like Dad's ashtray," I said of the Lagavulin. "Yeah," John said. "Pour me another."

There was no turning back. Smoky whiskies were as raw as rock yet refined as jazz. They also came with added cachet: centuries of history. Before coke, oil and natural gas became standard fuels to dry malted barley, distillers across Scotland relied on peat, an ancient form of decomposed vegetation. As sphagnum and other mosses rot in waterlogged bogs over thousands of years, anaerobic conditions trap carbon rather than releasing it as carbon dioxide, creating a combustible, pungent fuel.

Isolated from railways that eventually carried modern fuels across the Scottish mainland, Islay, a windswept island off the west coast, upheld the peat-reek tradition. It's home to Lagavulin, Laphroaig and Ardbeg, three of the smokiest whiskies on the planet, as well as to Bowmore, Bruichladdich and Caol Ila, all brands on heavy rotation on my home bar.

Besides smoke, peat can impart nuances of seaweed, salt, damp earth and iodine, a glorious mélange that gets the hyperboles flowing. Now I think of Lagavulin as an ashtray in a hospital ward by the ocean.

Rauchbier: Restless rejuvenators of Old World tradition, craft brewers in North America sadly have been slow on the uptake with this one. For good reason. It takes special effort. The name literally means "smoked beer" in German, and the style owes its essence to an involved process whereby malted barley is dried not in a conventional indirect-heat kiln but over open flame, the beer analogue to peated single malt. Dieu du Ciel in Montreal makes one called Charbonnière (Coalwoman). Samuel Adams in Boston brews up Bonfire Rauchbier. And fine German imports occasionally drift across the sea.

KICKASS CHICKEN WINGS

Ancho chili powder has a chocolaty taste and is not overwhelmingly hot. If you can't find it, substitute regular chili powder. Buy Italian passata for the tomato sauce or purée 1 cup of canned tomatoes with some of their juice. I grill the wings for a few minutes before adding the barbecue sauce, because otherwise the high sugar content causes the skin to burn.

Serves 4 to 6

1 cup tomato sauce
¼ cup cider vinegar
3 tbsp brown sugar
2 tbsp Dijon mustard
1 tbsp ancho chili powder
1 tbsp soy sauce
1 tbsp sambal oelek or other hot chili sauce
1 tsp chopped garlic
1 tsp chopped fresh ginger
4 lb (1.8 kg) chicken wings, separated at joint, wing tips discarded
2 tbsp vegetable oil
Salt and freshly ground pepper

Combine tomato sauce, cider vinegar, brown sugar, mustard, chili powder, soy sauce, sambal oelek, garlic and ginger in a small pot. Bring to a boil over high heat, stirring to dissolve sugar, and simmer for 10 minutes or until sauce thickens.

Preheat grill to medium-high and prepare a smoking pouch (see page 99). Place smoking pouch on the rear grill. Wait until the smoke swirls before adding wings.

Toss chicken wings with oil, salt and pepper. Place wings on grill, close lid and grill for 3 minutes. Flip wings and grill for another 3 minutes. Brush liberally with sauce and turn over again. Repeat brushing with sauce and turning every 3 minutes or until wings are cooked through, 12 to 20 minutes total, depending on their size.

PAIRING: **Pilsner**

It's heresy to suggest anything but beer for spicy wings, the go-to pairing for millions of North American sports fans, even though I prefer a rich red wine. Beer, counterintuitively, exacerbates spice by spreading the heat all over your palate. If beer's your preference, avoid light, industrial lager, which is too neutral and feeble. Opt instead for a bitter German or Czech-style pilsner, basically a quality-made lager with solid bitterness. The high hop content adds mouth-watering zip and citrus tang for refreshment. Wine-wise, I suggest jammy styles such as Australian shiraz and Californian zinfandel because the fruit gives a big bear hug to the spice and finds its way through the smoke.

BISTECCA FIORENTINA

This traditional steak of Florence is world-renowned. The best bistecca comes from the Chianina cattle bred in Italy for their rich flavour and relative leanness. The steak has a lot of character, with layers of flavour and a slightly buttery texture. Because the meat is so tasty it doesn't need many additions. Although some cattle farmers in North America are raising this particular breed, often the closest we can buy here is Angus, though some grass-fed breeds have a similar flavour. The steak is always the porterhouse cut and serves two or more people.

Serves 2 to 3

1 porterhouse steak (2 lb/900 g and 2 inches thick)
2 tbsp olive oil
Kosher salt and freshly ground pepper

Garnish:
1 tbsp olive oil (optional)
Maldon or other finishing salt

Preheat grill to high. Brush steak with oil and season with salt and pepper. Grill for 7 to 8 minutes per side for rare, turning once. Let sit for 10 minutes.
Carve off both the filet and the sirloin. Slice both the filet and the sirloin into ½-inch slices. Drizzle a little olive oil on steak if desired and season with Maldon salt. Serve the bone to the one who loves it best.
Bistecca is finished in different ways according to the household. Here are some alternatives:
Serve with lemon quarters.
Drizzle with a drop of balsamic vinegar.
Finely chop garlic and parsley and sprinkle on steak.
Serve with an arugula salad on the plate.

PAIRING: **Tuscan cabernet sauvignon or merlot**

A buddy and I once blissfully paired Florentine steak with Le Serre Nuove, the second wine of Ornellaia, the great super-Tuscan red. We were on an inner-city apartment balcony overlooking a parking lot, but who cares about the view when you've got good friends, great beef and a perfectly matched bottle of wine? Convention would dictate a classic Tuscan red based on the sangiovese grape, such as Chianti or Brunello di Montalcino. That's all in the past, though. I think tannic, richer cabernet sauvignon or merlot work better, and you'll find those French grapes in Tuscany now—they happen to be the main constituents of Le Serre Nuove.

SMOKED CAESAR

Classic cocktails tend to breed offspring, but rarely does the child outshine the parent. This descendant of the Bloody Caesar is an exception. It's much better than the original.

Not that the Caesar is a classic in the standard sense. It was born in the sixties, itself a mutation of the venerable Bloody Mary, with Mott's Clamato in place of tomato juice. The Smoked Caesar swaps out neutral vodka for robust, peaty Scotch from Islay, taming the fishy flavour while lending an essence of fire-roasted tomato. Brunch cocktail of the gods.

I owe my acquaintance with this drink to David Blackmore, global brand ambassador for glorious Ardbeg, the smokiest whisky in Christendom. (Acceptable substitutes include Lagavulin and Laphroaig, but don't tell David I said so.) I trust the people at Ardbeg won't mind if I add my own twist, a garnish of candied bacon. You can fall back on the conventional celery stick if time, energy and pork belly are not at hand.

1½ oz Ardbeg whisky
½ cup Clamato juice
1 tsp lemon juice
3 dashes hot sauce
Splash Worcestershire sauce
½ strip candied bacon (page 123)

Rim a tumbler or highball glass with salt. Fill with ice. Shake whisky, Clamato juice, lemon juice, hot sauce and Worcestershire sauce with ice and strain into glass. Drop in the candied bacon or a stick of celery.

CANDIED BACON

Preheat oven to 350°F. Place bacon strips (as many as you like) on a parchment-lined baking sheet. Lay another piece of parchment over top and cover with another baking sheet to keep it all flat. Bake for 10 minutes. Uncover and cool on baking sheet.

Dip bacon strips in simple syrup (1 part sugar dissolved in 1 part boiling water), then in brown sugar seasoned with cinnamon. Return to baking sheet and bake, uncovered, for 5 to 10 more minutes, until sugar has caramelized.

CREAMY

cream • milk • butter • buttermilk • eggs • yogurt
cheeses • chocolate • cream pies • scallops • polenta • bisques
mac and cheese • nut butters • cream puffs • dips • hummus
mayonnaise • crème brûlées • crème caramels • custards
panna cottas • ice cream • chocolate truffles • mousses • puddings
fools • creamy mashed potatoes • silken tofu • risottos • bananas
avocados • puréed and cream-style sauces and soups

WE TEND TO THINK OF FLAVOUR AS *distinct from texture, but that's a tidy abstraction. In the concrete world, you can't have one without the other, just as with colour and fabric in fashion (unless you happen to be into body paint). Invariably they play off each other, sometimes to the point where it's hard to discern where one ends and the other begins. So it is with cream, the flavour that walks like a texture—or vice versa.*

In strict scientific terms (hey, we cooks are chemists, after all), cream is a high-fat dairy emulsion. Two substances that normally don't mix, fat and water, bury their differences and tie the knot. Oils derived from plants can play the game too, as in avocados, coconut milk, chocolate, mayonnaise and peanut butter.

But one need not rely on fat or oil. Through sleight of hand, we can work up a rich, clingy texture with a spoon, fork or pulse of a Cuisinart. The starchy exterior of short-grained arborio or carnaroli rice, scraped away and dissolved through assiduous stirring in simmering stock, creates the thick consistency of Italy's glorious risotto. Mash a ripe banana and you've got a creamy paste with virtually no fat, a technique we sometimes rely on to add body to low-calorie recipes. Similarly, fleshy vegetables, such as squash and carrots, can be puréed into creamy fat-free soups.

There's yet another trick a wise cook can play to enhance the perception of creaminess without, paradoxically, changing actual texture. Sensory scientists have shown that complementary flavours associated with cream products, notably vanilla, sugar and molecules known as lactones found in plant fibres as well as milk, play a mind-bending trick, heightening our impression of richness—more flavours that walk like textures. Add vanilla to a dessert and it will taste smoother.

Even wines, especially chardonnay, can be described as creamy. Here the sensation is partly the product of a natural transformation known as malolactic fermentation that converts tart malic acid, the stuff found in apples as well as grapes, into softer lactic acid, found in milk. Let that wine mature in an oak barrel, a common practice for chardonnay as well as most reds, and you get a creamier sensation imparted by the oak's lactones and vanilla nuances. The same holds true of whisky, brandy and rum, all aged in wood. The longer the spirit matures in casks, the creamier it seems to get.

And there's beer, its creaminess dependent on the preparation of the base grain, type of yeast and even level of carbonation. Guinness stout, the Emerald Isle's ebony glory, is especially thick and rich thanks in part to the nitrogen that generates its fine effervescence. We think of it as cream of barley.

Menu 1

EUROPEAN UNITY

Fennel and Turnip Soup

Saffron Risotto with Scallops

Eton Mess

This European Union menu features a variety of techniques and cuisines. The creamy soup is essentially French, the scallops are Italian and the dessert is straight from Britain. Everything works together beautifully—a lesson for Europe.

FENNEL AND TURNIP SOUP

This soup is a perfect illustration of how something with no cream in it can still be creamy in texture. If you can find baby fennel you will need 3 bulbs. Shave off a few shards to use as a garnish rather than the basil. The bigger fennel is not tender or pretty enough to use for garnish.

Serves 4

- 2 tbsp vegetable oil
- 1 fennel bulb, trimmed and coarsely chopped
- 1 cup chopped white turnips
- 1 cup chopped onions
- 1 tsp crushed fennel seeds
- 4 cups chicken stock
- Salt and freshly ground pepper
- 2 tbsp sliced fresh basil

Heat oil in a soup pot over medium heat. Add fennel, turnips and onions and sauté for 5 minutes or until slightly softened. Stir in fennel seeds.

Add stock and bring to a boil. Reduce heat and simmer for 17 to 20 minutes or until vegetables are very tender. Season with salt and pepper.

Purée in a food processor or blender. Return to pot and simmer for 2 minutes. Serve scattered with basil or baby fennel shards for garnish.

PAIRING: **White Bordeaux**

Most white Bordeaux is a blend of sauvignon blanc and semillon, two grapes that get along like a burger and fries. The first provides citrusy tang, the second a more rounded, oily quality. They're good bookends for this herbal, creamy dream of a soup. Alternative: South African sauvignon blanc or chenin blanc.

RISOTTO

I learned how to make the definitive risotto in a small restaurant kitchen in Lake Como, in Italy. Here are some pointers that I learned from the chef.

First, the weight of the pot is all-important. A heavy pot retains heat and keeps the risotto cooking at a steady temperature without any fear of scorching. The best choice is copper, which can become the serving dish.

Stir the risotto regularly to release the starch from the rice grains. Keep the risotto simmering merrily on about a medium heat. At the correct temperature, it takes exactly 20 minutes from start to finish. Our chef watched the clock as he made his risotto and at precisely 20 minutes he removed the pot and the risotto was perfect. If, like some people, you prefer a less firm texture, add more stock and cook for 5 minutes longer.

The kind of rice you use is most important. Risotto's creamy texture can be obtained only when you use a rice that has the starch (called amylopectin) to bind the kernels together and at the same time leave the kernels al dente (with a bit of firmness) when cooked.

Carnaroli is the rice of choice for the best risotto. It has lots of soft starch for the creamy consistency but retains a good firm bite when cooked.

Arborio has large, plump grains that have a slightly nutty flavour when cooked. While the texture is stickier than carnaroli, it is the most readily available risotto rice.

Vialone nano has a short, stubby grain and a starch that does not dissolve as readily during cooking. This makes a looser risotto with a firmer bite to the rice, a style favoured in the Veneto region. It is excellent for vegetable risotto and cooks a bit more quickly than the other types.

Stock is essential because the rice absorbs its flavour. Although homemade stock is always best, I have used packaged low-sodium chicken or vegetable stock with good results. Ladle in the stock about ½ cup at a time. If you run out, switch to water.

SAFFRON RISOTTO WITH SCALLOPS

Risotto feels creamy because the starch in the rice melds with the liquid to create that texture. For a main course I usually serve 3 scallops per person, but if you use this as a substantial first course then just plop one on top of the rice. The fava beans have to be blanched after they're removed from the pods to make it easy to slip off the tough outer skin. Out of season, you can replace favas with peas or even soybeans (edamame).

Serves 4

1 lb (450 g) fresh fava beans, shelled
2 tbsp olive oil
½ cup chopped shallots
1 tsp chopped garlic
1½ cups risotto rice
½ cup white wine
½ tsp saffron threads
6 cups hot chicken stock
¼ cup grated Parmesan
1 tbsp unsalted butter, diced
1 tsp grated lemon zest
Salt and freshly ground pepper

Scallops:
12 jumbo scallops
Salt and freshly ground pepper
2 tbsp chopped fresh chervil

Blanch fava beans in a large pot of boiling water for about 2 minutes. Drain and run under cold water until cool. Peel and reserve.

Heat oil in a medium, heavy pot over medium heat. Add shallots and garlic and sauté until softened, about 1 minute. Add rice and continue to sauté until rice is coated with oil. Add wine, bring to a boil and cook, stirring, until the wine just about disappears.

Stir saffron into hot stock. Add ½ cup stock to rice and simmer, stirring, until it is absorbed. Continue to add stock ½ cup at a time, stirring until each addition is absorbed before adding more, until rice is al dente, 18 to 20 minutes. About 2 minutes before risotto has finished cooking, add fava beans to heat through. Stir in Parmesan, butter and lemon zest. Season with salt and pepper. Remove from heat.

Heat a heavy nonstick skillet over high heat while risotto is cooking. Season scallops with salt and pepper. When pan is very hot, add scallops and sear until caramelized on the bottom, about 2 minutes. Turn over, turn off heat and let sit in pan for 3 minutes.

Divide risotto among 4 soup plates. Place scallops on top and sprinkle with chervil.

PAIRING: **Soave**

You may remember Soave from the 1970s. Like Italian food in North America, it has vastly improved. Crisp and lemony, it happens to come from Veneto, risotto's homeland.

ETON MESS

Eton Mess is a famous dessert that has its origins at Eton College in England. In "Mess" legend, a cook broke a meringue she had made and, in trying to figure out some way to serve this to the students, she layered it with whipped cream and fruit. Perhaps a myth, but delightful anyway. This is the easiest, most decadent dessert. You can buy the meringues to make it extra easy.

Serves 4

Meringues:
2 large egg whites
½ cup granulated sugar
1 tsp lemon juice

Raspberry Sauce:
1 cup raspberries
3 tbsp superfine sugar
2 tbsp lemon juice

To finish:
1 cup whipping cream
1 tbsp granulated sugar
1 cup raspberries

Preheat oven to 275°F.

Beat egg whites in a bowl until frothy. Beat in sugar, 1 tbsp at a time, until incorporated. Continue to beat until egg whites are thick, stiff and very glossy (like shaving cream). Beat in lemon juice.

Spoon six 2-inch dollops onto a parchment-lined baking sheet. Bake for 1 hour or until crisp. Cool meringues, then break into large and small pieces. Reserve ¼ cup for garnish.

Combine raspberries with sugar and lemon juice in a food processor and process until smooth.

Beat whipping cream with sugar until it holds soft peaks. Reserve a few raspberries for garnish, then fold remaining raspberries and ¼ cup raspberry sauce into whipped cream. Place a spoonful of cream mixture in each of 4 parfait glasses. Top with some crumbled meringue and a drizzle of raspberry sauce. Repeat layers, finishing with reserved meringue and remaining raspberry sauce. Garnish with reserved raspberries.

PAIRING: **Black muscat**

This is one of the wine world's fetching rarities: a blue, almost black dessert wine. Crafted from an unusual dark-skinned variant of the muscat grape, it's a quirky specialty in, of all places, California, made notably by such producers as Quady, whose brand is called Elysium (Greek for "heaven"), and Rosenblum. Though black muscat is often paired with chocolate, its acid grip and deep flavour make it a ringer here.

Menu 2

SOPHISTICATED VEGETARIAN DINNER

Six-Minute Eggs on Fresh Field Greens

Mushroom Ragu with Polenta

The Composed Cheese Plate

This spring-like vegetarian menu incorporates several food trends, including "eggs everywhere." We're seeing eggs—boiled, poached, deep-fried—on salads, on pizzas, even topping fried chicken. Often menus feature what the French call *oeufs mollets*: a six-minute boiled egg. With its firm white and slightly runny yolk, it has the perfect texture for a salad. The mushroom and polenta pairing is a classic, offering comfort as well as sophistication. Composed cheese plates not only look elegant but take away any worry about last-minute prep—you buy the cheese and can make any accompaniments well ahead of time.

SIX-MINUTE EGGS ON FRESH FIELD GREENS

At her stylish Portland, Oregon, restaurant, Smallwares, Chef Johanna Ware made this six-minute egg as an hors d'oeuvre (cut in half and served as finger food), which I have integrated into a salad. Much is made today of preparing eggs by the sous vide method, in which the eggs are submerged in water at 62 to 65°F and slowly cooked for an hour. Yet I prefer this much quicker approach for a similar texture. Although Chef Ware coated her eggs in panko and then deep-fried them, it is not necessary. Another option is to garnish the salad with Parmesan shaved on top of the egg.

Serves 4

4 large eggs

Dressing for Eggs:
2 tsp honey mustard
½ tsp sriracha sauce

Salad:
8 cups fresh mixed field greens
¼ cup chopped chives
4 fresh tarragon leaves, coarsely chopped
1 tbsp olive oil
1 tsp lemon juice
Salt and freshly ground black pepper

Place eggs in boiling water and boil for exactly 6 minutes. Drain, run under cold water until cool enough to handle, then peel.

Stir together honey mustard and sriracha. Reserve.

Combine mixed greens, chives and tarragon in a large bowl. Whisk together olive oil and lemon juice. Season with salt and pepper. Toss dressing with greens.

Arrange greens on 4 plates. Dot each plate with mustard dressing. Cut eggs in half and place 2 halves on each salad. The yolks will be runny. Dot a little more mustard dressing on eggs. Sprinkle with pepper, if you like.

PAIRING: **Cava**

There's something you should know about eggs. They stink with most wines, which develop a sort of metallic flavour in their presence. Except, that is, for dry bubbly. Cava, Spain's attractively affordable Champagne-style sparkling wine, has a firm acid shell that no egg can crack. It's also lively enough to tiptoe with the light salad. Alternative: the Clammy Sammy, the tequila-based Caesar cocktail, page 275 in our "Salty" chapter.

MUSHROOM RAGU WITH POLENTA

Polenta is not a difficult dish to make, just time-consuming. This dish features the creamiest polenta and should be made with real cornmeal, not the instant kind. However, using instant cornmeal and adding extra cream gives me an approximation of the real thing. This recipe was inspired by a dish made by Jonathan Poon of Chantecler restaurant in Toronto.

Serves 4

Polenta:

1½ cups milk
1½ cups water
½ cup whipping cream
½ cup medium cornmeal
Salt

Mushroom Ragu:

6 dried shiitake mushrooms, stems removed
½ cup vegetable oil
½ cup all-purpose flour
Kosher salt
½ cup thinly sliced shallots
½ cup chopped shallots
8 oz (225 g) fresh shiitake mushrooms, stemmed and chopped
¾ tsp Chinese 5 spice powder
2 tsp light soy sauce
1 tsp dark soy sauce
2 tbsp chopped chives
¼ cup grated Parmesan

Combine milk, water and cream in a large pot and bring to a boil. Pour in the cornmeal in a stream, whisking to incorporate and prevent clumping.

Reduce heat to low. Simmer polenta, stirring often to prevent sticking, for 1 hour or until thick and creamy. Season with salt to taste. Keep warm until serving.

Cover dried shiitakes with hot water and let sit for 20 minutes or until softened. Strain, reserving liquid. Dice shiitakes.

Heat ¼ cup vegetable oil in a small skillet over medium-high heat. Combine flour and salt to taste in a small bowl. Add sliced shallots and toss to coat. Shake off excess flour. Fry in batches until crisp and golden. Drain on paper towels. Discard oil.

Heat remaining ¼ cup oil over medium-low in the same skillet or a sauté pan. Add chopped shallots and cook for 5 minutes. Increase heat to medium-high and add fresh and dried shiitake mushrooms. Cook, stirring often, until mushrooms are cooked through, about 3 minutes.

Add 5 spice powder. Stir together and cook gently for 2 more minutes or until flavours are combined. Add reserved mushroom liquid and soy sauces. Bring to a boil, reduce heat and simmer until thickened, 3 to 5 minutes.

Purée with a hand blender or food processor until sauce is still slightly chunky. Spoon over hot polenta.
Garnish with fried sliced shallots, chives and Parmesan.

PAIRING: **Barbaresco**

A slightly softer kid brother to Barolo, Barbaresco is a terrific cherry-like red with fall-foliage overtones that love to get in the sack with mushrooms. But in fairness, this is an accommodating dish where wine is concerned. Other suitable choices include Chianti, pinot noir, savoury southern French reds and even white Burgundy.

THE COMPOSED CHEESE PLATE

Cheese courses are a hot trend, becoming more popular in North American restaurants. For some people they replace dessert, but in Europe the cheese course is an integral part of the meal.

Stocking a large cheese trolley to roll around the dining room is too expensive today, so many smaller European and North American restaurants now serve composed cheese plates instead. These plates are designed to give the diner a taste of a particular cheese and are usually served with a salad, fruits or something sweet. The combinations are unlimited.

These plates are a natural for dinner parties at home. They are easy to put together, feature one great cheese and always look beautiful. They are served after the main course but before dessert. They also have the advantage of allowing your guests to finish that glass of great wine they were drinking with the main course (although Beppi would agree only if it was white).

Here are some cheeses you should be able to find at your local cheese shop, from soft or semi-soft to blue to firm and hard. These are just examples, though. Explore what's available, and substitute your favourites, particularly local varieties. Serve about 2 oz (55 g) of cheese per person. Remove cheese from the fridge at least 2 hours before serving to allow the flavours to fully develop.

Saint-André: Soft and irresistibly creamy, with a powdery-white, bloomy skin of mould. It's made in France from cow's milk. Like butter, only better.

Gruyère: A firm, yellow cow's milk cheese, named after the town of Gruyères in Switzerland. It has a marvellously nutty flavour and salty tang.

Humboldt Fog: Arguably the prettiest cheese in the firmament, this creamy-crumbly goat milk chèvre, made by Cypress Grove in California, features a line of edible dark ash on the inside of the soft rind as well as another ash vein running through the centre. A wedge looks like a piece of festive wedding cake.

Cabrales: This outstanding blue from northern Spain has a strong, tart flavour and may be made either entirely from unpasteurized cow's milk or from a combination of cow's, goat's and sheep's milk.

MUSTARD FRUIT COMPOTE

I use dried fruits because they are always available and their jewel tones set off the plates beautifully, but fresh fruit may be used instead. Use 2 lb of mixed dried fruits such as apricots, pears, prunes and cranberries (cut larger fruit in half). Try this compote with a wonderful runny triple-crème Brie or, even better, L'Ami du Chambertin, a cheese from Burgundy whose rind is washed with marc, the grape mash left over from wine-making. This recipe makes more than you'll need, but it keeps for 2 months, refrigerated. **Makes 6 cups**

- 3 cups granulated sugar
- 2 cups water
- 2 lb (900 g) mixed dried fruit
- 1 cup cider vinegar
- 2 (3-inch) cinnamon sticks
- ⅓ cup dry mustard
- 1 tbsp mustard seeds

Bring sugar and water to a boil in a large pot. Boil for 3 minutes. Reduce heat to a simmer and add fruit. Cook for about 15 minutes or until fruit is soft. Remove fruit and reserve. Add cider vinegar and cinnamon to pot. Return to a boil and boil for 5 to 8 minutes or until syrupy. Stir in mustard and mustard seeds. Return fruit. Cool.

Place in jars. Compote keeps, refrigerated, for 2 months.

PAIRING: **Monbazillac**

Creamy cheese slays red wine faster than an axe-wielding lumberjack on uppers. That's the first reason you want a sweet wine, which is bliss (trust me) with Brie. The second is the fruit. Monbazillac, from France, is sometimes called the poor man's Sauternes, made, like that vaunted dessert elixir, by letting the grapes shrivel into raisins in the presence of a beneficial vineyard mould. And while good versions can indeed be had at much less than half the price of a decent Sauternes, it often comes with a plus in the form of an intriguing, faintly smoky note. I'd call that rich, not poor.

ANCHOVY GOAT CHEESE BISCUITS

These are absolutely my favourite biscuits with cheese or anything else savoury. For a sweeter biscuit, replace the anchovies with ⅓ cup of chopped caramelized walnuts. Or make the dough without either the anchovies or the walnuts, divide it in half, and add 1 tbsp of chopped anchovies to one half and ¼ cup of caramelized walnuts to the other.

Makes about 30 biscuits

- 1 cup all-purpose flour
- ½ cup soft goat cheese
- ⅓ cup butter
- 2 tbsp chopped anchovies
- 1 garlic clove, crushed
- 1 egg yolk

Preheat oven to 350°F.

Combine all ingredients in a food processor and pulse until well combined. Turn dough out onto a floured work surface and gather into a ball. Roll out to ¼-inch thickness and cut out 2-inch rounds with a cookie cutter.

Place on a baking sheet and bake for 10 to 12 minutes or until pale gold. Cool on a rack.

CARAMELIZED WALNUTS

Serve with cheese or as an after-dinner nibble.

Makes 1 cup

- 1 tsp vegetable oil
- 1 cup walnut halves
- 1 tbsp granulated sugar
- 1 tbsp water
- ½ tsp kosher salt

Heat oil in a skillet over medium heat. Add nuts and toast, stirring occasionally, until they begin to turn golden. Stir in sugar, water and salt and cook until water has evaporated.

Spread nuts on a cookie sheet to cool and dry.

WINE AND CHEESE

Ripe cheese, crusty bread and a bottle of red—could there be a holier culinary trinity? Well, yes. The wine could be white. You may howl at the suggestion (my Italian-born father does so regularly), but red wine falls apart in the presence of most cheeses. Mind you, I'm hardly the first critic to crawl out on this limb. Many wine professionals, including the great Robert Parker, agree. Rajat Parr, another expert and the author of *Secrets of the Sommeliers*, told me this a few years ago: "Red wine can work with some cheeses, maybe. But about 95 per cent of cheeses out there are better with white wine."

Don't believe us? Then bend your ear to science. In a 2006 study, two researchers at the University of California at Davis, Hildegarde Heymann and Bernice Madrigal-Galan, served eight cheese styles with eight reds to a group of trained tasters. Their conclusion: in most cases, the cheeses demolished the wines, obscuring subtle fruit, tannins, acidity and oak.

How could centuries of European tradition be so wrong? In fact, it's not wrong at all when you scratch the surface. The harmony (or lack thereof) merely depends on whether you care more about cheese or wine. Acidity and tannins cleanse the palate, flattering fat-laden cheese, but red wine suffers collateral damage, losing structure and flavour. In short, it's a battle, and cheese wins.

To my taste, crisp whites like sauvignon blanc hold up better. Or try a vaguely sweet aromatic variety, such as gewürztraminer. Dessert wines are splendid with salty blue cheeses. And if, like my father, Tony, you must have red, consider raisiny Amarone or sweet Port.

Menu 3

SPRING HAS SPRUNG

Roasted Asparagus Salad with Green Mayonnaise

Lamb from Puglia

Lemon Meringue Tart

This is a delightful spring or Easter menu. When the first local asparagus becomes available, we eat it at every meal for a couple of weeks. Local asparagus is so nutty and green-tasting, so different from the bland imported kind we get during the off season. I had the lamb dish when we were in Puglia, in Italy, and loved the creaminess of the sauce—although there was no cream involved—with the richness of the lamb. The sweet-tart flavour of lemons always feels spring-like to me, and lemon meringue tart is the perfect dessert after this meal.

ROASTED ASPARAGUS SALAD WITH GREEN MAYONNAISE

Asparagus is a sexy vegetable and, for the most appeal, should be eaten with the fingers rather than a knife and fork.

Serves 6

- 2 lb (900 g) asparagus, preferably thicker stalks
- 1 tbsp olive oil
- Salt and freshly ground pepper
- ½ cup mayonnaise
- 1 cup chopped arugula
- ¼ cup chopped chives
- 2 tbsp lemon juice
- 2 tsp capers
- 1 tsp Dijon mustard

Preheat oven to 450°F.

Toss asparagus with olive oil. Lay asparagus on a baking sheet, season with salt and pepper and roast for 5 to 7 minutes or until crisp-tender. Cool.

Combine mayonnaise, arugula, chives, lemon juice, capers and mustard in a food processor and process until smooth. Season with salt. Place asparagus in a serving dish and spoon over sauce.

PAIRING: **Sauvignon blanc**

Some people love Paris in springtime. I love asparagus in springtime (preferably while sitting at a Parisian café watching asparagus-thin models strolling about during Fashion Week). The wine is as fresh as garden air and often hints at the spear-like vegetable, which is why it resonates so well here.

Peeling Asparagus: I often peel thick asparagus up to the head with a vegetable peeler—it is a different vegetable without its chewy skin. I don't peel the asparagus if it is destined for the barbecue or for roasting, because it needs the skin to protect the tender inner stalk. I also don't peel thin stalks.

RUMPUCCINO

As with socks under sandals, there's no defence for a creamy cocktail. The Grasshopper, the White Russian, the Brandy Alexander—classics, supposedly. But when you've got milk, booze and sugar, you've got . . . to lie down and go to sleep.

Unless, that is, the drink involves hot coffee. Because of its appearance, I think of this as a baby cappuccino. Or, rather, a very adult cappuccino. It's served in a little espresso cup and gets spiked with coffee's best friend, rum, inspired by one of my cousins in Italy who keeps a cellar full of rum. It's finished with a creamy cap (*cappuccino* means "little hood" in Italian), which you make by simply whipping up a little heavy cream.

Draw a double espresso into a small cup. Add a splash of dark rum. Top with ½ tsp whipped cream. Dust with chocolate or cinnamon, if you like.

LAMB FROM PUGLIA

Often called the breadbasket of Italy, Puglia is the stiletto heel of the country. Italians flock there in the summer to take advantage of the region's beautiful beaches and simple, flavourful food. Puglia is home to orecchiette pasta, burrata cheese, wonderful tomatoes and rich red wines. This lamb stew is a typical Easter dish from the region. The trick is to add the egg thickener just before serving, to prevent curdling. You can omit it if you prefer.

Serves 6

- 2 tbsp olive oil
- 2½ lb (1.125 kg) boneless lamb shoulder, cut in 1½-inch chunks
- Salt and freshly ground pepper
- 3 oz (85 g) pancetta, chopped
- 1 large onion, halved and thinly sliced (about 2 cups)
- 2 tsp chopped garlic
- 1 cup white wine
- 1 dried red chili
- ¼ cup chopped fresh flat-leaf parsley
- 1½ cups fresh green peas
- 3 eggs
- ½ cup grated Parmesan

Preheat oven to 300°F.

Heat oil in a Dutch oven or large skillet over high heat. Season lamb with salt and lots of pepper. Add lamb to oil in batches and fry until well browned on all sides, about 4 minutes total. Remove from pan and reserve.

Reduce heat to medium and add pancetta to pan. Cook for 2 minutes or until it renders its fat. Add onion and sauté for 2 minutes or until softened; add garlic and sauté for 1 more minute.

Stir in wine, chili and 2 tbsp parsley and bring to a boil, scraping up any brown bits. Simmer for 2 minutes to combine flavours. Return lamb and any juices to the pan.

Cover and bake for 1½ to 2 hours or until lamb is tender. Add green peas and return to oven, uncovered. Bake for 15 minutes or until peas are tender.

Reheat lamb when ready to serve. Beat together eggs, Parmesan and remaining 2 tbsp parsley. Stir egg mixture into lamb until incorporated and the sauce is smooth. Do not let boil. Season with salt and pepper and serve at once.

PAIRING: **Negroamaro**

There are two major red grapes grown in Puglia, primitivo and negroamaro. The first is just another name for zinfandel, the jammy-spicy signature of California. I'm a bigger fan of negroamaro, which better resists becoming syrupy sweet in the hot Mediterranean sun. And it works nicely here, not only for the geographical resonance. Plummy, herbal and often smoky, it orbits deftly around the gamy lamb, earthy pancetta and peas and parsley.

LEMON MERINGUE TART

This French version of lemon meringue pie is a bit lighter and more intensely lemony than the one we all know and love. My lemon curd is tarter than usual. Cook the meringue on a low heat rather than a high one. To avoid weeping meringue, make sure the filling is warm when you top it with the meringue. The cake crumbs will absorb any liquid and pretty much disappear. The lemon curd keeps for 2 weeks refrigerated or freezes for up to 6 months.

Serves 6 to 8

Lemon Curd:
4 egg yolks
½ cup granulated sugar
2 tsp grated lemon zest
⅓ cup fresh lemon juice
½ cup cold unsalted butter, cut in 8 pieces

Meringue:
4 egg whites
½ cup granulated sugar
Pinch kosher salt
1 tsp lemon juice
⅓ cup cake crumbs or challah crumbs

1 (9-inch) pastry shell, prebaked (page 170)

Preheat oven to 325°F.

Place egg yolks in a medium, heavy pot. Whisk in sugar, lemon zest and juice. Place pot over medium heat and whisk in butter. Cook, stirring constantly, for about 6 minutes or until curd thickens and all the butter is incorporated. Do not let boil. The curd should coat the back of a spoon. Cool slightly.

Fill pie shell with curd. Place on a baking sheet and bake for 10 minutes or until curd is warmed through.

Combine egg whites, sugar, salt and lemon juice in a heatproof bowl and set it in a larger bowl filled with hot water. Let egg mixture stand, stirring occasionally, for 5 minutes to warm up the whites. Remove bowl from water bath and beat with an electric mixer on high speed for 4 minutes or until meringue forms stiff peaks when beaters are lifted.

Sprinkle cake crumbs evenly over warm curd. Carefully spread meringue over top, spreading all the way to the pastry edge to seal it and trying not to incorporate any cake crumbs into the meringue itself. Use the back of a spoon to make lots of peaks and valleys in the meringue.

Bake until peaks are golden, about 15 minutes. Cool.

PAIRING: **Sparkling icewine**

Though hard to find, sparkling icewine merits the pairing here because, well, it's perfect. It covers the tart on two fronts: high sweetness to match the creamy filling, and high acidity and froth to click with the topping. Think of the bubbles as the wine's meringue. Alternatives: riesling icewine or late-harvest German trockenbeerenauslese.

CHOCOLATE CAJETA

This easy dessert is more intense and sophisticated than chocolate puddings or custards. It is rich, dense and delicious. It looks spectacular in tiny glasses. Small soufflé dishes or espresso cups work too. The milk chocolate texture is slightly different from the dark, making this both a taste and a texture delight.

Serves 8

Dark Chocolate Layer:

1 cup whipping cream
⅓ cup granulated sugar
¼ cup unsalted butter
1 tsp grated lemon zest
4 oz (115 g) dark chocolate, chopped

Milk Chocolate Layer:

¾ cup whipping cream
¼ cup granulated sugar
¼ cup unsalted butter
4 oz (115 g) milk chocolate, chopped

8 amaretti cookies

Bring cream, sugar and butter to a boil in a small pot, stirring constantly. Reduce heat and simmer, stirring occasionally, for 3 minutes. Remove from heat and stir in lemon zest and dark chocolate until mixture is smooth. Cool in pot for 15 minutes.

Bring cream, sugar and butter to a boil in a second small pot, stirring constantly. Reduce heat and simmer, stirring occasionally, for 3 minutes. Remove from heat and stir in milk chocolate until mixture is smooth. Cool in pot.

Spoon 2 tbsp dark chocolate mixture into each of 8 small tumblers or other small dishes. Chill for 30 minutes. Spoon 3 tbsp milk chocolate mixture into each glass. Chill for another 30 minutes. Divide remaining dark chocolate mixture among glasses and chill until set, about 1 hour. Garnish each with an amaretti cookie.

HOMEMADE RICOTTA WITH RHUBARB COMPOTE AND GRILLED BREAD

Creamy homemade ricotta is far superior to any that you can buy. And making it is easy; all you need is a pot, some cheesecloth and a few simple ingredients. It is rich, not too calorific and keeps for a few weeks. The longer the ricotta hangs, the drier it will become. I usually save the whey just in case it ends up a little too dry. Use buttermilk at the end to give a softer consistency, if you wish. If you don't want to make your own for this dish, make sure you buy a creamy ricotta. This fine dish is inspired by Chef Dan Kluger, of New York's ABC Kitchen. Serve it with grilled bread and savoury rhubarb as a first course. You won't be able to stop eating it!

Serves 6

Ricotta:
8 cups whole milk
1 cup whipping cream
1 tsp kosher salt
¼ cup lemon juice
2 tbsp buttermilk (optional)

Rhubarb Compote:
12 oz (340 g) rhubarb, cut in ½-inch pieces
¾ cup granulated sugar
¾ cup red wine vinegar
⅓ cup ruby Port
2-inch strip of orange peel, pith removed
1 tsp kosher salt
Pinch cayenne

To finish:
2 tbsp extra-virgin olive oil
Maldon salt
Coarsely ground black pepper
Grilled sourdough bread

Bring milk and cream to a gentle boil in a large pot. Reduce heat and simmer for 5 minutes. Add salt and stir to make sure it is well dispersed. Add lemon juice, stir once to combine, then remove mixture from heat. You should see it begin to curdle almost immediately. Let stand for 10 minutes.

Line a strainer with 2 layers of cheesecloth and set it over a very deep bowl or pot that will allow the ricotta to drain without touching the collecting whey. Pour milk mixture through cheesecloth. The whey will drip through. Let hang for 35 to 45 minutes or until soft curds form. You should have about 2 cups. Transfer ricotta to a bowl and refrigerate, covered, until needed.

Combine rhubarb, sugar, vinegar, Port, orange peel, salt and cayenne in a pot and bring to a simmer. Stir well, remove from heat and let sit at room temperature for 45 minutes. Drain in a coarse-mesh sieve for 15 minutes.

Purée rhubarb mixture in a blender until nearly smooth.

Mix ricotta with just enough buttermilk (if using) to make it smooth enough to spread when you're ready to serve.

Place about ⅓ cup ricotta in the centre of each plate and make a small well in the middle. Spoon a scant ¼ cup rhubarb compote into the well and then spread it out with the back of a spoon, swirling to combine with ricotta. Top each serving with 1 tsp olive oil. Sprinkle with salt and black pepper. Serve with slices of grilled bread.

PAIRING: **German riesling**

Wine-wise, this dish thrusts in more directions than an amusement park ride. There's fresh cheese, a natural for crisp white, while cream tends to favour buttery chardonnay. Port in the recipe might suggest a rich red, but there's cayenne also, which makes a case for an aromatic white such as muscat. On balance, I'd opt for off-dry riesling (halbtrocken) from Germany, gently sweet yet crisp, a wine that knows how to play the culinary diplomat.

BOURRIDE FROM MARSEILLE

Bourride is a Provençal specialty, a silky white-fish soup flavoured with aïoli and made with monkfish or cod and lots of white wine. It has a creamy texture, but from the aïoli, not cream. Finish it with a garnish of Provençal herbs, such as parsley, chives or chervil, and finely diced tomatoes for a luscious presentation.

Serves 4

2 lb (900 g) monkfish fillets
2 leeks, white part only, cleaned and sliced
1 carrot, sliced
1 cup sliced fennel
2 bay leaves
2-inch strip of orange peel
4 sprigs fresh parsley
2 sprigs fresh thyme
2 garlic cloves, sliced
4 cups fish or chicken stock
1 cup white wine
Salt and freshly ground pepper
1½ cups aïoli (page 157)
8 slices French bread, toasted
1 cup diced seeded tomatoes
Herbs for garnish

Slice monkfish into ½-inch rounds.

Combine leeks, carrot, fennel, bay leaves, orange peel, parsley, thyme, garlic, stock and wine in a large pot. Bring to a boil, reduce heat and simmer, uncovered, for 30 minutes. Strain broth into a clean pot. Season with salt and pepper to taste.

Bring broth to a simmer. Immerse fish and poach for 12 minutes or until tender. Remove fish, cover and keep warm.

Place 1 cup aïoli in a large bowl. Slowly add hot soup, whisking constantly. Return soup to pot and reheat gently. Do not let boil.

Place toast in soup bowls. Top with fish and ladle over soup. Garnish with diced tomatoes and a few herbs. Serve with extra aïoli or rouille.

PAIRING: **Dry rosé**

The world's best rosés hail from Provence, the regional inspiration for this sexy, delicately chunky soup. Crisp, strawberry-flavoured and subtly herbal, rosé picks up the herb garnish on the plate and will look marvellous on the table, its salmon hue matching the tomatoey pink of the dish. Download some Edith Piaf or Charles Aznavour onto the iPod and you'll be in French heaven.

AÏOLI

Aïoli is garlic mayonnaise frequently served as a dip for french fries. If you prefer not to use raw eggs, you can make a fake aïoli by replacing the eggs with ½ cup of full-fat mayonnaise and reducing the oil to 1 cup. To turn aïoli into rouille, add 2 tsp of chili flakes. Enjoy leftover aïoli as a dip for vegetables.

Makes about 1½ cups

2 small garlic cloves
1 tsp Dijon mustard
2 egg yolks
1 egg
1½ cups olive oil
1 tbsp lemon juice, or to taste
Salt and freshly ground pepper

Drop garlic down feeder tube with food processor running. Process until finely chopped. Add mustard, egg yolks and egg. Process to combine. With machine running, slowly add olive oil down feeder tube until mixture emulsifies. Season with lemon juice, salt and pepper. Refrigerate until needed.

YOGURT CHEESE

This is great to have on hand for healthy eating.

Place 2% yogurt in a cheesecloth-lined strainer set over a bowl. Let drip for about 4 hours or overnight. The resulting cheese is wonderful with fruit, sprinkled with brown sugar or as a spread for bagels or toast. Try it on top of pancakes too. To make maple mousse, add ½ cup maple syrup, 1 tsp grated lemon zest and 2 beaten egg whites to 2 cups yogurt cheese. Spoon into yogurt containers to take to work or into pretty dishes to serve after dinner. A great low-calorie treat.

CRÈME FRAÎCHE

2 cups whipping cream
¼ cup buttermilk

Whisk together cream and buttermilk. Cover with plastic wrap and let sit on the counter for 24 to 48 hours or until thickened. Crème fraîche keeps for 2 weeks, refrigerated. **Makes about 2 cups**

NUTTY

brown butter • lentils • millet • chia seeds • sesame seeds
peanut oil • chestnuts • hazelnuts • almonds • walnuts • pecans
pistachios • betel • kola • macadamias • soybeans • coconut
peanuts • cashews • Gruyère • Emmental • peanut oil • chickpeas
toasted rice • spelt • kamut • buckwheat • rye • jamón Ibérico
sunflower seeds • pine nuts • quinoa • almond milk
wild rice • tahini

THE HUMAN JAW WAS DESIGNED FOR *nut-munching. A study published in 2009 by researchers at the University of Bradford in England used computer models to analyze excavated teeth of* Australopithecus anamensis, *a hominid that lived in Africa four million years ago. Unlike apes, our early ancestors lacked hard enamel to protect against erosion from the acids in fruits, but their fearsome jaws could make swift work of hard foods, specifically nuts and—we'll spare you a flavour chapter on this one—such insects as termites.*

Nuts also came with useful calories and protein. Groundnut, a sort of peanut, likely was the jungle staple, though it must have taken serious foraging to score enough for nine innings of a ball game, never mind that cold beer and fino Sherry would not arrive until much later to fully civilize the snacking experience.

Australopithecus would have marvelled at the variety available in markets today: almonds, walnuts, peanuts, pecans, hazelnuts, pine nuts, pistachios, chestnuts, cashews and macadamias, to name the more popular ones.

Yes, we know, there will be protests from botanists over that list. Many so-called culinary nuts are imposters. Technically, cashews are seeds, each encased in a cute kidney-shaped shell that droops down from the cashew apple. The pistachio's edible meat is a seed too. Ditto the almond and walnut. Nutmeg qualifies as a seed, though it's grated as a spice. Peanuts belong to the legume family. Water chestnuts? No relation to the bona fide nut that grows on trees; they're tubers. The hazelnut is a true nut. Got all that?

It doesn't matter much in the end, because flavour is the key in the kitchen. How do we define nuttiness? Tough question. How about a satisfyingly rich but subtle flavour that makes you want to chew. It's sometimes, but by no means always, accompanied by a mild roasted note. In short, if it reminds you of any items in the above list, it's nutty.

Many other seeds can behave like nuts in cooking, particularly when toasted. The bonus is that they also happen to be safe for most people with nut allergies. Whole sesame seeds achieve a more delicate flavour and less mealy texture than ground or chopped nuts when applied as a crust to seared fresh tuna or Asian-style morsels of beef.

In the beverage world, coffee can taste nutty, as can beer, notably brown ales and other dark brews that rely on roasted barley malts. Sherry, chardonnay and older Champagnes frequently inspire wine critics to trot out the n-word. Whiskies, especially Irish, that rely heavily on unmalted barley, often do the same. And the flavour is especially prominent in spirits matured in casks that previously contained Sherry, such as Jameson Irish Whiskey and Macallan Scotch.

To enjoy nuts is human; to savour fine whisky and vintage Champagne, divine.

Menu 1

MODERN KOREAN

Silky Tofu Soup
Korean Beef Noodle Stir-Fry
Orange Almond Tart with White Chocolate Cream

Korean cooking is right on trend today. As Korea opens up and the food becomes better known, people are flocking to Korean restaurants. These establishments tend to specialize in one area—barbecue or tofu soup, for example—though they may have lengthy menus. A lot of Korean food has a nutty flavour because of the abundant use of sesame oil. While in Seoul, I went to a specialty restaurant that served just-killed octopus in spicy, sesame-laden broth. The octopus was so fresh that its residual nerve activity made it wriggle and writhe as soon as I put my chopsticks in the bowl. A stirring experience not to be repeated. The dessert is not Korean. It is nutty and has oranges, which I was served frequently in Korea. It's a fabulous end to any dinner.

SILKY TOFU SOUP

Traditionally this spicy, creamy soup is made one serving at a time in the ceramic bowl it is served in. The heat of the soup cooks the egg at the last minute. This recipe is vegetarian, but you can add clams and other seafood, or make a meat version with pork. If you have some Korean dumplings in your freezer, these are a welcome addition too. Korean hot pepper powder (gochugaru) is often added for extra heat. **Serves 4**

Seasoning Mix:
1 tbsp Korean chili paste (gochujang)
1 tbsp soy sauce
1 tsp chopped garlic
1 tsp sesame oil

Soup:
1 tbsp vegetable oil
1 cup finely chopped onions
1 cup slivered zucchini
2 cups thinly sliced napa cabbage
¼ cup sliced kimchi
4 cups vegetable or chicken stock
1 package (10 oz/300 g) silken tofu

Garnish:
2 green onions, sliced
4 eggs

Combine Korean chili paste, soy sauce, garlic and sesame oil in a small bowl.
Heat oil in a soup pot over medium heat. Add onions and zucchini and sauté for 2 minutes or until softened. Add seasoning mix, cabbage, kimchi and stock. Bring to a boil, reduce heat and simmer for 5 minutes or until vegetables are tender.
Warm 4 serving bowls.
Reduce heat to medium-low and add silken tofu a spoonful at a time, being careful not to break it up too much. Gently press it into the stock. Taste, adding more soy sauce or sesame oil as needed.
Spoon into bowls, scatter with green onions and break an egg into each bowl. Serve at once, having diners swirl their egg with a spoon or chopsticks.

PAIRING: **Grüner veltliner**

Kimchi, the fermented Korean staple based on vegetables and spices, is considered by many to be wine kryptonite. Too sour for wine, they say, and I'm inclined to agree. Put that together with spices as well as liquid (which always drowns wine) and you've got an extreme pairing challenge. My suggestion comes from, of all places, Austria. The country's signature—and fashionable—white delivers a pleasantly harmonious sour note as well as cooling fruitiness. Pacific Rim alternative: New Zealand sauvignon blanc.

IRISH WHISKEY

Lady Gaga is nuts about it, once referring to her favourite brand, Jameson, as her "long-time boyfriend." Rihanna spun a famous song around it: "Cheers (Drink to That)."

Irish whiskey and pop superstars—impressive! The talented young ladies and their followers have helped turn a once dusty category into one of the spirit world's fastest-growing segments. It makes perfect sense, actually. Delicate and smooth, Irish whiskey is a natural transition on life's road from neutral vodka for sweet cocktails to straight-sipping booze with flavour.

Dominant brand Jameson in particular oozes a rounded, nutty character thanks to time spent in casks previously used for Sherry, and it's unencumbered by the smoky nuances of more robust Scotches and bourbons. I, and Saint Patrick, will drink to that.

Gochujang, the Korean chili paste, is the new go-to seasoning for adding a spicy kick to any dish. Less hot than sriracha, it has a miso-like texture. Look for it in Asian grocery stores and some large supermarkets.

KOREAN BEEF NOODLE STIR-FRY

Korean cooking uses dark soy sauce and nutty-flavoured sesame oil to give a distinctive taste. Dark soy is thick but not too salty. The noodles in this dish are made with sweet potato starch, which is a good gluten-free option. They are also known as Korean glass noodles. Chinese chives are also sold as garlic chives. Kimchi, a fermented napa cabbage condiment, is served alongside nearly everything in Korea. **Serves 4**

1 New York sirloin steak (8 oz/225 g)

Marinade:
2 tbsp dark soy sauce
1 tbsp sesame oil
1 tsp chopped garlic
1 tsp granulated sugar
½ tsp freshly ground pepper

Noodles:
4 oz (115 g) sweet potato noodles
1 tbsp dark soy sauce
1 tbsp sesame oil

Vegetables:
3 tbsp vegetable oil
1 cup sliced onions
1 cup slivered carrots
3 oz (85 g) shiitake mushrooms, stemmed and sliced
6 cups baby spinach
4 green onions, cut in 2-inch lengths
1 tsp granulated sugar
1 tbsp dark soy sauce
1 tsp sesame oil

Garnish:
½ cup slivered Chinese chives

Cut steak into thin slices.
Combine soy sauce, sesame oil, garlic, sugar and pepper in a medium bowl. Stir steak slices into marinade and let sit for 15 minutes.
Bring a wok of water to a boil. Add noodles and boil for 8 to 10 minutes or until softened. Drain, transfer to a bowl and toss with soy sauce and sesame oil. Wipe out wok.
Drain beef. Heat wok over high heat, then add vegetable oil. Add onions, carrots and beef and stir-fry for 1 minute. Toss mushrooms into wok and stir-fry for another minute. Add spinach and green onions. Toss until spinach wilts. Stir in sugar, soy sauce and sesame oil. Add noodles and toss everything together with tongs.
Serve at once, garnished with a handful of Chinese chives and kimchi on the side.

PAIRING: **Red zinfandel**

A red with bold fruit and smooth tannins will give the spices here a friendly embrace. Zinfandel also often exhibits solid acidity, shaking hands with the kimchi.

ORANGE ALMOND TART WITH WHITE CHOCOLATE CREAM

Oranges are often served after a Korean meal, so this is my non-traditional take on that idea. The glazed orange slices are the perfect topping. Make sure you slice the oranges very thinly, otherwise the peel will be hard. You could buy a frozen pie shell for this tart.

Serves 6

Pastry:

1½ cups all-purpose flour
3 tbsp granulated sugar
½ tsp kosher salt
½ cup cold butter, diced
1 egg yolk
2 tbsp lemon juice

Topping:

Glazed orange slices (see note, page 171)
¼ cup apricot jam

Filling:

1 cup ground almonds
½ cup unsalted butter, at room temperature
½ cup granulated sugar
1 tbsp chopped candied orange peel (page 347)
2 eggs, beaten
Pinch kosher salt

White Chocolate Cream:

1 cup whipping cream
4 oz (115 g) white chocolate, chopped

Combine flour, sugar and salt in a food processor or large bowl. Scatter butter over flour. Pulse (or cut in) until mixture resembles coarse bread crumbs.

Beat together egg yolk and lemon juice. With machine running, pour egg mixture through feed tube. Pulse just until liquid is incorporated into flour. (Or add liquid and toss with your fingertips.) If dough seems dry, add a little more lemon juice.

Turn mixture into a bowl and knead gently until it forms a ball. Flatten into a disc. Wrap pastry in plastic wrap and chill for 15 minutes.

Preheat oven to 425°F.

Roll out pastry on a floured surface and fit into a 9-inch tart pan with removable bottom. Trim edges. Prick base with a fork, line with foil and fill with dried beans or pie weights. Bake for 15 minutes. Remove foil and beans and bake for 5 minutes longer or until pale gold. Cool.

Reduce oven temperature to 375°F.

Place ground almonds on a baking sheet and toast in the oven for 3 to 4 minutes or until golden. Cool.

Combine almonds, butter, sugar and orange peel in a food processor or by hand. Pulse until mixture is combined. Add eggs and salt and pulse to combine.

Spread almond filling in baked tart shell, smoothing the top. Bake for 25 to 30 minutes or until filling is set. Cool.

Arrange orange slices over top of tart. Melt apricot jam in a small pot over low heat. Strain out any chunks and brush top of tart with glaze.

Bring cream to a boil in a small pot. Pour over white chocolate in a bowl and stir until chocolate is melted. Cool. Stir together again before serving. Serve with tart.

PAIRING: **Muscat de Beaumes de Venise**

Two styles of wine are made in this southern Rhone Valley appellation: dry red and sweet fortified white. Look for the latter, usually found in half-bottles. I love the honeyed, often orange-like essence of this underrated dessert elixir. Alternative: a nutty liqueur, such as amaretto.

Glazed Orange Slices: Slice 1 navel orange into 1/8-inch slices. You will have about 12 slices. Boil 1 cup water with 1 cup granulated sugar for 2 minutes, stirring to dissolve sugar. Reduce heat, add orange slices and simmer very gently for about 45 minutes. Drain slices and cool on a parchment-lined rack. These are handy to have around. Refrigerate in the syrup.

CAVE SPRING
NIAGARA PENINSULA

Menu 2

A TAPAS MENU

Crushed Chickpeas with Jalapeños

Roasted Brussels Sprout Leaves

Seared Beef Filet with Brown Butter Mayonnaise

Kale and White Anchovy Salad

Shrimp Catalan

Nowadays, tapas are not necessarily Spanish. They come from all over the food map. At a Chinese restaurant in Barcelona, the dim sum was advertised as tapas because any small plates are often given that name! Tapas is a casual, fun way to entertain. Serve them while watching a movie or a football game. Book clubs and meetings love tapas too. You have to be organized, but you can also supplement with bought ingredients like prosciutto. Include plates of olives, crackers, perhaps the pâté in the "Sweet" chapter (page 303), and you have a feast. Each one of the following recipes makes a good first course for a dinner, and the dishes, though not necessarily made with nuts, all have a nutty feel. This tapas menu serves 4 to 6, depending on appetite, but each recipe will serve 4 as a starter.

TAPAS TIPPLES

If you are a fan of Spanish tapas, you are undoubtedly wise to Spain's passion for dry Sherry, the classic pairing in a country that elevated bite-size grazing to a performance art. I love dry Sherry, specifically fino and manzanilla, two styles with the bracing presence to stand up to any food, Spanish or otherwise.

As a great cocktail alternative, consider a modified dry gin martini using a ¼ oz splash of fino or manzanilla in place of dry vermouth. Gin is big in Spain and lends a refreshing herbal top note to everything, while the Sherry rounds things out with its salty-nutty overtone. The decadent combination turns a tapas dinner into a tapas fiesta. A toothpick-skewered olive adds a suitably Spanish exclamation point.

Not a fan of Sherry? Rosado—Spanish rosé—is the alternative choice of many a Spaniard today. This crisp, dry pink wine is more of a crowd-pleaser than love-it-or-hate-it Sherry, relatively moderate in alcoholic strength and brimming with berry-herbal refreshment.

I must confess a special weakness here for one of Lucy's dishes in particular, the kale and white anchovy salad. I grow a floppy forest of healthful lacinato kale in my garden. And if I could, I'd keep a saltwater aquarium filled with anchovies, their succulent flesh purported to possess aphrodisiac qualities. Put the two together and you've got a Mediterranean dish that's as good for your heart as it is for your libido. A dry Spanish rosado would make a splendid match, no question, but I'd give the nod to just about any zippy Mediterranean white, including albariño from Spain, inzolia from Sicily, assyrtiko from the Greek island of Santorini and vinho verde from Portugal. Acidity is an oily anchovy's best friend, and much as I adore the lingering fishiness on my breath, it's nice to keep the palate kissing-clean between bites. This is sexy salad, after all.

CRUSHED CHICKPEAS WITH JALAPEÑOS

This spicy pepper-laced nutty dip has more kick than hummus.

1 can (19 oz/540 mL) chickpeas, drained and rinsed
¼ cup chopped fresh parsley
2 tbsp chopped jalapeño peppers, or to taste
1 tsp finely chopped garlic
¼ cup olive oil
Salt and freshly ground pepper

Place chickpeas in a bowl and coarsely crush with a fork or potato masher. Add parsley, jalapeños, garlic and olive oil and stir together. Season well with salt and pepper.

ROASTED BRUSSELS SPROUT LEAVES

The leaves that fall off the Brussels sprouts when you trim the stem are perfect for this dish, although I usually take a few more rounds. The rest of the sprouts can be roasted or steamed for another meal. No matter how many of these you make, they disappear in minutes. The roasting brings out a nutty flavour.

Lots of Brussels sprout leaves
2 tbsp olive oil
Salt

Preheat oven to 350°F.
Toss leaves with oil and salt. Place on a baking sheet and bake for 6 to 10 minutes, tossing once, or until edges are brown and crispy.

SEARED BEEF FILET WITH BROWN BUTTER MAYONNAISE

This is a beef carpaccio–like tapas. Nutty brown butter makes a sensational mayonnaise.

1 filet of beef (1 lb/450 g)
½ tsp sea salt
Freshly ground pepper
2 tbsp butter
Brown Butter Mayonnaise (recipe follows)
1 cup fresh rye bread crumbs

Heat a skillet over high heat. Season meat with salt and pepper. Add butter to skillet, let it brown slightly, then add filet. Brown well on all sides. Remove from skillet and cool. Refrigerate until cold, then freeze roast for 15 minutes to make slicing easier. Slice into paper-thin slices and arrange on a platter. Drizzle with mayonnaise and sprinkle with bread crumbs.

BROWN BUTTER MAYONNAISE

This nutty sauce must be brought to room temperature before using, as it solidifies in the refrigerator.

Makes about 1 cup

¼ cup mayonnaise
1 tsp fish sauce
½ tsp grated lemon zest
1 tbsp lemon juice
3 tbsp olive oil
¼ cup brown butter (see note, below), cooled
Salt and freshly ground white pepper

Whisk together mayonnaise, fish sauce, lemon zest and juice. Slowly whisk in olive oil, then stir in brown butter. Season with salt and pepper.

Brown butter has a hazelnut flavour. It is often called beurre noisette because of its nutty taste. It is frequently served with plain fish and over steamed vegetables. To make brown butter, melt 1 cup unsalted butter over medium heat, stirring constantly. Keep cooking until butter turns light brown and smells nutty. Strain through a fine sieve or cheesecloth into a bowl. It keeps for a month in the fridge.

KALE AND WHITE ANCHOVY SALAD

Kale is today's superfood. Dinosaur, lacinato, Tuscan and black kale are all the same vegetable. The leaves are long and knobbly but have no curly edges. It is the best kale for any salad. White anchovies have a subtle tart flavour and are not as pungent as the dark ones, giving this salad a beautiful look with the dark kale and the white fish. If white anchovies are not available, use dark anchovies in oil, but soak them in milk for 30 minutes to remove some of the salt. Goat cheese is a tasty addition here too.

1½ cups cherry tomatoes, halved
1 tbsp olive oil
Salt and freshly ground pepper
1 bunch dinosaur kale, stems and thick ribs removed, thinly sliced (about 8 cups)
12 white anchovy fillets

Dressing:
¼ cup extra-virgin olive oil
2 tbsp chopped shallots
4 tsp white wine vinegar
1 tsp mustard

Preheat oven to 400°F.
Toss tomatoes with olive oil, season with salt and pepper, and place cut side up on a baking sheet. Roast for 10 to 15 minutes or until slightly browned and shrivelled. Reserve.
Whisk together olive oil, shallots, vinegar and mustard in a small bowl until combined. Season with salt and pepper.
Combine roasted tomatoes, kale and anchovies in a large bowl and toss with enough dressing to coat.

SHRIMP CATALAN

This zesty sauce gives a nutty, spicy flavour to the shrimp. The sauce is tossed with the shrimp and served hot, but you can also use it as a dip for cold shrimp.

1 large tomato
¼ cup fresh bread crumbs, toasted
¼ cup slivered almonds, toasted
2 tbsp pine nuts, toasted
2 tsp chopped garlic
½ tsp hot smoked Spanish paprika
¼ tsp chili flakes
3 tbsp olive oil
2 tbsp Sherry vinegar
3 tbsp chopped fresh parsley
Salt

Shrimp:
2 tbsp olive oil
½ cup chopped onion
1 lb (450 g) large shrimp, peeled
Freshly ground pepper

Place tomato, bread crumbs, almonds, pine nuts, garlic, paprika, chili flakes, oil and Sherry vinegar in a mini chopper or food processor. Process until a paste forms. Add parsley and pulse until combined. Season with salt. Reserve.

Heat oil in a large skillet over medium-high heat. Add onion and sauté for 3 minutes or until onion just begins to colour. Season shrimp with pepper, add to skillet and sauté for 2 to 3 minutes or until pink and just beginning to curl. Remove from heat, add sauce and toss. Serve warm or at room temperature.

Menu 3

AN END OF SUMMER DINNER

Gougères with Green Salad

Caramel-Pecan-Dusted Sea Bass with Cranberry Wine Sauce

Creamy Spinach

Hazelnut Meringue Roulade

This menu combines French and American influences, and the combinations are enticing. Gougères are classic French savoury cheesy cream puffs, while crusting fish with nuts is a typically American technique. The variety of lettuce available at the end of summer is staggering. Personally, I like mustard greens, arugula, mizuna and pea sprouts, but feel free to pick your favourites for the salad. Being the end of summer, passion fruit is everywhere.

GOUGÈRES WITH GREEN SALAD

These tasty little bites are good as an hors d'oeuvre, better when served with a salad. This recipe has a Burgundian twist to it. I first tasted these gougères in Beaune after a marathon wine tasting. Use a hard, gratable goat cheese, which gives the gougères a nutty twist. You can also make larger gougères to serve instead of bread with soups or saucy main courses.

Serves 4

1 cup water
6 tbsp unsalted butter, cut in pieces
1 tsp kosher salt
½ tsp dry mustard
Pinch nutmeg
1 cup all-purpose flour
4 large eggs
1 cup grated hard goat cheese
¼ cup freshly grated Parmesan
2 tbsp chopped chives

Egg Wash:
1 egg beaten with 1 tsp water and a pinch salt

Salad:
8 cups mixed lettuces
2 tbsp olive oil
2 tsp lemon juice
Salt and freshly ground pepper

Preheat oven to 425°F. Line 2 baking sheets with parchment paper.

Combine water, butter, salt, mustard and nutmeg in a medium pot. Heat over medium heat, stirring occasionally, until hot and butter has melted. Bring to a boil, then remove from heat. Add flour all at once and beat vigorously with a wooden spoon until the mixture comes together. Reduce heat to low and cook, stirring constantly, for 2 minutes. The flour will begin to coat the bottom of the pot.

Remove from heat and immediately add eggs, one at a time, beating after each addition until fully incorporated. Beat in goat cheese and Parmesan and keep beating until the dough is smooth and thick. Stir in chives.

Spoon mixture into a piping bag fitted with a large plain tip. Pipe mounds onto baking sheets about 1¼ inches wide and 2 inches apart. If the balls have little points, wet your finger and press them down. If you do not have a piping bag, use 2 wet tablespoons and drop mounds onto baking sheets; shape with wet hands. Brush with egg wash.

Bake for 20 minutes or until golden brown and puffed.

Combine lettuces in a bowl while the gougères are baking. Whisk together olive oil and lemon juice and season with salt and pepper. Toss lettuces with dressing.

Pile salad on plates and surround with 2 or 3 gougères.

PAIRING: **Sauvignon de Touraine**

When in Burgundy, I am accustomed to scarfing down a good fraction of my body weight in gougères. Cheesy, doughy, puffy, they are pillows of pure pleasure. Gruyère is the more common cheese for gougères, and a faintly nutty white Burgundy is perfect in that case. But the goat cheese here transports my thoughts farther north to the Loire Valley, where zesty sauvignon blanc is goat cheese's de rigueur partner. Sauvignon blanc also dances more ably with the light salad. Bargain-priced sauvignon from the district of Touraine (at half the cost of those from Sancerre, up the river) is just the ticket, though you could substitute pretty much any other sauvignon.

CARAMEL-PECAN-DUSTED SEA BASS WITH CRANBERRY WINE SAUCE

Mediterranean sea bass is a firm-fleshed, light-flavoured fish. It's often found whole, but fishmongers will fillet it for you. Substitute with halibut if desired, but cook about 4 minutes longer. The nutty coating has a sweet-hot taste that, when contrasted with the soft flesh of the fish, gives an unbeatable flavour and texture profile. Use medium or hot paprika.

Serves 4

¼ cup granulated sugar
2 tbsp water
1 cup pecan halves
¼ tsp smoked Spanish paprika
Pinch salt
4 sea bass fillets (about 6 oz/170 g each)
Salt and freshly ground pepper
Cranberry Wine Sauce (page 186)

Preheat oven to 450°F. Line a plate with parchment paper.
Combine sugar and water in a small pot. Bring to a boil over medium heat, reduce heat and simmer, without stirring, until melted sugar thickens and begins to turn brown, about 5 minutes. Add nuts, paprika and salt and cook, stirring, until nuts are well coated and sticky. Spoon onto the plate, separating nuts with a fork. Cool. Finely chop nuts.
Season sea bass with salt and pepper and place on an oiled baking sheet. Press nuts onto top of fish to form a crust. Bake for 8 minutes or until white juices begin to appear.
Serve with a drizzle of Cranberry Wine Sauce.

PAIRING: **Pinot noir**

Look to the sauce for your cue. It's made with red wine, which pulls this fish into pinot noir territory. The ideal red for fish, medium-bodied pinot keeps things light while delivering berry-like fruitiness to complement the smoky paprika in Lucy's sea bass. Delicate Oregon pinot as well as red Burgundy are the best options. If you prefer white, go with white Burgundy (a.k.a. chardonnay) or a chardonnay from another cool-climate region.

CRANBERRY WINE SAUCE

The right tart touch for the crunchy fish (page 185).

Makes 1/3 cup

½ cup red wine
½ cup cranberry juice
¼ cup cold unsalted butter, cut in pieces
Salt and freshly ground pepper

Combine red wine and cranberry juice in a heavy pot. Bring to a boil over high heat, reduce heat and simmer for 10 to 20 minutes or until thickened. Remove from heat and stir in butter a few pieces at a time until fully incorporated and sauce is emulsified. Season with salt and pepper.

CREAMY SPINACH

This decadent spinach is a superb accompaniment for many dishes. It is a good base for poached eggs, and I love it with steak, but it really shines with the sea bass because the richness complements the sweet nuttiness of the dish.

Serves 4

2 tbsp butter
8 cups packed baby spinach
(or 2 bunches regular, stemmed)
¼ cup mascarpone
2 tbsp whipping cream
⅓ tsp chili flakes
Salt and freshly ground pepper

Melt butter in a large skillet over medium heat. Add spinach and cook, tossing with tongs, for 2 minutes or until spinach is wilted. Stir in mascarpone, cream and chili flakes. Bring to a boil and cook, stirring, for 2 minutes or until sauce just coats the leaves. Season with salt and pepper.

HAZELNUT MERINGUE ROULADE

This memorable dessert can be made with roasted figs or with the passion fruit filling below. Roast figs at 350°F for 10 minutes.

Serves 6 to 8

Meringue:

2 cups whole blanched hazelnuts
8 egg whites
½ tsp kosher salt
1½ cups granulated sugar
1 tsp white vinegar
1 tsp cornstarch
Icing sugar for dusting

Filling:

1½ cups mascarpone
2 tbsp granulated sugar
2 tsp grated lime zest
2 tbsp lime juice
1 cup whipping cream
½ cup passion fruit pulp

Preheat oven to 350°F. Toast hazelnuts on a baking sheet until golden brown, about 6 minutes. Cool slightly. Rub hazelnuts in a tea towel to remove skins. Cool completely.

Reduce heat to 275°F. Line a baking sheet with parchment paper overhanging edges.

Place egg whites and salt in a large bowl and beat with an electric mixer until frothy. Gradually beat in 1 cup sugar, a few tablespoons at a time. Beat until thick and glossy, about 10 minutes with a hand mixer or 5 with a stand mixer. Beat in vinegar.

Whirl hazelnuts with cornstarch and remaining ½ cup sugar in a food processor until nuts are finely ground. Gently but thoroughly fold into egg whites. Scoop mixture onto prepared baking sheet and smooth into each corner. Level top.

Bake until lightly golden but still slightly soft, about 1 hour.

Turn meringue out onto a tea towel dusted with icing sugar. Cool a little, then gently remove parchment paper. Cover with another tea towel and cool completely.

Beat mascarpone with sugar, lime zest and lime juice in a medium bowl until fluffy, about 1 minute. Whip cream in a separate bowl until it holds soft peaks. Fold cream and passion fruit into mascarpone mixture.

Remove top tea towel from meringue. Spread mascarpone mixture evenly over meringue. Grasp the long ends of the tea towel and, starting from a long side and using the tea towel as a guide, roll up meringue like a jelly roll. Cut into slices to serve.

PAIRING: **Moscatel**

Some readers may be old enough to recall when cheap "muscatel" referred to the favourite intoxicant of people whom society used to call hobos. A sweet fortified wine, it delivered plenty of bang for the buck. Good moscatel, made in Portugal and Spain, spans a gamut of flavours, including orange, fig and nuts. Alternative: Vin Santo from Italy.

CHAMPAGNE COCKTAIL

In its ultimate form—bona fide French Champagne spiked with regal Cognac—this would be one to trot out for aperitif duty on New Year's. But that combination reminds me of the quip by British essayist Charles Lamb: "Brandy and water spoils two good things." Cognac and Champagne? Best when they can star independently.

Luckily, there are less stately versions of both, commonly known as sparkling wine and brandy. I'm partial to the drink over a plate of roasted nuts in autumn or winter, the bubbles and acidity stepping lively through the oil and salt as the spirit provides commensurate weight and golden colour.

There's history to this grand beauty, which has roots in the wine-based punches and cups of the early American cocktail canon rather than the land of Champers and yak (as rappers call their beloved Cognac). Mark Twain mentions it in *The Innocents Abroad,* published in 1869, the passage humorously underscoring that a cunning French barkeep advertising "all manner of American drinks" must be an imposter if he's never heard of a "champagne cock-tail."

The recipe: Drop a sugar cube into a champagne flute, soak with two or three dashes of Angostura bitters and gently crush the cube with a spoon. Add ¾ oz brandy and slowly top up with dry sparkling wine. Garnish with a small slice of lemon zest or a dried cranberry.

CARAMELIZED ONION AND CHEESE FONDUE

Cheese fondue can be made with a variety of cheeses. Try different combinations or use just one flavourful cheese, such as Taleggio or Comté. When using a less interesting cheese, flavour the fondue with herbs, olives, sun-dried tomatoes—whatever you fancy. In this recipe, Gruyère gives that nutty flavour that always goes so well with onions.

Serves 4

- 2 tbsp butter
- 2 cups chopped onions
- Pinch salt
- Pinch sugar
- 1 cup ale
- 1 tbsp Dijon mustard
- 12 oz (340 g) Gruyère, shredded
- 4 oz (115 g) white cheddar, shredded
- 1 tbsp cornstarch
- ½ tsp freshly ground pepper

Dippers:

- Belgian endive leaves
- Breadsticks
- Crusty Italian bread, cut in bite-size pieces
- Blanched cauliflower pieces
- Cooked mini red potatoes
- Pear or apple wedges

Melt butter in a wide, heavy pot over medium heat. Add onions and salt and sauté for 1 minute. Reduce heat to medium-low, sprinkle in sugar, and cook onions, stirring occasionally, for 15 minutes or until golden. Reduce heat to low and stir in ale and mustard.

Toss Gruyère and cheddar with cornstarch. Add a handful of cheese to onions, stirring until cheese is completely melted. Add remaining cheese a handful at a time, stirring until melted between each addition. Season with pepper.

Transfer to a fondue pot. Reheat over low heat until dippable.

PAIRING: **Grüner veltliner**

For regional authenticity's sake, you could seek out a fruity white chasselas from Switzerland, fondue's homeland. But it's hard to come by. For fondue, I equally prefer Austrian grüner veltliner, a dry white with a lovely yin-yang of round, stone-fruit character and electric acidity. You'll welcome that acidity when tucking into a cauldron of molten cheese. And you'll be on trend too. Grüner veltliner has become a darling of savvy sommeliers, particularly in such culinary capitals as San Francisco, where it sometimes goes by the hip (or hippie) nickname groo-vy. Alternative: pilsner beer.

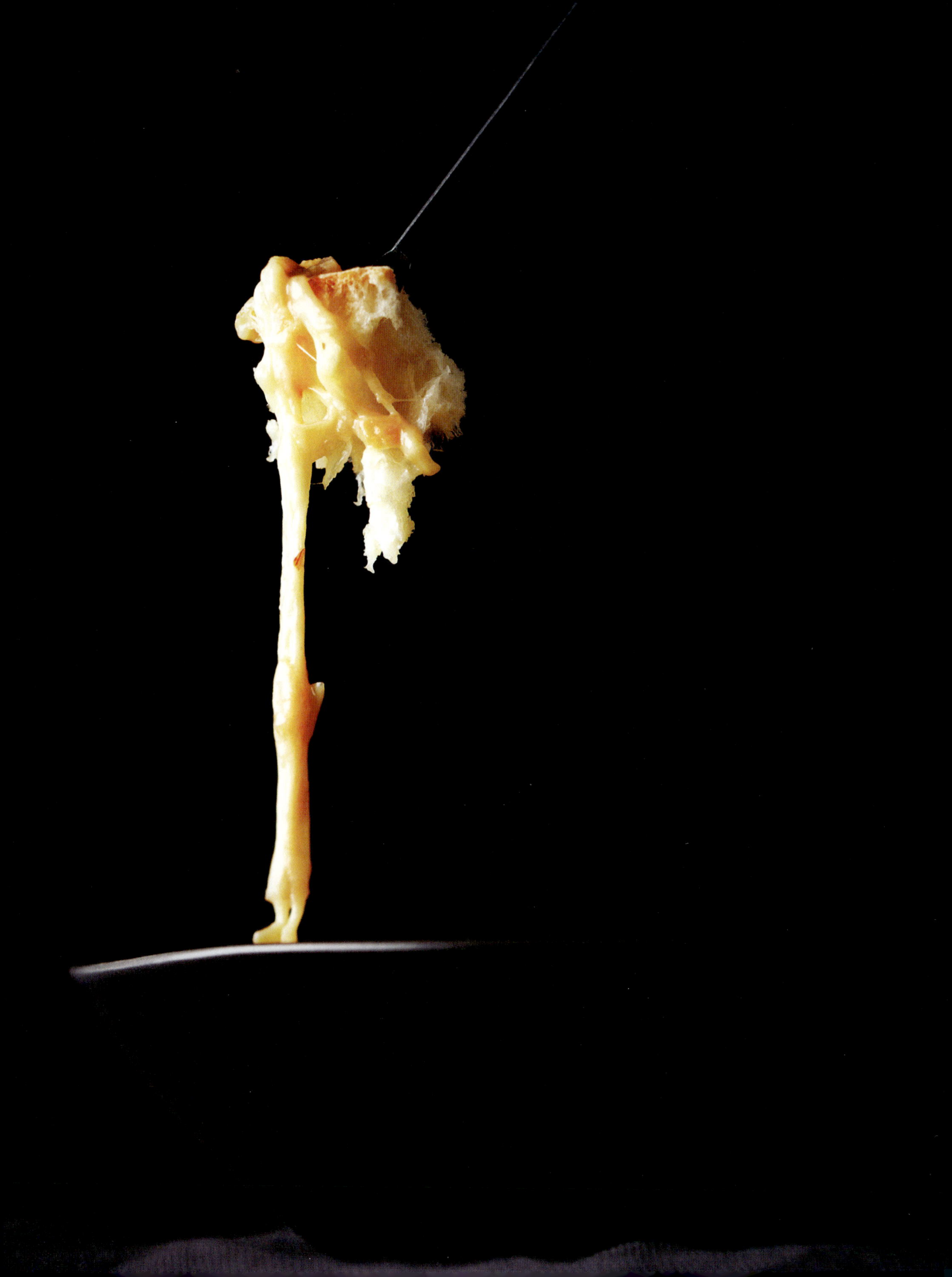

EARTHY

potatos • beets • mushrooms • eggplant

miso • rutabagas • turnips • jerusalem artichokes

radishes • truffles • parsnips • onions • garlic • beans

Brie • Muenster • Époisses de Bourgogne • Taleggio

buckwheat • barley • truffles • Brussels sprouts

brown rice • quinoa • celery root • leeks • yams

black beans • chickpeas • romano beans • liver • bison

THE FRENCH HAVE AN EXPRESSION—

don't they always have an expression?—for a taste of the earth: gout de terroir. *It's not so much an expression as a literal description, but it seems to taste better in French. Mainly it's trotted out in passionate exchanges about wine, where it's code for such nuances as stone, chalk, graphite and damp soil. A soupçon of mineral or a whiff of dirt is nirvana to grape geeks, notably devotees—like us—of that ultimate expression of pinot noir, red Burgundy. Wines imbued with terroir are seen as more authentic, less manipulated, purported evidence that the vintner treated the grapes with a delicate hand and stepped aside to let the ground do the talking.*

This can all seem a bit strange to a non-drinker. One can taste earth without splurging on a decent Burgundy. Just sink your teeth into a humble radish, beet, mushroom, turnip or rutabaga. There's no danger you'll encounter even a hint of grape to spoil the nirvana.

But there's more to earthiness, as we define it here, than mere soil, rocks or roots. People sometimes use the term to convey the gutsy quality of organ meats or the farmhouse flavour of charcuterie, not least French andouille sausages, which often use gastrointestinal portions of the pig that give off—sorry, we've got to say it—a certain fecal aroma prized by devotees. Wine can smell that way too, an essence captured by the euphemism "barnyard" that refers to the waft of manure found in rustic reds. In subtle doses, we lovers of old-school pinot find it pleasing, like a drive next to a cow pasture with the windows down. Above a certain threshold, though, it's off-putting, evidence the winemaker needs to invest in new barrels—or move the cows out of the cellar.

It doesn't take a wine geek to appreciate the appeal. African-American musicians coined the term *funky* to refer to a hip-swinging groove emphasizing bass and drums. Before it came to be synonymous with rhythm and blues, it literally meant a strong sweaty odour, more specifically the smell of sex. How's that for another dimension in our definition of earthy? A sexy bass note—*goût de boudoir*.

That brings a few other enticingly pungent ingredients into the picture: truffles and certain cheeses, such as Muenster, Brie, Camembert and wonderfully stinky Époisses de Bourgogne, for example.

There's lots of latitude when foraging for a suitable beverage to wash down all that dirt and sweat. Earthy flavours present the perfect canvas for a variety of reds. Besides pinot noir, Italy's nebbiolo grape, found in regal Barolo and Barbaresco, delivers an uncanny nuance of truffle or mushroom. So do Tuscan reds, often imbued with a note of underbrush.

But don't feel compelled to stick strictly to the theme when playing match game. Rich reds with berry-like flavour can make splendid complements. A stroll down a dirt road is always more fun when you can pick a few berries along the way.

RED AND GREEN: CHINA'S SIGNATURE COCKTAIL

China has given so much to the world. Science. Philosophy. Art. Food! Frankly, those *har gow* dumplings on the dim sum cart alone make it a superpower in my books. But cocktails? This is the land where a person can order expensive red wine with Coke (in the same glass) and not get laughed out of the bar.

Yet all is forgiven because of this: Johnnie Walker Red and green tea. Simple but sublime. The tea's earthy-herbal essence locks with the earthy-peatiness of the Scotch. (Other brands don't work so well.) Important: the tea must be unsweetened; sugar would wreck the spirit.

I prefer one part Red to three parts green for the best balance. Typically consumed cold, it's also nice warm with a slice of chocolate cake.

JOHNNIE WALKE
Red Labe
BLENDED SCOTCH WHIS
ISHED 1820
40% alc

Menu 1

AN ARGENTINIAN ODYSSEY

Sweet Potato and Black Bean Empanadas

Argentinian Short Ribs

Jerusalem Artichoke and Potato Purée

Dulce de Leche Flan

Argentinian food has many Mediterranean influences. The techniques, spicing and flavours of both Spain and Italy are common, and pasta, pizza and rice-based dishes are on many menus. But it is the asado, or barbecue, which started with the cowboys on the pampas, that is the backbone of meals all over Argentina. Argentinians eat meat every day, and although you may wonder about the health benefits of doing so, their meat is very different from ours. It is less fatty, grass fed, full of omega-3s and butchered differently. The meat itself is chewier than we are used to, and it has huge flavour. Added flavourings are often simple, sometimes no more than salt and pepper, while oregano, cilantro and parsley are popular herbs. In this menu, I've braised the short ribs instead of grilling them, but the earthy flavour is all Argentinian. Empanadas are the South American equivalent of dumplings, except they are baked. Fillings vary all over the country, some meat, some vegetarian. Mine are vegetarian, from Familia Zuccardi in Mendoza (home of the popular Fuzion wine), where I attended a class in empanada making. Dulce de leche is the ubiquitous sweet caramel filling used in many desserts. Here it is incorporated into a Spanish-like flan.

SWEET POTATO AND BLACK BEAN EMPANADAS

When I was in Chile and Argentina, these empanadas were invariably served naked as a first course. I like to serve a salsa with them, or plate a small salad of bitter lettuce with the empanadas on top. Here a sweet potato and bean filling gives an earthy flavour. Although this recipe makes larger ones, you can also make tiny hors d'oeuvres. Cut out 2-inch rounds with a cookie cutter and fill with a heaped teaspoon of filling. These empanadas reheat at 350°F for 8 to 10 minutes. You may have a bit of filling left over—it's great inside a quesadilla. You can buy empanada pastry at South American grocery stores if you don't have time to make your own.

Makes about 12 empanadas

Filling:

1 sweet potato
½ cup canned black beans, drained and rinsed
1 tbsp vegetable oil
1 tbsp chopped seeded jalapeño pepper
½ tsp ground cumin
½ tsp ground coriander
4 tsp lime juice
¼ tsp chili flakes, or to taste
Salt and freshly ground pepper
2 cups shredded provolone (6 oz/170 g)
¼ cup queso fresco or pressed cottage cheese (2 oz/55 g)

Pastry:

2½ cups all-purpose flour
¾ cup lard or organic shortening, cut in small cubes
1 tbsp granulated sugar
1 tsp kosher salt
½ tsp turmeric
1 egg yolk
1 tbsp white vinegar
4 tbsp cold water

Egg Wash:

1 egg yolk beaten with 2 tbsp cold water

Preheat oven to 350°F.

Place sweet potato on a baking sheet and bake for 1 hour or until soft. Scrape out flesh. You should have about ½ cup.

Crush beans with a potato masher but make sure that they still have some texture.

Heat oil in a medium skillet over medium heat. Add jalapeño and sauté for 30 seconds or until beginning to pop, then add cumin and coriander and sauté for 30 seconds longer or until fragrant. Add sweet potato and black beans. Stir in lime juice and chili flakes. Season with salt and pepper to taste. Remove from heat and cool completely. Stir in provolone and queso fresco. Reserve.

Place flour, lard, sugar, salt and turmeric in a food processor and pulse until mixture has the texture of coarse bread crumbs. Add egg yolk and vinegar and pulse just to mix. Dough should not come together. Add water, 1 tbsp at a time, and pulse until dough sticks together but does not form a ball on the blades.

(If it does, it will be tougher, but proceed anyway.) Turn out onto a work surface and knead into a ball. Divide in half, wrap each half in plastic and chill for 30 minutes.

Preheat oven to 400°F.

Roll out one half of dough on a lightly floured surface to about ⅛-inch thickness. Cut out 4-inch rounds with a cookie cutter. Gather scraps together and re-roll as needed to use up dough. Repeat with other half of dough.

Brush egg wash over edges of pastry. Place 1 heaping tbsp of filling in centre of each pastry circle. Fold over pastry, press edges to seal and use a fork to crimp edges.

Place on a parchment-lined baking sheet, prick with a fork and brush with remaining egg wash. Bake for 12 to 15 minutes or until pastry is golden. Serve hot or at room temperature.

PAIRING: **Torrontes**

It was Chile's late president, Salvador Allende, who, upon election in 1970, promised a peaceful, Chilean-style socialist revolution, not with guns but "with red wine and empanadas." He must have been thinking about meat-filled empanadas, because these vegetarian delights beg for white. Chile's South American neighbour Argentina has just the thing: torrontes. A national signature grape, along with red malbec, it's dry and exotically perfumed, with punchy peach and white-table-grape flavours and moderate acidity, perfect assets to lift the earthy sweet potato and soften the spices.

ARGENTINIAN SHORT RIBS

This is a superb, full-flavoured stew for entertaining. Argentinian short ribs are on the long bone, not divided into sections as other short rib cuts are.

Serves 6

1 tbsp chopped garlic
1 tbsp chopped fresh oregano
1 tbsp chopped fresh thyme
1 tsp dry mustard
1 tsp hot paprika
1 tsp chopped jalapeño pepper, or to taste
½ cup red wine
2 tbsp red wine vinegar
4 tbsp olive oil
6 Argentinian short ribs on the long bone
Salt and freshly ground pepper
1 cup chopped red onions
1 tsp diced jalapeño pepper
2 cups canned diced tomatoes
2 cups beef stock, homemade or store-bought
1 tbsp Worcestershire sauce
3-inch strip of orange peel

Combine garlic, oregano, thyme, mustard, paprika, chopped jalapeño, wine, vinegar and 2 tbsp olive oil in a bowl. Arrange short ribs in a single layer in a large dish (or two). Pour marinade over ribs. Marinate, covered and refrigerated, for 12 hours.

Preheat oven to 300°F.

Remove ribs from marinade, reserving marinade. Pat ribs dry and season with salt and pepper.

Heat remaining 2 tbsp oil in a large skillet or Dutch oven over high heat. Working in batches, brown meat well on each side, about 2 minutes per side. Reserve.

Spill out all but 1 tbsp oil. Reduce heat to medium. Add onions and diced jalapeño and sauté until softened, about 2 minutes. Stir in tomatoes, stock, Worcestershire sauce and reserved marinade. Bring to a boil, scraping up any bits on bottom of pot. Add short ribs and orange peel (or place all ingredients in a casserole dish).

Cover and bake for 2 to 2½ hours or until ribs are fork-tender. Remove short ribs to a baking sheet.

Increase heat to 400°F.

Skim any fat from sauce. Place over medium heat and reduce until slightly thickened, about 5 minutes.

Roast short ribs for 15 minutes. Return to sauce.

PAIRING: **Malbec**

Once popular in Bordeaux and still the dominant grape in Cahors in southwest France, heat-loving malbec found more hospitable, sunny skies in Argentina's vast Mendoza region. Full-bodied and robust, it loves fatty beef. It also won't let a bit of spice shackle its gaucho spirit.

THE ASADO

The asado is the quintessential Argentinian barbecue. It is a long process, in which a huge fire is allowed to die down to smouldering embers while meats are roasted either on the grill or on stakes. Meats, sausages, blood sausages (the famous Argentinian morcilla), offal and sometimes chicken are all cooked simply and served with only a chimichurri sauce and a salad as accompaniments. The meat is seasoned with salt, never marinated or oiled, and set directly on the grill (or if it is a whole goat, staked by the hottest end of the fire). Doing an asado at home is easy and fun for everyone. Adventurous eaters can try sweetbreads and blood sausage; others can stick to steak. Not much Argentinian beef is exported, so typical recipes need to be adapted slightly. If you have a charcoal grill, the taste will be more authentic.

JERUSALEM ARTICHOKE AND POTATO PURÉE

The Jerusalem artichoke is not an artichoke at all but a tuber with an artichoke taste. They are wonderful combined with other roots to make purées and are equally good roasted or quickly sautéed. Feel free to increase the amount of butter and cream in this recipe, depending on your cholesterol levels! Serve beside or under the short ribs.

Serves 6

8 oz (225 g) Jerusalem artichokes, peeled and cut in ¾-inch chunks
1 lb (450 g) Yukon Gold potatoes, peeled and cut in 1-inch chunks
¼ cup butter, melted
¼ cup whipping cream
Salt and freshly ground pepper

Place artichokes in a large pot with enough salted cold water to cover. Bring to a boil and boil artichokes for 10 minutes. Add potatoes and cook for another 10 minutes or until the vegetables are very soft. Drain well, reserving ½ cup cooking water. Return potatoes and artichokes to pot and place over low heat to evaporate any water clinging to vegetables. Remove from heat and mash.

Use an electric mixer to beat in butter, cream and enough cooking water to make a soft purée. Season well with salt and pepper. Reheat over medium heat, stirring constantly.

A BRAISING PRIMER

Braising and stewing are interchangeable terms; both mean long, slow cooking in liquid, usually in the oven to ensure even heat. The result is tender meat and a rich sauce. Braises are a staple in all cultures and are an essential comfort food. They started off as food of the peasants—the wealthy got the best cuts and roasted them, and the poor ended up with the tough ones.

Stewing meats are cut from hard-working muscles, which have built up both flavour and toughness. A slow cooking in liquid makes them tender and tasty. Already tender cuts, on the other hand, will dry out if stewed. The best cuts for stewing are beef chuck, shoulder, shanks, brisket and short ribs; veal shoulder and breast; pork butt and shoulder; lamb shoulder, shank and breast.

Choose the right pot. Too large a pot causes the gravy to evaporate too quickly; too small means the meat cooks unevenly. Cubed stewing meat should sit in one or two layers, and one piece of meat should fit snugly inside. A Dutch oven is perfect for braising, as it can go from the stovetop to the oven. If you don't have a Dutch oven, start in a skillet and transfer to a casserole dish with a tight-fitting lid.

Cut the meat—and the vegetables too—into uniform pieces for even cooking. Sear meat in oil over high heat. Work in batches: crowding the pan lowers the temperature and results in greyish meat. The added liquid can vary from stock to tomato juice to wine. Don't use water—it makes weak gravy. You can thicken the stew with flour, cornstarch or arrowroot, but my preference for thickening the sauce is to boil down the liquid. That way you get a more intense flavour.

Use gentle heat to cook the meat slowly in the oven; 300 to 325°F is perfect for stews and braises. The liquid should barely simmer—reduce the heat if it boils. Turning the heat up will toughen the meat's fibres. The meat is done when it can be pierced with a fork. Add vegetables such as potatoes, carrots and whole small onions about 45 minutes before the meat is cooked. Wait to add tender vegetables such as zucchini, cabbage, mushrooms or peas until about 15 minutes before the end of cooking time.

It is easiest to remove fat by chilling the stew overnight, spooning the solidified fat from the surface. Braises reheat beautifully and taste even better the next day.

DULCE DE LECHE FLAN

This flan provides a double hit of caramel in both the topping and the custard. The small amount of corn or maple syrup prevents crystallization. You can also bake this in an 8-cup soufflé dish. You can buy the dulce de leche if you wish.

Serves 6

Flan:
- 2½ cups milk
- 1 cup dulce de leche (page 211)
- 4 large eggs
- 4 large egg yolks
- 1 tbsp vanilla

Caramel:
- ½ cup granulated sugar
- 3 tbsp water
- 1 tbsp corn or maple syrup

Combine milk and dulce de leche in a large pot. Whisk over medium-high heat until milk is hot and mixture is uniform. Remove from heat.

Beat eggs and yolks together in a large bowl. Add milk mixture to eggs in a slow steady stream, whisking constantly so that eggs don't curdle. Add vanilla. Reserve.

Preheat oven to 325°F.

Combine sugar, water and syrup in a heavy pot. Stir over medium-high heat until sugar has dissolved. Bring to a boil and boil for 5 to 7 minutes, until caramel is golden. Immediately pour caramel into a 10-cup stainless steel bowl. Moving quickly, swirl bowl so that caramel coats bottom. Let bowl sit until caramel has hardened.

Pour in custard. Place bowl in a deep metal baking pan. Pour hot water into baking pan until it comes halfway up side of bowl. Cover bowl with a sheet of parchment paper. Bake for 45 to 50 minutes or until custard is set but still has a slight wiggle in the centre. Remove from water bath and cool. Refrigerate until set, about 3 hours.

Unmould onto a rimmed serving plate. If caramel sticks to bowl, place directly on stove over very low heat for 1 minute or until loosened. Serve with fruit, if desired.

DULCE DE LECHE

Here is a foolproof method for making your own dulce de leche. It is always better than the bought version. Refrigerated, it keeps for months. Use as a filling for cookies, cakes and meringues or drizzle over fruit desserts.

2 cans (14 oz/398 mL each) sweetened condensed milk

Preheat oven to 425°F. Scrape condensed milk into a glass pie plate or shallow baking dish and cover tightly with foil. Place dish in a roasting pan and pour in boiling water until it comes halfway up side of baking dish. Carefully transfer to oven and bake until golden brown, about 1 hour 15 minutes. Remove from oven, uncover and cool. Store in a covered container in the refrigerator.

PAIRING: **Tokaji**

I would have suggested late-harvest torrontes, but you'd be hard pressed to find a sweet Argentine wine at your local wine purveyor. Hungarian tokaji fits the bill beautifully, though. A storied dessert elixir with roots dating back at least to the seventeenth century, it's analogous to Bordeaux's famous Sauternes, the product of concentrated juice from grapes partially desiccated by a benevolent fungus called noble rot. Taste the caramel flan, sip the golden, honeyed nectar and prepare to be amazed.

Wine-and-Dessert Rule: Food-and-wine pairing is no dictatorship, but one law comes close to absolute: the wine should be sweeter than the dessert. Sugar in food cancels fruitiness in wine, causing the latter to taste sour and unbalanced. Most important, fight the impulse to serve dry champagne with dessert, and that includes strawberries. Take it from Frédéric Heidsieck, global sales manager for Louis Roederer, maker of the iconic Cristal Champagne. "I prefer to have my strawberries with a dessert wine," he once told me. "Champagne is a beautiful balance between sugar and acidity. If you put some sugar in your mouth, then you are in trouble. Some people like to have strawberries and chocolate, and it's even worse."

MINERALITY: WINE ON THE ROCKS

Okay, so it's not even a proper English word. *Minerality*? The suffix *ity* forms nouns from adjectives, as in *drinkability* from *drinkable*. *Mineral* is already a noun. But I digress. Wine geeks trot it out incessantly as the ultimate praise. Fruit? Texture? Who cares when you've got a wine with . . . minerality!

It's a catch-all (I use it myself for convention's sake), covering such perceived nuances as chalk, flint, slate and wet stone, hallmarks of the world's most elegant wines. I'm a chalk addict. But, no, there's none in your glass, despite what that dinner-party bore insists while pontificating about the limestone bedrock in Burgundy. At a Geological Society of America conference in 2009, rock scientists declared that the mineral content in wine is well below the threshold of human perception. There's way more calcium in Evian.

True, minerality is often (though hardly always) linked to wines grown on stony soils, but the perceived flavour more than likely comes from acidity and the by-products of yeast during fermentation.

NIAGARA PENINSULA

Menu 2

A FIRST NATIONS DINNER

Beet and Blue Potato Salad with Local Blue Cheese

The Just-Right Bison Burger with Homemade Ketchup

Bannock

Pear, Apple and Cornmeal Crunch

First Nations people ate only what grew or could be hunted locally, much the way we strive to eat today. We nod to that way of life in this menu. Bison, also known as North American buffalo, was once a staple food for aboriginal people, but was hunted nearly to extinction in the nineteenth century. It is slowly coming back, with new herds being raised in the west. It is a nutrient-rich, lean and flavourful meat. When ground, it is meatier than regular hamburger, with an earthier taste. Bannock, an aboriginal flatbread, is basically a fried bread. Once you've eaten one, you can't stop. Pears and apples were an important part of the First Nations diet, and cornmeal was a staple. I have combined them for a sensational dessert.

BEET AND BLUE POTATO SALAD WITH LOCAL BLUE CHEESE

This salad is colourful and tasty. Local blue cheeses can be found all across Canada and the United States. I love ones from Quebec. Beets and maple syrup play a role in Quebec cuisine, but vibrantly hued blue potatoes originated in Peru. Their texture is like a sweet potato. **Serves 6**

4 medium beets
Salt and freshly ground pepper
8 oz (225 g) blue potatoes, unpeeled
1 head romaine lettuce
1 cup diced red onions
2 tbsp chopped fresh dill
4 oz (115 g) local blue cheese, diced or crumbled

Vinaigrette:
2 tbsp red wine vinegar
1 tsp Dijon mustard
½ tsp maple syrup
⅓ cup olive oil
2 tbsp chopped fresh dill

Preheat oven to 400°F.

Place a large piece of foil on a baking sheet. Place beets in the centre. Season with salt and pepper. Sprinkle with 2 tbsp water. Fold foil over beets to enclose, sealing package tightly. Roast beets for 1 hour to 1 hour 15 minutes or until easily pierced with a fork. Cool. Peel and dice beets.

Add potatoes to a pot of cold water. Bring to a boil, reduce heat and simmer for 15 to 20 minutes or until tender. Drain and cool under running water. Peel potatoes and cut into quarters.

Tear romaine into bite-size pieces. Place on a platter. Layer red onions, beets and potatoes over lettuce. Sprinkle with dill and blue cheese.

Combine vinegar, mustard and maple syrup. Whisk in olive oil, dill and salt and pepper to taste. Sprinkle over salad and toss together right before serving.

PAIRING: **Demi-sec Vouvray**

You may be tempted to serve this hearty salad on its own rather than as a side to the bison burgers. Sweet, tangy and earthy, it represents a tall order where drink is concerned. Demi-sec Vouvray from France covers the bases: tart, nectar-like and often with a whisper of mineral. Off-dry German riesling is another good option, as is New Zealand pinot gris. Should you prefer red with this "blue-on-blue" course, try jammy-earthy California pinot noir.

THE JUST-RIGHT BISON BURGER WITH HOMEMADE KETCHUP

Serve these flavourful but lean burgers on bannock with homemade ketchup (both recipes follow), with sliced red onions, sliced tomatoes, Dijon mustard, pickles and coleslaw. Use ground chuck if bison is unavailable.

Serves 4

1½ lb (675 g) ground bison
1 tsp kosher salt
½ tsp freshly ground pepper
2 tbsp vegetable oil

Preheat barbecue to high.

Season ground bison with salt and pepper. Form into 4 patties, each about 1 inch thick. Brush patties with oil.

Grill for 5 to 7 minutes per side or until desired degree of doneness.

PAIRING: Nk'Mip Qwam Qwmt Merlot

The name is a mouthful, just like the bison burger. Nk'Mip (pronounced inka-meep) is North America's first aboriginal-owned-and-operated winery, located in the town of Osoyoos in British Columbia's Okanagan Valley, just over the border from Washington State. It's a territory of wild sagebrush, parched landscapes and sunny weather for vines, which translates into perfectly ripened, full-bodied reds. Bison meat is lean but assertive in flavour, no time for wimpy wines. And, hey, this is a burger, with tangy-spicy ketchup and Lord knows what else you'll pile on this bison's back. Nk'Mip's top-level merlot delivers a wagonload of fruity richness. Alternative: jammy red zinfandel from California.

TOMATO KETCHUP

This is not a knock-off of bottled ketchup. It has a layered texture and taste, an edge of tomato but with other flavours folded in. It is a must-have with burgers. Use it as a dip or a condiment for plain grilled meats. Made with canned tomatoes, it is a year-round pleasure. This will keep, in a covered container in the fridge, for a month or more.

Makes about 3 cups

1 can (28 oz/796 mL) tomatoes
1 Thai red chili, seeded and chopped (or 1 tbsp chili flakes)
1 tsp chopped garlic
¾ cup brown sugar
¾ cup red wine vinegar
2 tbsp fish sauce

Purée half the tomatoes and all their juice with the chili and garlic in a food processor. Chop remaining tomatoes.

Combine puréed tomatoes, sugar, vinegar and fish sauce in a large pot. Slowly bring to a boil over medium-high heat, stirring constantly. When mixture comes to a boil, reduce heat to a simmer and add chopped tomatoes.

Simmer gently, uncovered and stirring occasionally, for 30 to 40 minutes or until ketchup is dark red and jam-like. Pour into a bowl, cool and refrigerate.

BANNOCK

Bannock is a Native fried bread that will become a staple in your cooking. My first real bannock, at Lil'wat Cultural Centre in Whistler, BC, was a wonderful surprise, rich, crisp and tender inside. Use these as your hamburger buns. You can adjust the size as needed. Leftover bannock can be eaten on its own or with peanut butter, jams, maple syrup or honey.

Makes 8 to 12 bannocks

- 4 cups unbleached all-purpose flour
- ¼ cup granulated sugar
- 3 tbsp baking powder
- 2 tsp kosher salt
- 2 to 3 cups cold water
- Vegetable oil for frying

Sift together flour, sugar, baking powder and salt. Stir in enough water to form a sticky dough.

Heat ¼ inch of vegetable oil in a large skillet over medium heat.

Ladle a scant cup of dough into the hot oil for each bannock, shaping a circle about 4 inches wide.

Fry patties until golden brown on each side and puffed up, about 2 to 3 minutes per side. Transfer to a rack and repeat with remaining dough.

PEAR, APPLE AND CORNMEAL CRUNCH

There is energizing crunchiness in the topping from the Demerara sugar, cornmeal and almonds. Combined with the soft juiciness of the fruit, it will become a standard in your kitchen. To make this gluten-free, replace the flour with rice flour. Toast almonds at 375°F for 3 to 4 minutes or until golden brown. **Serves 4**

3 Pink Lady or other cooking apples, peeled, cored and diced
2 Bartlett pears, peeled, cored and diced
¼ cup granulated sugar
1 tsp grated lemon zest
2 tbsp lemon juice
2 tbsp apple juice
¼ tsp cinnamon
¼ tsp ground star anise
1 tbsp all-purpose flour

Topping:
½ cup Demerara sugar
½ cup cornmeal
½ cup all-purpose flour
½ tsp kosher salt
½ cup unsalted butter, cut in pieces, at room temperature
½ cup sliced almonds, toasted

Preheat oven to 375°F.

Place apples and pears in a bowl and toss with sugar, lemon zest and juice, apple juice, cinnamon and star anise. Butter a 6-cup gratin dish and pile in fruit. Bake for 15 minutes or until fruit starts to soften. Remove from oven, sprinkle flour over fruit and toss to coat.

Combine sugar, cornmeal, flour, salt and butter in a food processor. Process until mixture is clumpy. Add almonds and stir to combine. Sprinkle topping over fruit. Bake for 30 minutes or until fruit is soft and bubbling and topping is golden. Serve with ice cream.

PAIRING: **Dark rum**

To be fair, there are abundant sweet-wine options here, from German auslese riesling to late-harvest gewürztraminer, even moscato d'Asti, the low-alcohol crackling Italian white I love so much (there's polenta in the crunch, after all). But a wee nip of oak-aged rum (you might have an underused open bottle lying around?) would sing with the Demerara sugar. There's even a superb brand called El Dorado labelled "Demerara" because it comes from the banks of Guyana's Demerara River, source of the sugar's name. If that seems rich, try a tiny splash in your coffee.

Menu 3

A VEGETARIAN HOLIDAY DINNER

Cream of Lentil Soup with Horseradish

Chestnut-Stuffed Portobello Mushrooms

Shallot and Brussels Sprout Compote

Barley Pilaf

Apple Amaretti Parfait

Vegetarians often have to sacrifice at holiday celebrations. They can eat the veggie side dishes but usually do not get special attention when turkey or roast beef is the crowning glory. We are fixing this with a menu that will satisfy vegetarians and carnivores alike. These are familiar holiday flavours, just packaged differently. Barley and portobello mushrooms have an earthy attitude, giving this menu lot of oomph.

CREAM OF LENTIL SOUP WITH HORSERADISH

With a touch of Middle Eastern spicing but a modern French finish, this soup is an outstanding starter to this meal. Sometimes I embellish it with a few strands of grated fresh horseradish. **Serves 6**

- 1 green apple, peeled, cored and chopped (about 1 cup)
- 1 cup du Puy or brown lentils
- ½ cup chopped onions
- 1 tsp ground ginger
- 1 tsp ground cumin
- ½ tsp grated lemon zest
- 4 cups vegetable stock or water
- Salt and freshly ground pepper
- ¼ cup whipping cream
- 2 tsp horseradish

Combine apple, lentils, onions, ginger, cumin, lemon zest and vegetable stock in a pot. Bring to a boil over high heat. Reduce heat to low, cover and simmer for 40 minutes or until lentils are soft.

Purée mixture in a food processor until smooth (or use a hand blender). Season with salt and pepper. Return to pot.

Stir together cream and horseradish. Stir into soup and reheat when needed.

PINOT NOIR

Sometimes when I enthuse to Lucy about how this syrah or that chardonnay would flatter food she's prepared, she'll adopt a quizzical stare. No words necessary. I've learned what she means. "Prove to me it would be better than pinot noir." To her credit, I'm occasionally at a loss.

Lucy adores pinot. Fortunately, I do too. It's a shame we're not married, because, from where I see it, we've got the perfect recipe for bliss. She cooks; I uncork the pinot.

Great pinot noir is one thing above all else: graceful. More specifically, it's medium bodied and crisp, with a texture as supple as 1500-thread-count Egyptian cotton and flavours that call to mind a seductive combination of forest berries, plums, cinnamon and earthy beetroot. Throw in the best floral perfume and a nuance of stony mineral and you've just chanced upon a fine red Burgundy, pinot's greatest expression.

It's the world's most versatile red, able to span the canyon between delicate fish and hearty braised beef, a chief reason Lucy loves it so much. Pinot gets along handsomely with earthy foods, though it's at its elegant best with medium-weight proteins, such as grilled salmon, roast poultry and, my personal favourite match, pan-seared rare duck breast.

Bad pinot noir, on the other hand (and there's more of it than good), is a waste of time. If it doesn't taste like cheap candy, it's sharp and thin. Expect to pay at least $20 for a good one from New Zealand's Central Otago and Martinborough regions, $25 and up for the fine offerings from Carneros and the Santa Rita Hills in California, and $40 or more for great red Burgundy. There are occasional bargains to be had, but pinot and penny-pinchers inevitably end up in divorce.

CHESTNUT-STUFFED PORTOBELLO MUSHROOMS

Think of chestnut-stuffed turkey and transfer that thought to mushrooms, which are meaty in their own way. The chestnuts add a rich earthiness to this dish and make the mushrooms that much more meat-like. Look for the largest, juiciest-looking portobellos for this dish. If your mushrooms are smaller, you may have extra stuffing; stir in half a beaten egg and bake in a gratin dish alongside your mushrooms. **Serves 6**

12 large portobello mushrooms
½ cup olive oil

Chestnut Stuffing:
¼ cup butter
1 cup chopped onions
1 cup chopped celery
1 tsp cracked fennel seeds
1 tbsp chopped garlic
2⅓ cups vacuum-packed peeled roasted chestnuts (about 14 oz/400 g), chopped
4 cups fresh bread crumbs
½ cup chopped fresh flat-leaf parsley
⅓ cup unsweetened apple juice
Salt and freshly ground pepper

Rich Red Wine Sauce (page 227)

Preheat oven to 425°F.

Cut off mushroom stems flush with caps and chop. You should have about 1½ cups.

Heat 2 tbsp olive oil in a large skillet over high heat. Working in batches, add mushroom caps to pan and fry for 1 to 2 minutes per side or until just beginning to soften. Transfer gill side up to a baking sheet. Repeat with remaining mushroom caps, adding more oil to pan as needed. Reserve.

Melt butter in the same skillet over medium heat. Add onions, celery and fennel seeds and sauté for 10 minutes or until slightly caramelized. Add garlic, chestnuts and chopped mushroom stems and sauté for 2 minutes or until mushrooms are juicy. Remove from heat.

Stir bread crumbs and parsley into stuffing mixture. Add enough apple juice to moisten stuffing well. Season well with salt and pepper. Divide stuffing into 6 portions and place on top of each of the mushroom caps on the baking sheet. Top with remaining 6 mushroom caps, gill side down, to make a kind of sandwich. Do not totally enclose the stuffing. Roast for 15 minutes or until mushrooms are tender and stuffing is crisp around the edges. Serve drizzled with Rich Red Wine Sauce.

PAIRING: **White Burgundy**

Try this inventively woodsy, earthy dish with a nutty, mineral-laden white Burgundy (such as Macon or, if budget permits, Puligny-Montrachet) and bask in the subtle decadence. The wine is great for the Brussels sprouts too. Alternative: If you prefer red, uncork a Chianti.

RICH RED WINE SAUCE

Pomegranate juice gives a wonderful colour to this sauce as well as a subtle flavour. This is similar to a beurre blanc sauce but made with red wine.

Makes ½ cup

- ½ cup red wine
- ½ cup pomegranate juice
- 2 tsp light soy sauce
- ½ tsp granulated sugar
- ¼ cup cold unsalted butter, cut in pieces
- Salt and freshly ground black pepper

Combine red wine, pomegranate juice, soy sauce and sugar in a heavy pot. Bring to a boil over high heat, reduce heat and simmer for 10 to 20 minutes or until thickened. Remove from heat and stir in butter a few pieces at a time until fully incorporated and sauce is emulsified. Season with salt and pepper.

SHALLOT AND BRUSSELS SPROUT COMPOTE

Brussels sprouts are a traditional holiday vegetable and are having their moment as a trendy one. This is the perfect side dish for the mushrooms.

Serves 6

- 6 large shallots, unpeeled
- 8 garlic cloves, unpeeled
- 2 tbsp butter
- 1 tbsp vegetable oil
- 8 oz (225 g) Brussels sprouts, cut in half
- Salt and freshly ground pepper
- 1 tbsp chopped fresh parsley

Add shallots and garlic to a pot of cold water. Bring to a boil and boil for 2 minutes. Drain, then remove skins. Cut shallots in half lengthwise if large.

Heat butter and oil in a heavy sauté pan (one with a lid) over medium heat. Add garlic and shallots and sauté for 1 minute. Add Brussels sprouts and toss everything together. Cover, reduce heat to medium-low and cook, stirring occasionally, for 8 to 10 minutes or until vegetables are tender.

Season with salt and pepper and sprinkle with parsley.

Shallots are an elongated or round member of the onion family. They sometimes have two or three clove clusters. They are not as strongly flavoured as onions—in fact, they impart a slight sweetness to dishes and are most often used in salad dressings and for flavouring sauces.

BARLEY PILAF

Barley is full of nutrients, and its nutty texture offers a contrast to the mushrooms. The truffle oil enhances the earthiness of the barley, but it is not necessary.

Serves 6

2 tbsp olive oil
1 cup chopped onions
½ cup chopped carrots
1 tsp chopped garlic
1 cup pearl barley
3 cups vegetable stock or water
Salt and freshly ground pepper
1 tbsp butter
2 drops truffle oil (optional)

Heat oil in a medium, heavy pot over medium heat. Add onions, carrots and garlic and sauté until onions soften, about 2 minutes. Add barley and sauté until coated with oil.

Add stock and bring to a boil, stirring. Cover and simmer for 30 minutes or until barley is tender but still has a slight bite. Season with salt and pepper and stir in butter and truffle oil (if using).

Truffle oil varies hugely in quality. Cheap oils are flavoured with artificial truffle flavouring, the more expensive ones with real truffles. If you are going to buy it, splurge on the good stuff. Truffle salt is another good standby in the kitchen. A little sprinkle on eggs or a steak brings out and complements their flavour. Again, the more expensive, the better.

APPLE AMARETTI PARFAIT

After such a large meal, serving a simple dessert is the best. We used Jonagold apples, but Pink Lady, Cortland or Mutsu would all be fine. This is an easy make-ahead dessert, and it looks great too: the apples have a pinkish hue from poaching in the pink syrup.

Serves 6

- 2 cups rosé wine
- 2 cups apple juice
- 1 cup granulated sugar
- 4 star anise
- 3 thin slices peeled fresh ginger, smashed
- 2-inch cinnamon stick
- 4 apples, peeled, cored and quartered
- 1 cup mascarpone
- 1 cup whipping cream
- 1 cup coarsely crushed amaretti or gingersnaps
- ½ cup slivered almonds, toasted

Combine rosé, apple juice, sugar, star anise, ginger and cinnamon stick in a pot wide enough to hold apples in one layer. Bring to a boil over high heat, stirring to dissolve sugar. Boil for 2 minutes.

Reduce heat to medium-low, add apples and cover them with a circle of parchment paper to promote even cooking and help them stay submerged. Poach for 15 to 20 minutes or until apples are soft and saturated with flavour. Remove with a slotted spoon.

Increase heat to high and bring juice to a boil. Boil until syrup is reduced to about ¾ cup and is thick and syrupy, 15 to 20 minutes. Return apples to pot and turn to coat with syrup.

Stir together mascarpone and ¼ cup syrup until well combined. Beat whipping cream until soft peaks form. Fold half of whipped cream into mascarpone mixture.

Layer some amaretti crumbs, some mascarpone cream and 2 apple quarters in each of 6 parfait glasses, then repeat layers. Top with remaining whipped cream and drizzle with a little syrup. Scatter over toasted almonds.

PAIRING: **Quarts de Chaume**

A wine nerd's wine, Quarts de Chaume is an offbeat but eye-popping gem made from the white chenin blanc grape in the Loire region of France. Often syrupy sweet and laced with flavours of honey, baked apple and custard, it comes with a piercing edge of acidity that not only balances the wine but livens up the cream in this parfait. Or look for any white from the surrounding area of Coteaux du Layon. Alternative: spiced harvest ale from a microbrewery.

20-HOUR LAMB SHOULDER ROAST

This is the best lamb shoulder dish I have ever made. It is based on a lamb shoulder I had in Paris that was cooked sous vide. Here I use the same low oven temperature and a heavy pot. The lamb is succulent but retains some texture. Try it—it is amazing. Everyone who makes this recipe raves about the ease of cooking and the superb taste. Cook about 12 fingerling potatoes separately and add them to the sauce before serving.

Serves 4

- 1 shoulder of lamb on the bone (4 lb/1.8 kg)
- Salt and freshly ground pepper
- 4 sprigs fresh rosemary
- 6 garlic cloves, peeled and root end removed
- 1 cup chopped onions
- 1 cup beef or chicken stock
- ½ tsp dark soy sauce (optional)
- 2 tbsp chopped fresh parsley

Preheat oven to 160°F.

Season lamb well with salt and pepper. Place in a heavy ovenproof pot that the roast fits snugly. Scatter over rosemary and garlic. Cover, place roast in oven and cook for 15 hours.

Add onions and stock and cook for another 5 to 6 hours or until lamb is very tender.

Remove lamb from pot and skim fat from sauce. Place pot over high heat. Bring sauce to a boil and reduce until flavours have intensified, 8 to 10 minutes. Stir in soy sauce for colour, if desired.

Remove string from lamb. Heat a nonstick skillet over high heat. Place lamb fat side down in pan and sear for about 2 minutes or until browned and crispy. Turn lamb and continue to brown all sides.

Place lamb and sauce in a covered serving dish. When ready to serve, reheat at 300°F for 30 minutes. Sprinkle with parsley before serving.

CRANBERRY GINGER CHUTNEY

I had a request from a reader for a different cranberry sauce. Here's one flavoured with lime, ginger and lime leaves. If you can't find lime leaves in Asian markets, you can leave them out. This colourful, refreshing, unusual chutney is splendid with our vegetarian menu or a holiday turkey and is also terrific with cheese. It keeps for a month, refrigerated. Give some away as gifts if you have too much. **Makes about 5 cups**

2 tbsp grated orange zest
1 tbsp grated lime zest
1 navel orange, peeled and diced
1 lime, peeled and cut in half crosswise
2 cups granulated sugar
½ cup water
½ cup dried cranberries
1 tbsp finely chopped fresh ginger
1-inch piece cinnamon stick
6 lime leaves
1½ lb (675 g) fresh cranberries

Place orange and lime zest, diced orange and lime in a food processor and process until finely chopped.

Place sugar and water in a large pot and bring to a boil over high heat, stirring occasionally until sugar has dissolved. Cook, without stirring, until sugar has begun to caramelize and is a light gold, about 8 minutes.

Stir in orange/lime mixture, dried cranberries, ginger, cinnamon stick and lime leaves. Cook for 1 minute, then stir in fresh cranberries. Reduce heat to medium and continue to cook, stirring occasionally, for about 12 minutes or until most of the cranberries have exploded. Cool.

Remove lime leaves and cinnamon stick. Place chutney in jars and refrigerate for up to 3 weeks.

GRILLED ARGENTINIAN SHORT RIBS

My favourite meat at steak houses in Argentina was the grilled short ribs. You had to order them very rare, otherwise the meat was too chewy. The richness and meatiness of the taste can't be beat, but be sure to start with well-marbled meat.

Serves 4

4 short ribs on the long bone
Salt and freshly ground pepper
2 tbsp olive oil

Preheat grill to high.

Season short ribs with salt and pepper. Brush with oil. Place on grill, close lid and sear on both sides, turning once.

Reduce heat to low and continue to grill, turning once, for about 15 minutes or until medium-rare. Season with more salt and pepper and serve with chimichurri sauce (page 236).

CHIMICHURRI SAUCE

This typical South American sauce probably originated in Nicaragua but is today served everywhere. It is particularly popular in Miami, where it is served in upscale Latino restaurants as everything from a dip for sweet potato fries to a topping for toasted bread for a nibble. Traditionally served with grilled meats, it is the kind of sauce that each household makes to its own taste, so feel free to add more or less of what you like. You can substitute cilantro for oregano or use both. It keeps for 2 weeks in the refrigerator.

Makes about 1 cup

4 medium garlic cloves, peeled
1 cup packed flat-leaf parsley leaves
2 tbsp fresh oregano leaves (or 2 tsp dried)
¼ cup lemon juice
1 tsp chili flakes
½ cup olive oil
Salt and freshly ground pepper

Purée garlic in a food processor by dropping cloves down the feeder tube while the processor is running. Add parsley, oregano, lemon juice and chili flakes and process until chunky. Transfer to a bowl and whisk in olive oil. The sauce will thicken. Season with salt and pepper.

DULCE DE LECHE TARTLETS

Makes 4 tartlets

½ lb frozen butter puff pastry, thawed
1 oz (28 g) dark chocolate (at least 63% cocoa), melted
½ cup dulce de leche (page 211)
½ cup whipping cream, lightly whipped

Preheat oven to 400°F.

Roll out puff pastry on a lightly floured surface to ⅛-inch thickness. Cut out 4 rounds with a 4-inch cookie cutter. Press into individual tartlet pans or muffin cups. Prick the base. Line with foil and fill with pie weights or dried beans.

Bake for 15 minutes or until pastry is set. Remove foil and weights and bake for 5 minutes more or until golden and cooked through. Remove tart shells from pans and cool on a rack.

Brush insides of each tartlet shell with chocolate. Let sit until firm.

Spoon 2 tbsp dulce de leche into each tartlet shell. Serve at room temperature topped with whipped cream.

SALTY

natural salts • sea salt • sea vegetables • breads and rolls
cold cuts • cured meats • cooked pastas • soups • crackers
soy sauce • salad dressings • Parmesan • blue cheeses • feta
Asiago • ricotta • Pecorino • Roquefort • cured olives • capers
potato chips • bottarga • gravlax • club soda • brined poultry
seaweed • salted anchovies • sun-dried tomatoes • pickled foods
marsh samphire • saltwater crab • fish sauce

HERE'S A BRAINTEASER FOR YOUR NEXT *dinner party amusement: Who was the most important cook ever? Auguste Escoffier? Antonin Carême? Julia Child? Alice Waters? Ferran Adrià? Mario Batali? David Chang? Fine candidates all, but we'd nominate someone else: the cave dweller who first sprinkled salt on a piece of fish or mastodon steaks. We're not alone here. In a conversation years ago with Ferran Adrià, the Spanish molecular gastronomy pioneer, Beppi prevailed on the master to name his all-time favourite ingredient. "Salt," he said without a pause. "It's the most magical ingredient in the world." He took the words out of our mouths. Imagine cooking without salt. It's like reading in the glow of a Bic lighter: salt is the culinary light switch, amplifying and sharpening everything.*

Our Flintstone ancestors learned that lesson early on. As far back as the early Neolithic period, roughly 12,000 years ago, humans were mining salt caves and harvesting sea salts. Their initial goal may have been to preserve meat and fish (as with prosciutto and salt cod today), but Fred and Barney surely would have soon discovered that a pinch of the white stuff turned bland into grand. Perhaps they also felt more vigorous after a sprinkle or two, because salt, though justly maligned for overuse in processed foods, helps regulate fluid balance. Without small dietary quantities, animal life would cease. Worse, french fries would be boring.

Sodium chloride, the main culinary form of crystalline minerals we call salts, was so prized in ancient times it was equivalent to money. *Salarium*, Latin for "salary," was the Roman soldier's allowance for buying *sal*.

Fear not. We won't throw a sack of Sifto at you in this chapter. We will, though, give the mineral more room to strut its stuff, as in braised winter greens and mushroom salad with miso, the salty Japanese seasoning made from fermented rice, soybeans or barley.

We'll certainly cover the prepping technique known as brining, which involves soaking proteins in salty water before the meat is cooked. The salt acts to transport water into the meat's cells, resulting in a juicier roast.

There is, to be sure, no salt added to wine. But we think some grapes can exhibit a quality that could be described as saline. Sangiovese, the great red variety responsible for Chianti and Brunello di Montalcino, often comes across with a salty finish, though what you're perceiving likely is the wine's acidity. It's similar with many whiskies from Scotland's west coast and the exceedingly dry style of Sherry called manzanilla, redolent of the maritime breeze around the sea estuary of Spain's Guadalquivir River. Which brings us to a cardinal pairing rule: salt loves acidity. Sodium's dry tingle begs for a mouth-watering beverage.

Salt also likes to cozy up to sweetness. In cooking, it's been dubbed the trail-mix effect because of the harmony of salted nuts and grains with dried fruit. Italians might insist on the *prosciutto e melone* effect. Ham and sweet melon—it's a simply perfect way to start a meal, with or without a cooking quiz.

Menu 1

A SUSHI-FREE JAPANESE MEAL

Mushroom Miso Salad

Japanese Chicken Curry

Cucumber Pickles

Napa Pickles

Triple Ginger Cake

The meaning of the word *curry* has long been debated, but it seems to have descended from the Tamil word *kari*, which means "spiced gravy." The Japanese first tasted curry when the British arrived in Japan in the nineteenth century. Many of them came via India and brought curry with them. However, the Japanese form of curry is richer, sweeter and thicker than Indian curry and it uses lots of turmeric for its distinctive yellow look. It is served with Japanese short-grain rice. Japanese pickles are a fine accompaniment, as their saltiness provides a balance with the heat of the curry. Mushrooms and miso are a natural combination, and the miso dressing brings out the mushrooms' meaty, woodsy flavour. The ginger cake gives a hit of tangy flavour at the end of the meal. It is so luscious you won't be able to stop eating it.

MUSHROOM MISO SALAD

Healthy miso dressing is useful in the kitchen. Apart from salads, it is a winning addition to grilled fish, sautéed spinach and as a marinade for chicken. Use a mixture of mushrooms—it really does not matter which ones.

Serves 4

Dressing:
2 tsp white miso
1 tbsp lemon juice
2 tbsp vegetable oil
2 garlic cloves, finely chopped
2 tsp finely chopped fresh ginger
1 tbsp white wine
Salt and freshly ground pepper

Mushrooms:
1 tbsp vegetable oil
8 shiitake mushrooms, thickly sliced
8 oyster mushrooms, cut in half
8 oz (225 g) brown or white mushrooms, thickly sliced

Garnish:
2 tbsp flat-leaf parsley leaves
1 tsp sesame oil

Whisk miso with lemon juice and vegetable oil in a medium bowl for the dressing.
Heat vegetable oil in a medium skillet over medium-high heat until just before smoking.
Toss in all mushrooms and stir-fry until slightly brown, 3 to 4 minutes. Stir in garlic and ginger. Pour in wine and cook until it disappears, about 30 seconds. Season with salt and lots of pepper. Stir in miso dressing, combine well and remove from heat. Stir in parsley leaves and sesame oil. Serve warm.

PAIRING: **White Burgundy**

If you've been blessed with the means and foresight to have tucked away an old white Burgundy (or live with someone who has), exhume it now. There's a mushroom note in that chardonnay-based wine and (if you're lucky) insane balance that will get along handsomely with this soulful salad. Alternative: vintage Champagne.

MISO GINGER VINAIGRETTE

Here is an alternative, more assertive, vinaigrette for the Mushroom Miso Salad. Serve over cooked or raw spinach, sliced cucumber or steamed broccoli, asparagus or cauliflower.

¼ cup white miso
¼ cup rice vinegar
1 tbsp grated fresh ginger
1 tsp granulated sugar
½ tsp sesame oil
A few drops hot sauce

Combine miso, rice vinegar, ginger, sugar, sesame oil and hot sauce in a bowl. Refrigerate until needed.

JAPANESE CHICKEN CURRY

You can buy Japanese curry powder but it's just as easy to make your own with our recipe. Serve the curry with rice or udon noodles and Japanese pickles (recipes follow). The grated apple gives sweetness to the sauce.

Serves 4

- 1½ lb (675 g) boneless, skinless chicken thighs
- Salt and freshly ground pepper
- 4 tbsp vegetable oil
- 1 cup thinly sliced onions
- ½ cup coarsely grated peeled apple
- 2 tbsp Japanese curry powder (page 248)
- 1 tbsp chopped fresh ginger
- 1 tbsp chopped garlic
- 2 tbsp all-purpose flour
- 2 cups chicken stock
- 4 cups baby spinach
- 2 tbsp finely chopped fresh cilantro

Cut chicken thighs into 2-inch pieces. Season with salt and pepper. Heat 2 tbsp oil in a large skillet over medium-high heat. Add chicken in batches and sear for 1 to 2 minutes per side or until lightly golden. Reserve.

Reduce heat to medium. Add remaining 2 tbsp oil and onions to skillet and sauté for 2 minutes or until onions are softened. Add apple, curry powder, ginger and garlic and sauté for 1 minute or until fragrant.

Stir in flour and cook, stirring, for 1 to 2 minutes to cook out floury taste. Stir in stock a little at a time until well combined. Bring to a boil, stirring. Reduce heat and simmer for 2 minutes to thicken. Taste and adjust seasoning.

Return chicken and any juices to skillet and cook in sauce for 10 minutes or until meat is cooked through. Stir in spinach and cook for 1 minute or until spinach wilts. Garnish with cilantro just before serving.

PAIRING: **Dry riesling**

No, you don't have to drink sake here just because of the dish's heritage. That said, I do love Japan's highly underappreciated rice beverage—mainly the cold stuff, not the inferior warm brew. It works with this dish because it works with most foods, but riesling shines just as brightly, if not more so. The below-the-radar sweetness adds a smile to the delicate and complex spicing, while the vibrant acidity dances with the pickles. Alternative: Austrian grüner veltliner.

JAPANESE CURRY POWDER

This curry powder gets its traditional deep yellow colour from the turmeric. It is not a hot curry; it is more textured, with layered flavour.

Makes 4½ tbsp

- 2 tbsp turmeric
- 1 tbsp ground coriander
- 1 tsp ground cumin
- ½ tsp ground cardamom
- ½ tsp cinnamon
- ½ tsp ground ginger
- ½ tsp freshly ground pepper
- ¼ tsp cayenne pepper
- ¼ tsp ground cloves
- ¼ tsp ground fennel

Combine all spices in a small bowl and stir until uniform. Curry powder keeps well in a sealed container.

CUCUMBER PICKLES

I use a mandoline for even slices. You can make this with zucchini too.

Makes about 2 cups

1 large English cucumber, thinly sliced
1 tbsp kosher salt
¼ cup rice vinegar
2 tbsp mirin
2 tsp granulated sugar

Toss cucumber slices with kosher salt. Place in a colander and let sit in the sink or over a bowl for 15 minutes or until cucumbers are wilted and much of their water has been extracted.
Press on cucumbers to squeeze out remaining liquid and pat dry with paper towels. Transfer to a bowl.
Add rice vinegar, mirin and sugar and toss to combine.

There is an art to Japanese pickling. Use very fresh ingredients, and pickle lightly and quickly. Use salt and add ginger, soy, sesame oil, shiso leaves and chilies. Extra flavour is sometimes added by using an umami ingredient such as granules of dashi or dried Japanese mushrooms. Serve with any kind of Japanese food, but pickles are especially fine at breakfast. You can, of course, buy them at Japanese and Korean stores.

NAPA PICKLES

The first time I made these they were a disaster, as I thought they had to pickle for a few days. I ended up with wet, limp cabbage. This is a much simpler recipe. If you don't have instant dashi granules, use a bit of a vegetable stock cube. Shichimi togarashi is a Japanese hot pepper mix. If you can't find it in Asian markets, use chili flakes.

Makes about 3 cups

1 tbsp kosher salt
8 cups coarsely chopped napa cabbage
1 tsp shichimi togarashi
½ tsp dashi granules (optional)
1 tsp grated lemon zest
1 tsp sesame oil

Sprinkle salt over cabbage in a large bowl. Mix in the togarashi, dashi (if using), lemon zest and sesame oil. Transfer to a plastic bag and massage cabbage with the other ingredients through the plastic for a few minutes. Squeeze air out of the bag, seal bag and marinate for 1 hour. Remove cabbage from plastic bag and drain well.

TRIPLE GINGER CAKE

This cake has real zing with the four kinds of ginger, plus a wasabi hit. It is moist and light. Don't be concerned if the centre sinks slightly—it will still be perfect.

Serves 8

- 1½ cups + 2 tsp flour
- 1 tsp baking powder
- 1 tsp baking soda
- ½ tsp kosher salt
- 1 tbsp wasabi powder
- 2 tsp ground ginger
- ½ tsp ground cardamom
- 1 cup golden raisins
- ½ cup unsalted butter
- ½ cup dark brown sugar
- ½ cup maple syrup
- ¼ cup chopped pickled ginger
- 3 tbsp finely chopped crystallized ginger
- 2 eggs
- ½ cup milk

Syrup:

- ½ cup granulated sugar
- ½ cup water
- 1 tbsp grated fresh ginger

Preheat oven to 350°F. Butter an 8-inch square cake pan and line bottom with parchment paper.

Sift together 1½ cups flour, baking powder, baking soda, salt, wasabi powder, ground ginger and cardamom into a large bowl. Stir raisins with remaining 2 tsp flour in a small bowl and reserve.

Place butter, brown sugar, maple syrup, pickled ginger and crystallized ginger in a medium pot over medium heat. Gently heat, stirring, until butter is melted and sugar is dissolved. Remove from heat.

Beat eggs with milk in a medium bowl using an electric mixer.

Add butter mixture to flour mixture and stir together. Beat in egg mixture. Batter will be very thin. Sprinkle floured raisins onto batter and fold in gently with one or two strokes. Spoon into prepared pan and bake for 30 minutes or until a cake tester comes out clean.

Combine sugar, water and grated ginger in a small pot over medium heat while cake is baking. Stir until sugar is dissolved. Increase heat to medium-high, bring to a boil and boil for 4 or 5 minutes or until slightly syrupy. Pour through a sieve into a small bowl. Reserve syrup.

Cool cake in pan for 10 minutes. Run a sharp knife along the inside of the pan. Turn cake out of pan, peel off parchment and set cake right side up on a rack over a baking sheet. Use a skewer to punch holes all over top of cake. Brush with ginger syrup. Cool cake completely. Cut into squares and serve with a dollop of lemon ice.

PAIRING: **Prosecco with elderflower liqueur**

This dessert would be lovely with warm green tea. But if a celebratory end-of-meal cocktail suits the mood, try adding a splash of sweet elderflower liqueur, such as St-Germain from France, to a flute of prosecco, the dry Italian sparkling wine.

Menu 2

ITALIAN SIMPLICITY

Antipasto

Buffalo Mozzarella and Pickled Fennel

Garganelli with Prosciutto and Peas

Veal Scaloppine with Tomato Caper Sauce

Cassata Parfait

Italian cuisine is simplicity itself. Use excellent products, eat four smaller courses and enjoy the tastes and textures of quality seasonal, local ingredients. Eat your starch separately. Let the main ingredient in the main course be the star, and provide a sauce and perhaps a vegetable with it. This kind of cooking is a millennium away from fusion, pan-Asian and the hot—but I think cooling—modernist cuisine. This type of Italian cooking proves itself in New York, where Mario Batali has taken the city by storm with his excellent chain of Italian restaurants. Babbo and the fish restaurant Esca, famous for its crudo (and where I first tasted tuna prosciutto), are great places to try. To illustrate the essence and flavour of Italian food, here are some simple dishes for a perfect Italian dinner.

ANTIPASTO

Most Italian meals start with an antipasto, often a selection of cured meats and cheeses. Today, there is great choice to buy, as both butchers and restaurants are making their own cured meats and sausages. You also won't go wrong buying a few imported Italian products. Serve with some good sliced bread or breadsticks. A simple platter will consist of prosciutto, several kinds of cured sausages and perhaps a hunk of Parmesan or other Italian cheese. Garnished with some olives, a few pickles and a good relish, this is the perfect start to a dinner party.

PAIRING: **Aglianico**

Wine keeners are all atwitter over aglianico, the most regal native grape of southern Italy. Its greatest expression is found in volcanic hills near Naples in the Campania region, where I was once served a glass with samples of *salumi*, prosciutto and cheese in the cellars of Mastroberardino, producer of the most storied and longest-lived aglianicos. "See Naples and die" goes an Italian expression, meant to convey the city's magnificence. To which I'd add: don't leave without sampling the cold cuts and aglianico. The wine (pronounced with a silent *g*) is full bodied and gutsy, with astringent tannins that seem to dissolve in the presence of fatty-salty food. And the vise grip of acidity cleanses the palate, making room for more . . . antipasto!

CHAMPAGNE AND CHIPS

My list of carnal weaknesses is embarrassingly long, but if I had to settle on just three, Champagne and Lay's Classic Potato Chips would rank at No. 2 and No. 3, respectively. (No. 1 has nothing to do with food, except for whipping cream in a supporting role, so I'll leave it out for decorum's sake.)

As luck would have it, the wine and chips make for a heavenly combination. Bubbles dance with salt, acidity mops up the oil, and the Champagne's ambrosial nuances of fruit, yeasty dough, roasted nuts and dry chalkiness are cast into compelling relief by the plain, earthy, delicate chips. Don't miss this perfect high-low pairing if the budget permits Champagne, or try it with more affordable Spanish Cava, Italian prosecco or Crémant d'Alsace. Think of it as snack, crackle and pop.

BUFFALO MOZZARELLA AND PICKLED FENNEL

This dish is a composed salad, in which the elements are arranged separately on the plate rather than tossed together. Until you've tried pickled fennel, you don't know what a treat you are missing. Leave the fennel in the pickling liquid for up to a week if you're not using it right away. **Serves 4**

Pickled Fennel:
1 fennel bulb
1 cup water
½ cup white wine vinegar
¼ cup granulated sugar
1 tbsp kosher salt
½ tsp fennel seeds

Salad:
2 cups cherry tomatoes
2 tbsp olive oil
Salt and freshly ground pepper
2 tbsp fresh rosemary leaves
½ head escarole lettuce, washed and torn
2 tbsp extra-virgin olive oil
2 tsp lemon juice
1 large ball buffalo mozzarella, sliced
Maldon salt

Cut fennel in half lengthwise and cut out the core. Cut fennel in quarters, then thinly slice crosswise or shave on a mandoline. Place in a bowl.

Combine water, vinegar, sugar, salt and fennel seeds in a pot. Bring to a boil, reduce heat and simmer for 2 minutes.

Pour over fennel and marinate for 30 minutes or until softened. Drain and refrigerate until needed.

Preheat oven to 400°F.

Toss tomatoes with 1 tbsp olive oil and season with salt and pepper. Spread on a baking sheet and roast for 10 to 12 minutes or until browned and just crinkling. Set aside to cool.

Heat remaining 1 tbsp olive oil in a small skillet over medium-high heat. Add rosemary and sauté for 30 seconds or until crispy. Drain on paper towels.

Toss escarole with extra-virgin olive oil and lemon juice and season with salt and pepper to taste. Divide escarole among 4 plates. Lay a few slices of buffalo mozzarella on the side of each plate along with one-quarter of the roasted tomatoes and about ¼ cup pickled fennel. Sprinkle fried rosemary leaves around plates, and decorate with a little more extra-virgin olive oil and Maldon salt.

PAIRING: **Falanghina**

I am still waiting for this stellar white Italian grape to have its day in the fashion spotlight. A signature of the Campania region around Naples—where buffalo mozzarella reigns supreme—it is crisp yet more characterful than (yawn) pinot grigio.

GARGANELLI WITH PROSCIUTTO AND PEAS

This recipe is a traditional one from Emilia-Romagna, where butter is often used instead of olive oil. Garganelli are small squares of pasta that have been rolled into tubes. Substitute penne if you can't find it. The prosciutto adds just the right amount of saltiness to the dish. **Serves 4**

½ lb (225 g) garganelli
⅓ cup butter
1 cup chopped onions
3 oz (85 g) prosciutto, sliced into strips
4 oz (115 g) fresh or frozen peas
Salt and freshly ground pepper
1 cup grated Parmigiano-Reggiano

Cook pasta in a pot of lightly salted boiling water until al dente. Drain, reserving 1 cup pasta cooking water. Return pasta to pot.

Place a skillet over high heat with half the butter while the pasta cooks. Add onions and prosciutto. Sauté, without allowing onions to colour, for about 5 minutes. Reduce heat to medium-low. Stir in peas and season with salt and pepper. Add ¼ cup reserved pasta cooking water and simmer until peas are just tender, 3 to 4 minutes.

Stir remaining butter and half the Parmigiano into the pasta.

Add pasta to sauce and stir together. If it is too dry, add a little extra cooking water. Serve with remaining Parmigiano for sprinkling.

PAIRING: **Soave**

Emilia-Romagna—vaunted home of Parmesan, prosciutto di Parma and balsamic vinegar—is something of a wine underachiever by Italian standards. The signature is much-maligned lambrusco. Red, fizzy and often sweet, cheap versions were popular during the disco era and went by such brand names as Riunite and Chiarli Castelvetro. If you can find a good dry lambrusco (they exist), by all means deploy it with this quill-shaped pasta. Better yet, look for a tangy Soave from Veneto or, harder to find, any white labelled Colli Piacentini from Emilia-Romagna. Prefer red? Try the sangiovese di Romagna I suggest for the veal dish that follows.

Italian packaged pasta always states the cooking time. Start your timer when the water has returned to a boil and you will have perfect al dente pasta.

VEAL SCALOPPINE WITH TOMATO CAPER SAUCE

Here is a mouth-watering way to serve veal. Make sure the veal is sliced thin for the best texture. Ask the butcher to do it for you or place between two pieces of parchment paper and pound with the bottom of a pot. The anchovies disappear in the sauce, leaving just a background hint of flavour. If fresh tomatoes are not very flavourful or juicy, use 1 cup canned tomatoes without juice instead.

Serves 4

Sauce:

¼ cup white wine
3 plum tomatoes, seeded and chopped
3 anchovy fillets, chopped
1 tbsp capers
1 tbsp butter

Veal:

2 tbsp olive oil
2 tbsp butter
8 slices veal scaloppine
Salt and freshly ground pepper
½ cup all-purpose flour seasoned with salt and pepper
2 tbsp chopped fresh parsley

Combine wine, tomatoes and anchovies in a small pot. Bring to a boil, reduce heat to medium-low and simmer for 5 to 8 minutes or until thickened. The anchovies will have practically disappeared by this point. Stir in capers and butter. Reserve and keep warm.

Heat olive oil and butter in a large skillet over high heat. Season scaloppine with salt and pepper. Dip scaloppine into flour and shake off excess. Place in skillet, in batches if necessary, and cook until browned, about 30 seconds per side.

Place the scaloppine on plates and pour over the sauce. Sprinkle with parsley.

PAIRING: **Sangiovese**

The delicate meat and tangy sauce need a red with dancing shoes, nothing too heavy. I love the subtle suggestion of mouth-watering saltiness in sangiovese, the grape of Chianti and also the ingredient in much-improved and underappreciated sangiovese di Romagna. Bargain alternative: montepulciano d'Abruzzo.

CASSATA PARFAIT

This splendid dessert takes just a few minutes to assemble but tastes as if you spent the whole day in the kitchen. The flavourings can change to suit your taste: omit ginger and add nuts, for example. **Serves 4**

¼ cup chopped candied orange peel (page 347)
¼ cup orange liqueur
2 cups ricotta
½ cup granulated sugar
¼ cup whipping cream
3 oz (85 g) dark chocolate (at least 64% cocoa), chopped
2 tbsp chopped preserved ginger

Topping:
1½ oz (42 g) dark chocolate (at least 64% cocoa), chopped
1 tbsp coffee
2 tbsp unsalted butter
4 pieces candied orange peel (page 347)

Soak chopped orange peel in liqueur for 30 minutes.
Beat ricotta until smooth. Beat in sugar and cream. Fold in orange peel with liqueur, chocolate and ginger. Chill.
Melt chocolate with coffee over low heat. Remove from heat and beat in butter. Cool until slightly thickened but still thin enough to pour. Swirl into ricotta mixture. Spoon into parfait glasses. Top with a piece of candied orange peel. Chill until thickened, about 2 hours.

PAIRING: **Verduzzo friulano**

Permit me to suggest a hard-to-come-by wine that enjoys lofty status among my relatives in northeast Italy. The white grape verduzzo is fashioned into both dry and sweet styles, and you'll want the latter here. Deep gold in colour, it bursts forth with honeyed aroma and flavours that can suggest honey, tinned peaches, candied orange and licorice—a lovely medley for this creamy, vibrant parfait. Alternatives: recioto di Soave, also from northeast Italy, or the sweet fortified wines of Marsala in Sicily or Madeira from Portugal.

FINO SHERRY

As bracing as a stiff wind on the open sea, as versatile as a set of pearls, yet less fashionable than elbow patches on tweed, fino Sherry is the most underappreciated wine on Earth. Distinctive for its salty tang, it's the consummate aperitif and can pair with just about anything, from soup to nuts (especially soup and nuts). Best of all, it's the greatest wine bargain this side of a stolen case of Pétrus.

Bone-dry and straw-coloured, fino bears only passing resemblance to the brown, heavily sweetened oloroso and cream sherries of Granny's "medicine" cabinet. For starters, it's lighter, at about 15 per cent alcohol versus 18 to 22, and stays fresh only for a couple of days once uncorked (sorry, Granny). And it positively must be served chilled.

The secret to fino's complexity lies in a magical formula. It starts out as a dry white wine, made from palomino grapes, then gets spiked with neutral spirit until it reaches the desired strength. Once fortified, it's transferred to a large barrel filled only about five-sixths of the way up. Thanks to the air pocket and the warm, humid climate around the southern Spanish city of Jerez de la Frontera, a foamy coating of wild yeast called *flor* forms on the surface. The yeast acts as an air barrier, preventing excessive oxidation while imparting tangy, doughy flavours of its own. Manzanilla is the name given to an especially salty fino style made in the seaside town of Sanlúcar de Barrameda, where cooler temperatures result in a fresher, more delicate profile.

Fair warning: fino and manzanilla are acquired tastes. If you're like me, you might even detect an aroma of petrol, as though you were slurping briny oysters near a gas station. What can I say? Glorious.

Menu 3

BRINING: A CELEBRATORY MENU

Oysters with Horseradish Gelée

Herb and Spice Roast Rack of Pork

Braised Winter Greens

Orzo

Warm Chocolate Caramel Cakes

The resurgence of pork—especially pork with pedigrees like Berkshire—inspired the main dish, a brined roast rack of pork that's tender and juicy. As a side, try creamy starches such as polenta over more traditional mashed potatoes and combine cold-weather greens such as rapini and spinach or escarole and watercress. Oysters are the salty, sophisticated first course for any dinner, and the Warm Caramel Chocolate Cakes are one of my finest sweet, salty, chocolaty desserts.

OYSTERS WITH HORSERADISH GELÉE

This is a simple, stylish first course. The zesty gelée cubes make a distinctive sparkly topper for oysters. You can use prepared horseradish in the gelée, but use 1 tbsp; the gelée will be cloudy. Or you could be really lazy and just sprinkle a few drops of horseradish on the oysters. **Makes enough gelée for 12 oysters**

2 tsp gelatine
2 tbsp water
1 cup dry white wine (preferably muscadet)
2 tsp grated fresh horseradish
12 freshly shucked oysters

Heat gelatine and water in a small pot, stirring until gelatine is melted. Stir in wine and horseradish. Pour into a 9- × 5-inch loaf pan lined with plastic wrap. Chill until firm.
Turn out of pan, remove plastic and cut into little cubes to top freshly shucked oysters.

PAIRING: **Muscadet**

Raw oysters shine with lean, crisp (and very cold) whites. In France, that means Chablis if you've got the dough, Champagne (if you've got more dough) and muscadet. I'm a $12 muscadet man. The wine hails from the western end of the Loire River, near the Atlantic coast. Leaner than a supermodel on a cleanse diet, it holds hands with the subtle, briny oysters. And unlike prima donna Chablis, it won't throw a tantrum in the presence of spicy horseradish. Alternative: the Clammy Sammy cocktail on page 275.

HERB AND SPICE ROAST RACK OF PORK

Make sure the butcher frenches the bones on the rack of pork for you (that is, cuts away the fat from the bones, leaving the meat). It makes an outstanding presentation. **Serves 6 to 8**

Brine:
16 cups water
1 cup kosher salt
½ cup brown sugar
1 head garlic, cut in half crosswise
2 tsp peppercorns
2 bay leaves
3 sprigs fresh rosemary

Sauce:
¼ cup orange juice
2 cups chicken stock
2 tbsp balsamic vinegar

Pork:
1 rack of pork (6 bones), frenched
1 tbsp chopped fresh sage
1 tbsp cracked fennel seeds
1 tsp cracked coriander seeds
1 tbsp cracked pepper
1 tsp grated fresh ginger
1 tsp grated orange zest
Salt

Place 4 cups water in a large pot. Add salt, sugar, garlic, peppercorns, bay leaves and rosemary and bring to a boil. Remove from heat, add remaining 12 cups water and cool completely. Add pork to brine and refrigerate for 24 hours.

Remove pork from brine (discarding brine), rinse and pat dry. Refrigerate for 2 hours to dry off, then bring back to room temperature.

Preheat oven to 450°F. Place pork bone side down on rack in a roasting pan. Combine sage, fennel seeds, coriander seeds, pepper, ginger, orange zest and salt and rub all over pork. Roast for 15 minutes. Reduce heat to 325°F and roast for 1 hour longer or until a thermometer reads 150°F for a pink roast. (Time will vary depending on the thickness of the rack.) Let sit for 15 minutes while making sauce.

Drain fat from roasting pan and add orange juice. Bring to a boil over medium heat, stirring up all the little bits from the bottom of the pan. Add stock and bring to a boil. Stir in balsamic vinegar. Reduce heat to medium-low and simmer until sauce is slightly thickened, about 4 minutes.

Slice rack of pork into thick chops and serve with sauce.

PAIRING: **Beaujolais**

I adore crisp, light Beaujolais with roast pork, the cheerful berry-like fruit bringing its own juicy touch to the delicate meat. Tangy orange sauce brings the wine's assets into sharper focus.

BRINING

Brining is essentially soaking meat in salt water. What it does is make the meat juicier and tastier. I believe in brining pork, which can be dry, and poultry that is not free range or kosher (which is basically pre-brined).

The ratio of water to salt is the key. I find that using 16 cups of water to 1 cup kosher salt (which is less "salty") works the best. I add sugar and spices as well, although I cannot vouch that they really become embedded in the flavour of the meat. I heat 4 cups of water with the salt and sugar to dissolve them, and then mix in the rest of the water. Brines need to be cool before they're used.

I recommend Diamond Crystal brand of kosher salt. It is the best for both brining and cooking, although any coarse salt will do. If you look in any chef's kitchen, you'll find a box of it.

Use any container that will allow the pork to be completely immersed in the brine. Measure the volume of the container and make up that amount of brine. You will not need it all.

Brining timing is a matter of how much salt you use in the solution. The saltier the solution, the shorter the brining time. For my solution, brine for about 6 hours at room temperature or for 24 hours in the refrigerator. Rinse off the brine, pat dry and place the meat on a baking sheet in the refrigerator for at least 2 hours or overnight to dry out.

BRAISED WINTER GREENS

Use escarole, frisée, endive, Swiss chard, beet greens, collard greens or a mixture of all of them, removing about 2 inches of tough stem ends if necessary. These greens are slightly bitter but they mellow out when cooked.

Serves 4

- 1 lb (450 g) winter greens
- 3 tbsp olive oil
- 1 cup sliced leeks
- ½ cup vegetable or chicken stock
- Salt and freshly ground pepper

Bring a pot of salted water to a boil. Add greens and boil for 2 minutes or until greens are just tender. Drain well. Chop coarsely.

Heat oil in a large skillet over medium-high heat. Add leeks and stir-fry for 1 minute. Add greens and stock. Season with salt and pepper. Cover, reduce heat to low and cook for 5 minutes or until greens are full of flavour and tender.

ORZO

The slight sweetness in the pork dish matches perfectly with a starch that has a little fire in it. If you don't like heat, omit the chili flakes.

Serves 4

- 2 cups orzo
- 2 tbsp butter
- 1 tsp chili flakes
- Salt and freshly ground pepper

Bring a large pot of salted water to a boil. Add orzo and boil for 7 minutes or until tender.

Drain, return to pot and stir in butter, chili flakes, and salt and pepper to taste.

THE (UNCONVENTIONAL) TRUTH ABOUT TANNINS

Wine myths get around faster than cheesy cat videos on YouTube. Here's a major slice of baloney found in countless treatises on food-and-wine matching: salt exacerbates tannins. Who makes this stuff up?

Tannins are bitter, dusty compounds found in grape skins, seeds, stems and oak barrels. They're prevalent in full-bodied reds, such as cabernet sauvignon. Now, if you happened to read the introduction to our "Bitter" chapter (hey, no worries, you've been busy cooking!), you'll know that salt suppresses bitterness.

Having been brainwashed with the tannins-battle-salt lie in wine school, I saw the light after a conversation with Tim Hanni, a vaunted Master of Wine (and professionally trained chef) based in Napa. He's done more to bury food-pairing bunkum than anyone. Try his simple experiment if you've got money to burn: Grill two steaks, one without salt and one with a liberal dusting. Sample each with a tannic young red (Bordeaux is ideal). The first steak leaves the wine's tannins in fighting form, while the salted cut mellows and softens the wine.

WARM CHOCOLATE CARAMEL CAKES

This is the most sensuous and exciting dessert. The combination of rich chocolate cake with heady caramel sauce spurting from the centre is a sensation. Instead of making your own salted caramel, you can buy good-quality caramels and use them the same way in the recipe, but add a sprinkle of Maldon salt. You can make the cakes ahead (or reheat leftovers): heat for 5 minutes at 350°F and serve at once.

Makes 8 cakes

- 8 salted caramels (page 272), cooled
- 6 oz (170 g) dark chocolate (preferably 70% cocoa), chopped
- ⅔ cup unsalted butter (plus extra for moulds)
- ⅓ cup granulated sugar (plus extra for moulds)
- 3 eggs
- 3 egg yolks
- ⅓ cup all-purpose flour
- Maldon salt or fleur de sel

Roll 1 tbsp caramel into a ball; repeat to make 8 balls. Freeze for at least 1 hour.

Preheat oven to 350°F. Butter and sugar 8 nonstick moulds or muffin cups.

Melt chocolate and butter together in a heavy pot over low heat. Remove from heat. Cool slightly.

Beat together sugar, eggs and egg yolks in a large bowl with an electric mixer until thick and creamy, about 4 minutes.

Pour in chocolate mixture and continue beating for 2 to 3 more minutes or until silky and thickened. Fold in flour.

Fill moulds one-third full with batter. Place a frozen caramel and a few flakes of Maldon salt in centre of each, then fill with more batter to ¼ inch from top of mould. Bake for 13 to 14 minutes or until edges are just cooked.

Cool for 5 minutes in moulds. Invert onto plates. Serve with crème fraîche or lightly whipped cream.

PAIRING: **Banyuls or Rivesaltes**

Lightly fortified sweet wines from southern France, these elixirs like to huddle around decadent chocolate cake almost as much as I do. Banyuls, my top choice here, is mainly red and offers up intense berries. Muscat de Rivesaltes is white and sings with orange and honey. Alternatives: Late Bottled Vintage Port or cabernet franc icewine.

SALTED CARAMELS

Always a treat, salted caramels are the perfect sweetmeat after a dinner. This is a soft caramel, adapted from a recipe by Jacques Pépin, but if you refrigerate it, it becomes harder. These are perfect to use in the Warm Chocolate Caramel Cakes (page 271). Lyle's golden syrup, which you can find at the supermarket, is made with cane sugar, not beet, giving it a distinctive caramel flavour. **Makes about 18 caramels**

¼ cup unsalted butter, cut in pieces
½ cup whipping cream
1 tsp fleur de sel
1 cup granulated sugar
¼ cup Lyle's golden syrup
3 tbsp water

Oil a loaf pan and line the bottom with parchment paper. Cut a second sheet of parchment paper and place crosswise across the pan, allowing the ends to drape over the sides. This will help you lift the caramel out later.

Place butter, cream and fleur de sel in a small pot. Heat over medium heat until butter is melted. Reserve.

Combine sugar, golden syrup and water in a medium, heavy pot. Bring to a boil over medium-high heat. Boil until a candy thermometer reads 320°F—the caramel will be dark and boiling rapidly. Carefully stir in cream mixture—the caramel will boil up. Bring back to a boil and cook until a candy thermometer reads 245°F, about 3 minutes longer.

Pour caramel into prepared pan but do not scrape out any that is left behind in the pot. Sprinkle with a little extra fleur de sel. Cool to room temperature, then refrigerate for 1 to 2 hours, until set. Remove from loaf pan and cut into rectangles or squares with an oiled knife. Wrap in wax paper or cellophane if desired.

CLAMMY SAMMY

For this one, I'm indebted to Sammy Hagar, former lead singer of the rock band Van Halen. An entrepreneur with many sidelines, Sammy founded Cabo Wabo Tequila, an excellent premium brand, which he subsequently sold for close to $100 million. Ka-ching!

The name above is my own. Sammy calls it the Cabo Almeja, apt (if hard to pronounce), since *almeja* is Spanish for "clam" and tequila comes from Mexico. Beware: it's powerful, a sort of cross between the Bloody Caesar and a Margarita.

Pour 2 oz good tequila and 1 oz Clamato juice over ice. Shake and strain into a rocks-filled tumbler rimmed with salt. Garnish with a lime wheel or celery stalk.

Menu 4

TRUCK-STOP TREATS

Lobster Rolls

Belgian Baked Fries

Spicy Mango Slaw

Caramel Pecan Popcorn

Right now lobster rolls are served everywhere, from trucks to upscale restaurants. Lobster has a natural saltiness that makes it a favourite with everyone. The first lobster roll I had was in Maine near the sea, and it is still the bar I try to reach. In Belgium, fries are an art. The big difference between Belgian fries and french fries is the squared-off ends of the Belgian ones, which makes them good for stacking. Caramel Pecan Popcorn is always the finest snack.

LOBSTER ROLLS

These will wow your guests. They are full of lobster sandwiched inside buttery rolls. What could be better? I buy my lobster precooked and taken out of the shell by my favourite fishmonger, Gus. Cut each roll in half if you want to serve them as an appetizer.

Serves 4

- 3 cooked lobsters (1½ lb/675 g each)
- ½ cup chopped fennel
- ¼ cup butter
- 1 tsp chopped garlic
- 4 hot dog rolls
- 4 red leaf lettuce leaves

Mayonnaise:

- ½ cup mayonnaise
- 2 tbsp chopped shallots
- 2 tbsp chopped chives
- 1 tbsp chopped fresh parsley
- 2 tsp chopped fresh chervil or tarragon
- 1 tbsp lemon juice
- 1 tsp Dijon mustard
- 2 tbsp olive oil
- Salt and freshly ground pepper

Remove lobster meat from shells and coarsely chop. Transfer to a bowl.

Combine mayonnaise, shallots, chives, parsley, chervil, lemon juice and mustard. Stir in olive oil. Season with salt and pepper.

Add fennel to lobster meat and toss with enough mayonnaise to moisten.

Melt butter with garlic in a large skillet over medium heat. Slice open rolls, leaving them attached along a long side. Add to butter and fry until buns are golden brown, about 1 minute per side. Place a lettuce leaf in each roll and heap with lobster filling. Serve immediately.

PAIRING: **Sauvignon blanc**

Naked boiled lobster loves to sink its claws into chardonnay, the oeno-analogue of melted butter. All-dressed, as in this recipe, though, it craves more zip. Sauvignon blanc tingles with just the right acidity and herbal aromatics to party with the zesty mayo. The spicy mango coleslaw tips the balance further in favour of a punchy, fruit-forward New World sauvignon blanc from New Zealand, Chile or South Africa. Alternative: dry riesling.

BELGIAN BAKED FRIES

These are spicy to give contrast to the rich lobster roll. Serve only a few per person, as they are meant as a garnish. If there is leftover mayonnaise from the lobster roll, you could add some spicy paprika to it and use it as a dip.

Serves 4

1 lb (450 g) Yukon Gold potatoes (3 medium), peeled
3 tbsp olive oil
¼ tsp hot smoked Spanish paprika
Salt

Preheat oven to 450°F.

Slice ends off each potato and then trim sides so you have a square potato. Cut into batons about 3 inches by ½ inch.

Combine oil and paprika in a bowl. Add potatoes and toss to coat. Season with salt. Spread out on a parchment-lined baking sheet. Bake for 10 minutes. Turn and bake 10 minutes longer or until golden brown and cooked through.

French Tarragon: Perennial French tarragon is the best of all culinary herbs. Never confuse it with the coarser, tasteless Russian tarragon. A reputable greengrocer will be selling the French kind. Its enticing and distinctive flavour is suggestive of anise or licorice. Essential in such famous butter sauces as béarnaise, hollandaise and mousseline, tarragon also adds a beguiling touch to omelettes, marinated meats and poultry stuffing. It is excellent sprinkled over chicken or fish and perks up otherwise dull green salads. Steep fresh tarragon in wine vinegar and use the concoction as a basis for salad dressings. At its best from late June until the end of September, tarragon suffers in the heat. Dry it to preserve it.

SPICY MANGO SLAW

This spicy slaw can be used as a side for fish and chips too. It elevates the dish from ordinary to something special.

Serves 4

4 cups thinly sliced napa cabbage
2 large mangoes, peeled and slivered
1 cup thinly sliced red onions
½ cup fresh mint leaves, thinly sliced

Dressing:
1 tsp grated lime zest
⅓ cup lime juice
2 tbsp chopped fresh cilantro
2 tbsp fish sauce
2 tsp finely chopped seeded green chili (or to taste)
2 tsp finely chopped garlic
2 tsp brown sugar

Combine cabbage, mangoes, onions and mint in a bowl or on a platter.
Whisk together dressing ingredients and toss with slaw just before serving.

CARAMEL PECAN POPCORN

A fun dessert or nibble. Serve over caramel ice cream and add a brownie with it too. The popcorn will keep for up to a week stored in an airtight container.

Makes 14 cups

- 12 cups popped corn
- 2 cups pecan halves
- 1¼ cups packed light brown sugar
- ¼ cup unsalted butter
- ¼ cup pure maple syrup
- 2 tsp vanilla
- 1 tsp white vinegar
- ½ tsp kosher salt
- ¼ tsp baking soda

Preheat oven to 250°F. Line 2 baking sheets with parchment paper. Toss popcorn and pecans on tray. Keep warm in oven while preparing caramel.

Stir brown sugar, butter and maple syrup in a pot over medium-low heat until butter is melted. Increase heat to high and boil mixture until a candy thermometer reads 255°F (just past softball stage), about 4 minutes. While boiling, occasionally brush the sides of the pot with a pastry or silicone brush dipped in cool water. Remove from heat and carefully stir in vanilla, vinegar, salt and baking soda (mixture will bubble). Slowly pour syrup over popcorn and pecans, then gently stir to coat completely.

Bake, stirring occasionally, until caramel feels dry, about 1 hour 20 minutes. Using a metal spatula, scrape mixture from bottom of baking sheets to loosen. Cool completely on baking sheets.

PAIRING: **Late-harvest white**

Kendall-Jackson, the large premium California vintner, scored a delicious hit at the Sonoma County Harvest Fair a few years ago, pairing caramel popcorn with late-harvest chardonnay. The eye-opening match took home best-in-show honours and became a staple offering on the winery's Wine Center menu. If you can't find late-harvest chardonnay, look for late-harvest riesling or vidal. Alternative: spiced rum and Coke (the one and only time I'll ever condone rum and Coke).

HERRING TARTARE

A quick appetizer served with toast.

1 jar (about 10 oz/300 g) pickled herring
1 red onion, finely chopped
1 tart apple, peeled, cored and finely chopped
2 tbsp chopped fresh dill

Drain pickled herring well. Chop into small dice. Combine with red onion and apple. Stir in dill.

PAIRING: **Akvavit**

The signature flavoured spirit of Scandinavia, akvavit primarily gets its essence from caraway or dill. Sometimes it's matured in oak, which, along with the herbs, imparts a golden colour. It's a matter of time before the spirit follows Scandinavian cuisine into the limelight, and this recipe is as good a reason as any to explore the bracing, herbaceous flavour. Akvavit weighs in at 40 per cent alcohol, so you drink it in a shot glass. Stash the bottle in the freezer and serve it cold. Alternative: cold vodka.

LYLES GOLDEN
Délicieux sirop

SWEET

sugar • parsnips • peas • scallops • cream • honey

bananas • dates • carrots • berries • grapes • mangoes

watermelon • pineapples • apples • vanilla • peaches • prunes

apricots • maple syrup • toffee • chocolate • jam • fennel

beets • raisins • caramel • walnuts • dried fruits

THE LINE BETWEEN SWEET AND SAVOURY

has been getting deliciously blurry, some might even say wacky. How's this for a mind-bender: toasted foie gras marshmallows and smoked-vanilla ice cream ribboned with veal chocolate sauce? Trust us, it's better than it sounds. It's just one of the flavours conjured up by wunderkind Tyler Malek at Salt & Straw, a chain of "farm-to-cone" ice cream parlours in Portland, Oregon. The constantly evolving menu—which has also included Citra hops with apricot, chèvre with marionberry habanero jam, and honey-balsamic strawberries with cracked pepper—stands at the cutting edge of one of modern gastronomy's more pervasive trends, extreme ice cream.

The movement began innocently enough in fine restaurants, with such now seemingly timid flavourings as basil and Parmesan, followed, perhaps most famously, by Chef Heston Blumenthal's bacon-and-eggs ice cream at The Fat Duck in England. One thing seems certain: dessert isn't just for dessert anymore.

To be fair, though, it's an evolution, not a revolution. Sweet and savoury have been bunking together for a long time. It was an inspired (and probably at the time avant-garde) cook who first thought to serve spring rolls with plum sauce, duck with cherries, ham with pineapple, or to weave honey into a mustard vinaigrette. Sugar balances acidity and salt and tames spice, while fruity flavours add something more—for example complementing the earthy, gamy quality of many meats.

Sweetness is not just a flavour; it's a biological imperative. The body craves it, a hallmark of energy-dense foods (fruits, quintessentially) that sustained our primate ancestors in the lean days between wild-boar hunts (and presumably put a spring in their step when the animal was charging in the wrong direction). That's why there always seems to be room for dessert, an impulse to store more energy. And, yes, have no fear, there will be a few enticing desserts in the pages that follow.

Some of us regularly consume fruit with savoury items without thinking about it—in the form of wine. It may be sweet, as in Sauternes with foie gras (another glorious sweet-savoury combination), or off-dry riesling with smoked fish. But even when technically dry, wine contains below-the-radar natural grape sugar, which is never fully consumed by yeast during fermentation. Australian shiraz, though seemingly dry, ranks up there on the residual-sugar scale, as do many other wines produced in such New World regions as California, Chile, Australia, Argentina and British Columbia's Okanagan Valley, where ample sunshine cranks up grape ripeness.

In most cases, these New World styles taste fruitier than their European counterparts. They also can represent more suitable options when fruit or sugar feature prominently in a dish. That's because sweetness in food overwhelms and cancels subtle sweetness in the glass, causing the wine to taste sour and weak without enough fruit flavour to fill the void.

SWEETNESS IN COOKING

I am not a sweet person. Whether in savoury or sweet recipes, my tendency is to cut back the sugar. Over the years, though, I have found that a little sugar improves many dishes. Too acidic a sauce? Add sugar. A Thai or Vietnamese dish lacks balance? Add sugar. Of course, sugar is not the only sweetener. I use maple syrup in salad dressings, as it combines more easily. Honey is used extensively in eastern European cooking. In Asian kitchens, palm sugar sweetens many a dish. If you over-sweeten, adding something salty or acidic helps right the balance: fish sauce, lemon or lime juice, soy sauce, salt or vinegar.

The one sweetener I try to avoid is corn syrup. It is really an artificial sweetener and is an ingredient in a huge number of processed foods, where it replaces more expensive cane sugar. The presence of corn syrup in so much of what we eat and drink has been red-flagged, as its prevalence coincides with an increase in obesity rates. Research is under way to see whether we metabolize it differently from other sweeteners. Maple syrup is a good substitute in any recipe calling for corn syrup, as is the English Lyle's golden syrup, which is thicker but not sweeter.

Sweet spices are something Indian cooks use frequently to balance flavours in their dishes. The main sweet spices are allspice, anise, cinnamon, cardamom, cloves, ginger, mace and nutmeg. Indian garam masala, sometimes added at the end of cooking, is a mixture of sweet spices with a hit of heat. Sweet herbs include sweet cicely and some basils.

To sweeten without sugar or spices in savoury dishes, cook down onions, long and slow, until they release their essential sweetness. This method is the basis of many Indian curries but adapts to numerous other cuisines.

I truly do not understand the use of artificial sweeteners unless you have health problems. Why put a processed ingredient into your system when you can just use less of a natural one? And I can always taste them in cooking. Stevia is the hot new natural sweetener. Obtained from a plant grown in Brazil, it is now being added to soft drinks and other products. Research is ongoing about its safety, and it will be years before there are any answers, but it is approved for sale in Canada and the US. A little goes a long way.

Menu 1

A ROSH HASHANAH DINNER

Carrot, Ginger and Coriander Soup

Sweet-Spicy Garlic Chicken

Radish and Orange Salad

Honey Marmalade Cake

In ancient times there was no New Year as we know it today. The early Persians and Babylonians marked the New Year in spring, when everything turned green, but the Jews calculated it as the time closest to the gathering of the fruits in the fall. The new moon nearest to that time became the New Year, or Rosh Hashanah. It is the beginning of the holiest time in the Jewish calendar. Food plays a tremendously important role in the New Year celebrations. The table is laden with delicacies that represent the hope of a sweet future. Honey, raisins, carrots and apples are eaten in many combinations. My family always starts the New Year with apples dipped in honey before we sit down to dinner. No sour, bitter or black dishes are served because they could bring bad luck. The egg bread, or challah, is baked in a special round to bring never-ending good luck and it is always studded with raisins for a sweet year. This menu is more North African in approach than more standard types of Rosh Hashanah dinners. The sweet in the soup and the chicken are balanced with Moroccan-type spice. Honey cake, the traditional finish for a Rosh Hashanah dinner, is tarted up here with marmalade.

CARROT, GINGER AND CORIANDER SOUP

You can add ¼ cup whipping cream to this spiced, wholesome soup at the end if it is not being served at the holiday dinner. Add other root vegetables such as parsnips, if you like. **Serves 8**

- 2 tbsp olive oil or butter
- 1 cup chopped onions
- 1 tsp ground coriander
- Pinch cayenne pepper
- 2 lb (900 g) carrots, chopped (about 5 cups)
- ½ cup chopped peeled potatoes
- 2 tsp grated fresh ginger
- 6 cups chicken stock
- 2 tsp honey
- ½ cup packed fresh cilantro leaves
- Salt and freshly ground pepper
- Cilantro sprigs

Heat oil in a large pot over medium heat. Add onions and sauté for 2 minutes or until softened. Stir in coriander and cayenne and cook for 1 minute longer or until fragrant. Add carrots, potatoes and ginger and cook for 2 minutes or until ginger is softened. Add stock and honey and bring to a boil. Cover, reduce heat to low and simmer for 20 minutes or until vegetables are soft. Add cilantro leaves and cook for 2 minutes or until wilted.

Transfer to a blender (or use a hand blender) and purée until smooth. Return to pot and adjust seasoning to taste, adding more stock if the soup is too thick. Serve garnished with cilantro sprigs.

PAIRING: **Gewürztraminer**

I'm forever seeking excuses to uncork gewürztraminer, the musky, spicy white grape with the soft, round centre and exotic allure of a belly dancer. Big on grapey flavour, it's invariably nuanced with ginger and rose petals. Some find it bold, but don't judge it harshly till you've sat down to the soup. Technically dry, most gewürztraminers exhibit the opulence to match the sweetness here as well as to frame the subtle aromatic spices. The Alsatian producer Willm makes a good kosher offering, and the Yarden brand from Golan Heights Winery in Israel does a fine job too. Alternative: oaky New World chardonnay.

SWEET-SPICY GARLIC CHICKEN

This traditional and easy family dish is loved by children because of its sweetness and by adults because of its familiar comfort level. Serve with roasted vegetables such as parsnips, carrots, fennel and Brussels sprouts. Use chicken breasts or thighs instead of whole chickens, if desired.

Serves 8

- 2 tsp ground fennel or anise seeds
- 1 tsp ground allspice
- 1 tsp ground ginger
- ¼ tsp cayenne
- Salt and freshly ground pepper
- ¾ cup all-purpose flour
- 2 chickens (2 to 3 lb/900 g to 1.35 kg each), each cut into 8 portions
- ¼ cup vegetable oil
- 1 cup hot chicken stock or water
- ¾ cup fresh orange juice
- ¼ cup honey
- 2 tbsp grated fresh ginger
- 2 tbsp lime juice
- 1 tbsp chopped garlic
- 1 tbsp Dijon mustard
- 1 tbsp soy sauce
- 2 tbsp chopped fresh mint

Combine fennel, allspice, ground ginger, cayenne, salt and pepper with flour. Coat chicken pieces with seasoned flour.

Preheat oven to 375°F.

Heat oil in a large skillet over medium-high heat. Add chicken pieces in batches and fry until golden brown on each side, about 3 minutes per side. Place chicken in a roasting pan or large gratin dish as the pieces are browned.

Stir together stock, orange juice, honey, grated ginger, lime juice, garlic, mustard and soy sauce. Pour over chicken. Bake, uncovered and basting occasionally, for 40 to 45 minutes or until chicken is cooked through.

Transfer chicken to a platter. Place roasting pan on stovetop and simmer just until sauce is thick enough to coat the back of a spoon, 1 to 2 minutes.

Serve chicken with sauce separately. Sprinkle with mint.

PAIRING: **Australian semillon or semillon-chardonnay**

Maybe you didn't finish the gewürztraminer I suggested for the soup (I would have). Boldly fruity and aromatic, it would sing here, resonating with the spices, ginger and fragrant fennel. Australian semillon, another underrated white, is even better, hugging the spices with a honeyed character while shaking the mustard's hand with lively tang. On the red front, consider a soft, luscious Spanish garnacha. Prefer to keep things kosher? Try a ripe French offering from the southern Languedoc region (Herzog and Fortant make inexpensive kosher selections). Other kosher alternatives: shiraz from Israel (Dalton and Galil Mountain are reliable brands) and Five Stones Shiraz from Australia. A honey beer would be nice too, if not as kosher.

Sweet Spices: Allspice, star anise, cinnamon, cardamom, cloves, ginger, mace and nutmeg are all considered sweet spices, although they have no relationship to sugar. Their fragrance imparts a sweet flavour to food.

RADISH AND ORANGE SALAD

Refreshing, sweet orange balances the crunchy, spicy radish. You can add chopped red onions to this salad. The flavours meld with the flavours in the chicken.

Serves 8

4 navel or blood oranges
2 bunches radishes, sliced (about 2½ cups)
2 tbsp lemon juice
2 tbsp olive oil
2 tbsp chopped fresh mint
Salt

Cut peel and white pith from oranges and thinly slice oranges into rounds. Cut in half and transfer to a bowl.

Add radishes and toss with lemon juice and olive oil. Add mint and season with salt.

HONEY MARMALADE CAKE

Honey cake is the traditional sweet end to the New Year's dinner, symbolizing sweetness for the coming year. I love marmalade, so I incorporated it, making a terrific cake even better because it adds an orange zing. This may be baked in two loaf pans, but reduce baking time to 55 minutes. The cake keeps well in an airtight container.

Serves 12

- 3½ cups all-purpose flour
- 2 tsp baking powder
- 1 tsp baking soda
- 1 tsp kosher salt
- 1 tsp ground ginger
- ½ tsp cinnamon
- 1 cup strong coffee
- ¾ cup honey
- ½ cup Seville orange marmalade, peel finely chopped
- 4 large eggs
- 1½ cups light brown sugar
- 1 cup vegetable oil
- 1 cup grated unpeeled apple

Preheat oven to 300°F. Grease and flour a 10-inch Bundt pan.

Combine flour, baking powder, baking soda, salt, ginger and cinnamon in a medium bowl.

Stir together coffee, honey and marmalade in a separate bowl.

Beat eggs in a large bowl until frothy, about 2 minutes. Gradually beat in sugar. Add vegetable oil and beat until combined. Beat in half of flour mixture and all of honey mixture. Stir in remaining flour mixture and apple. The batter will be quite thin.

Pour batter into prepared Bundt pan and bake for 1 hour or until cake is springy to the touch and a cake tester comes out clean.

Cool in pan for 15 minutes. Unmould, cover and leave in a cool place for 24 hours to allow flavours to mellow.

PAIRING: **Moscato d'Asti**

Sweet, gently sparkling moscato d'Asti would bring lift and a fruity underpinning to this honey of a cake (Bartenura is a fine kosher Italian brand). Alternative: sweet fortified muscat de Beaumes de Venise from France's Rhone Valley or Carmel Shaal Late-Harvest Gewürztraminer from Israel.

APEROL SPRITZ

In my ancestral region of Italy, from whence this blessed drink hails, Venetians often simply call it the Spritz. Or, more phonetically, *spreetz*. The liqueur's brand name is redundant. Substitute an imposter and the deceit stands out faster than a Prada logo spelled with two *d*'s. It's in the colour. Nothing delivers the electric-orange dazzle of Aperol, except maybe for orange Kool-Aid.

A kinder, gentler cousin of Campari, Aperol—at just 11 per cent alcohol—is sweeter and less bitter, with a dominant orange flavour. Ubiquitous in Italy, it was developed in Padua in 1919 and found traction here only recently thanks to a distribution push by its relatively new parent, none other than Gruppo Campari. If you want to amaze guests with a light, and newly trendy, cocktail, put on the Spritz. It's hard to screw this one up, but Italians put sexy flair into the ceremony. (Of course they do—they're Italian.)

Half slice of orange
3 parts prosecco
Splash of sparkling water
2 parts Aperol

Place 3 ice cubes and a half slice of orange in a tumbler. Pour in prosecco (or any other dry sparkling wine) until the froth reaches the rim (that should be about 3 oz). Wait for the froth to subside, then add 1 or 2 oz (I like 2) of sparkling mineral water or club soda. Then top up with Aperol—about 2 oz—using a circular motion to prevent it from pooling at the bottom.

APEROL
DAL 1919

Menu 2

ICEWINE EXTRAVAGANZA

Chicken Liver Pâté in a Foie Gras Style

Arugula Salad with Stilton and Redcurrant Vinaigrette

Maple-Glazed Salmon with Beets, Ricotta and Dill

Brûléed Rice Pudding with Icewine-Soaked Raisins

At *Food & Drink* magazine, we challenged chefs to come up with a menu in which each dish could be paired with icewine. The results were impressive, and this menu reaffirms that icewine may indeed be the perfect accompaniment to courses other than dessert.

CHICKEN LIVER PÂTÉ IN A FOIE GRAS STYLE

This spreadable pâté is rich and sinful with its infusion of butter and cream. To give it an even more foie gras–like quality, I have made a slightly sweet sauce for it. This is a perfect holiday dinner appetizer. Serve it in slices as a first course or spoon it onto toasted brioche and serve with a drizzle of the dark-hued gelée. It will keep for 5 to 7 days as long as it is well sealed, and I have frozen it for a short time successfully, although it becomes slightly more granular. Defrost in the refrigerator overnight.

Serves 6 to 8

½ cup unsalted butter, at room temperature
½ cup chopped onion
1 tsp chopped garlic
1 lb (450 g) chicken livers, cleaned and cut in half
2 tsp fresh thyme leaves (or ½ tsp dried)
1 star anise
Salt and freshly ground pepper
1 tbsp Sherry vinegar
1 tbsp Cognac
¼ cup whipping cream
Cracked black pepper

Gelée:
¼ cup redcurrant jelly
2 tbsp icewine or other sweet wine
2 tbsp chopped dried cherries

Melt ¼ cup butter in a large skillet over medium-high heat. Add onion and sauté for 1 minute, then add garlic and sauté for 30 seconds. Add chicken livers, thyme, star anise, salt and pepper and sauté for 4 to 6 minutes or until chicken livers are browned on the outside but still pink in the centre. Add vinegar and Cognac and bring to a boil. Transfer mixture to a food processor. Leave in the star anise, as it gives a subtle undertone to the pâté.

Add cream and remaining ¼ cup butter and process until smooth. Add more salt and pepper if needed. Line a small buttered loaf pan or pâté mould with plastic wrap. Spoon in pâté mixture and smooth top. If there is some left over, spoon it into a buttered small container and save for another occasion. Cover with plastic wrap and refrigerate until needed.

Combine redcurrant jelly, icewine and cherries in a small pot. Stir over medium heat until jelly is melted. Cool. Turn pâté out of pan, top with some cracked black pepper and serve with a drizzle of gelée.

PAIRING: **Cabernet franc icewine**

Lucy calls this a sinful appetizer. I call it heaven. But let's take her word for it and sin some more, with icewine. Earthy, creamy foie gras is a magnet for sweetness, like peanut butter in search of jam. Sauternes from France is the classic match. Icewine is sweeter and more opulent still, yet with powerful acidity to cut through the fat and leave the palate cleansed of all that sin.

ARUGULA SALAD WITH STILTON AND REDCURRANT VINAIGRETTE

This salad has it all: spicy arugula, salty rich Stilton and the sweetness of the vinaigrette. Think of it as a cross between a salad and a cheese course.

Serves 4

- 8 cups baby arugula
- 4 oz (115 g) Stilton, crumbled
- 2 tbsp slivered fresh mint

Vinaigrette:

- 1 tsp redcurrant jelly, melted
- 1 tbsp red wine vinegar
- 3 tbsp vegetable oil

Toss arugula with Stilton and mint in a large bowl.

Combine redcurrant jelly, vinegar and vegetable oil. Toss half of vinaigrette with salad.

Place salad on 4 plates and drizzle extra vinaigrette around the side of the salad.

PAIRING: **Sparkling rosé**

Assuming you'll serve this salad on its own between the pâté and the salmon, you may not want to unleash a separate wine. In fact, it could stand on its own, the vinaigrette a built-in palate cleanser. But if you're up for it, here's a trick. Crack open a dry sparkling wine and add to each flute a ½-oz splash of the cabernet franc icewine from the pâté course. Acid from the bubbly meets the vinaigrette on its terms, and the berry sweetness of the icewine salutes the salty cheese and jelly. Or opt for the next-best thing, a sparkling rosé.

MAPLE-GLAZED SALMON WITH BEETS, RICOTTA AND DILL

This salmon is marinated in maple syrup for sweetness and then quickly roasted to make a light but intensely flavoured main course after the rich pâté. Use golden beets if available, because their colour does not bleed onto the cheese, although red ones are fine too. This recipe is adapted from Chef Stephen Treadwell, whose eponymous restaurant Treadwell's is located in Niagara-on-the-Lake, Ontario. He deep-fries his own beet chips, but we bought a package of vegetable chips and picked out the beet ones. **Serves 4**

¼ cup maple syrup
½ tsp hot sauce
4 salmon fillets (6 oz/170 g each)
1 lb (450 g) golden beets, cleaned
2 tbsp olive oil
Salt and freshly ground pepper
¼ cup Banyuls vinegar or Sherry vinegar
1 tbsp lemon juice
2 tbsp chopped fresh dill
1 cup ricotta
Deep-fried beet chips
Chervil sprigs

Combine maple syrup and hot sauce. Pour over salmon, skin side down. Marinate for 1 hour in the fridge.

Preheat oven to 350°F.

Toss beets with 1 tbsp olive oil and season with salt. Wrap tightly in foil, place on a baking sheet and bake for 1 hour or until fork-tender.

Increase heat to 450°F.

Whisk together vinegar, lemon juice and remaining 1 tbsp olive oil. Season with salt and pepper.

Unwrap beets. When cool enough to handle, peel and dice. Toss with half the dressing. Cool completely. Stir in dill.

Remove salmon from syrup and pat dry. Season with salt and pepper. Line a baking sheet with foil, place salmon skin side down on baking sheet and roast for 4 to 5 minutes, then broil for 1 to 2 minutes or until top is golden and salmon is just cooked through.

Divide beet salad among 4 plates. Dot with ricotta and top with salmon. Spoon a touch of the remaining dressing around each plate. Garnish with deep-fried beet chips and some chervil sprigs.

PAIRING: **New World chardonnay or pinot noir**

Rich flesh, maple syrup and sweet-earthy beets—there are two great options here. On the white side: oaky New World chardonnay, with a thick, buttery texture and lush tropical fruit. On the red: fruit-forward pinot noir from such New World locales as California and New Zealand, subtly jammy yet light enough not to drown the fish.

BRÛLÉED RICE PUDDING WITH ICEWINE-SOAKED RAISINS

This is the best, richest rice pudding ever! The tarragon gives an unusual background flavour to the rice that is unbeatable. You may also soak the raisins in icewine syrup, which is much less expensive. You can include bits of caramelized apples with the raisins, if you wish.

Serves 4

- ½ cup arborio rice
- 1 cup milk
- 1 cup whipping cream
- 2 sprigs fresh tarragon, tied together with kitchen string
- ½ vanilla bean, cut in half lengthwise, seeds scraped out with the edge of a knife
- 3 egg yolks
- ⅓ cup granulated sugar
- ¼ cup raisins
- 2 tbsp icewine
- Granulated sugar for brûlée topping

Combine rice, milk and cream in a large pot. Add tarragon and vanilla bean and seeds and bring to a boil. Reduce heat to low and simmer, stirring occasionally, for 20 to 30 minutes or until rice is soft and mixture is reduced and thickened.

Place egg yolks and sugar in a large bowl. Beat with an electric mixer on high speed for 1 to 2 minutes or until pale and very thick. Add cooked rice mixture to yolks and stir to combine.

Return mixture to pot and cook over low heat, stirring constantly, for about 12 minutes or until thickened. Do not let boil or pudding will curdle.

Pour rice pudding into a clean bowl and cool until warm to the touch. Remove tarragon and vanilla bean.

Combine raisins and icewine in a small pot. Bring to a boil. Remove from heat and let raisins sit for 10 minutes or until plump.

Divide raisins among 4 individual ramekins or espresso cups. Fill with warm rice pudding. Sprinkle each ramekin with an even layer of sugar (about 2 tsp each). Caramelize with a blowtorch or by placing ramekins under a preheated broiler for 1 to 2 minutes or until golden. Chill for 1 hour before serving.

PAIRING: **Vin Santo**

This sounds a little like risotto crossed with crème brûlée, my kind of dessert. So let's go to Italy for one choice, Vin Santo, the raisin-like white dessert wine made from dried grapes. From France, consider Banyuls, a fortified sweet wine from the southern Roussillon area. Alternative: late-harvest vidal or riesling, the less sweet baby brother of icewine.

ICEWINE

There's sweet irony in a glass of Canadian icewine. A country once deemed too frigid for tender European grape varieties (a fallacy shown the door decades ago), Canada proved not only that its summers were sufficiently warm to yield quality wine but also that its famous winters could go one better. This intense, syrupy elixir, made from the rich juice of grapes left to shrivel on the vine until December or January, is a national signature.

Global recognition came in 1991, when an Inniskillin vidal took home the Grand Prix d'Honneur at Vinexpo in France. New entrants rushed in. More medals followed. And those distinctive slender (and expensive) bottles soon became duty-free-shop fixtures proudly sold around the world (especially in Asia, where sweet wines go over particularly well).

Brimming with opulent flavours of tinned peaches, apricots, honey, mango and caramel, icewine has a finish longer than the Trans-Canada Highway. It's just the thing for intense desserts, even foie gras. Frankly, I prefer it as dessert unto itself.

Picked in the darkness during the first sustained plunge in temperature, grapes are gently pressed, permitting the still-fluid—and concentrated—juice to seep out while water (roughly 80 per cent of a grape's content) remains trapped inside the skins as ice. The yield is roughly one-fifth that for dry table wine, which helps account for the price, often $75 for a half-bottle.

Canada did not invent icewine. It's been made for centuries in Germany and Austria, where it's known as *eiswein*. But the requisite temperatures there come around only every few years, whereas the Great White North can play the game without fail every winter. Like scores of other European immigrants, the wine has found a more prosperous home in the New World.

Menu 3

EASY-PEASY BRUNCH

Double-Baked Soufflés with English Cheddar
Sticky Toffee Bacon
Walnut and Endive Salad
Isle of Mull Oatcakes
Grapefruit Compote
Millionaire Bars

Brunch is one of those meals that is a pleasure to be invited to, but no one wants to get up in the early morning to prepare and then be tired once guests arrive. If you are hosting, a little planning makes a big difference. Here are some foolproof brunch tips and a menu that is mostly make-ahead.

- Set the table the day before.
- Buy good croissants, bagels and baguettes. Buy smoked salmon for an accompaniment, good butter, cream cheese, and jam for those who want some sweetness. Serve with Beppi's brilliant Aperol Spritz cocktail (page 298).
- The bars can be made up to 4 days earlier. The oat biscuits can be made 2 days before. You can bake the soufflés the day before, then reheat to trembling heights before serving; the grapefruit compote may also be made the day before. The bacon should be on the baking sheet the night before, ready to go. That won't leave you much to do the morning of. Easy peasy, as my kids say.

DOUBLE-BAKED SOUFFLÉS WITH ENGLISH CHEDDAR

If you are intimidated by soufflés, fear not: these ones are extremely easy to make. The secret? Make them ahead of time and reheat to billowing heights. English cheddar has a sharper bite than ours, but you can easily substitute Canadian. You could make this in a variety of dishes, such as small cast-iron pots, extra-large muffin pans or large individual ramekins.

Serves 6

Vegetables:

3 tbsp butter
¼ cup finely grated Parmesan
3 leeks, white and light green part only, thinly sliced (about 2½ cups)
4 cups packed baby spinach
Salt and freshly ground pepper

Soufflés:

5 tbsp butter
5 tbsp all-purpose flour
2 cups milk
1 tbsp chopped fresh thyme (or ½ tsp dried)
1 tsp dry mustard
1½ cups shredded English cheddar
6 eggs, separated

Topping:

6 tbsp whipping cream
½ cup grated Parmesan

Preheat oven to 375°F. Use 1 tbsp butter to grease six 1¼-cup soufflé dishes (4 inches wide) and dust insides with Parmesan to coat.

Heat remaining 2 tbsp butter in a large skillet over medium heat. Add leeks and sauté for 3 minutes or until limp. Add spinach and cook for 1 to 2 minutes or until wilted and dry. Season with salt and pepper, scrape into a large bowl and reserve.

Heat 5 tbsp butter in a medium pot over medium heat. Slowly stir in flour and cook, stirring, for 2 minutes. Slowly whisk in milk. Add thyme and mustard and bring to a boil, stirring until smooth and thick. Remove from heat, add cheddar and stir until melted and combined. Add soufflé base to leek mixture and stir to combine. Cool slightly. Beat egg yolks in a small bowl and stir into mixture. Season with salt and pepper.

Beat egg whites with an electric mixer until they hold soft peaks. Stir one-quarter of egg whites into cheese base to lighten it, then gently but thoroughly fold in remaining whites.

Divide soufflé mixture among prepared dishes. Place soufflé dishes in a roasting pan and pour in hot water until it comes halfway up the sides of the dishes. Bake for 20 to 22 minutes or until soufflés are well risen and golden on top.

Remove soufflés from water bath and cool on a rack for 10 minutes. Loosen sides of soufflés with a sharp knife, then turn out onto a parchment-lined baking sheet. (If making ahead, cover loosely and refrigerate for up to 1 day. Bring soufflés to room temperature before baking.)

Preheat oven to 400°F.

Pour 1 tbsp cream on top and down sides of each soufflé. Sprinkle tops with Parmesan. Bake for 16 to 18 minutes or until puffed and golden. Serve immediately, topped with Sticky Toffee Bacon (page 314).

PAIRING: **Sparkling wine**

Food with airy bubbles. You guessed where this match was going to go, didn't you? Sparkling wine is classic for almost any soufflé, and it works especially well here, the salty-nutty zip of the cheeses (in both the soufflé and oatcakes) playing straight into the arms of a nutty, minerally, crisp bubbly. The wine's high acidity also stands strong against the vinaigrette in the accompanying salad. And this is brunch, after all, the bubbly hour. Alternative: pale or amber ale. (Hey, they've got bubbles!)

Fruit Ice Cubes: Okay, so it's come to my attention that not everybody on the planet drinks alcohol. Understandable. But what to offer said guests while the rest of the shindig benefits from that precious pinot noir you schlepped back from Oregon? Club soda? Yes, actually, club soda is good, but served with a fitting twist. Pinot tastes like berries, so here's how you can play with the theme and make everybody feel included. Take an assortment of fresh strawberries (sliced into quarters), raspberries, blackberries and blueberries and insert a quarter strawberry plus one each of the rest into each slot of an empty ice-cube tray. Top up with water and freeze. When it's party time, drop three or more cubes into each glass and fill with club soda. Should you desire a citrusy, herbal sauvignon-blanc effect, use quarter slices of lemon, lime or cucumber. It's a fine way to gussy up a long drink, such as gin and tonic, too.

STICKY TOFFEE BACON

Use parchment paper or foil on the baking sheet, otherwise you will spend the entire day trying to clean it up.

Serves 6

1 lb (450 g) thickly sliced bacon
4 tbsp maple syrup
1 tbsp cracked black pepper

Preheat oven to 425°F.

Lay bacon strips, snugly but not overlapping, on a rack over a parchment-lined baking sheet. Brush with 2 tbsp maple syrup and top with all the pepper. Bake for 10 minutes or until fat has rendered. Brush with remaining 2 tbsp maple syrup and bake for another 10 to 12 minutes or until bacon is crisp and slightly caramelized. Serve on top of soufflés.

WALNUT AND ENDIVE SALAD

This sturdy salad matches beautifully with the cheese soufflés because of the mustard dressing. You can put the salad together and make the vinaigrette ahead of time, but do not dress the salad until just before serving.

Serves 6

2 tbsp butter
1 cup walnut pieces
1 tbsp brown sugar
3 heads white Belgian endive
3 heads red Belgian endive

Vinaigrette:
1 tbsp chopped shallots
2 tsp Dijon mustard
2 tsp white wine vinegar
2 tsp balsamic vinegar
½ tsp maple syrup
¼ cup olive oil
Salt and freshly ground black pepper
½ cup pomegranate seeds

Melt butter in a medium skillet over medium heat. Add walnuts and sauté for 2 to 3 minutes or until beginning to smell toasty. Sprinkle with sugar and cook for another minute or until sugar has dissolved and coated walnuts. Cool on a baking sheet.

Slice endives and place in a bowl. Add walnuts and toss.

Whisk together shallots, mustard, white wine vinegar, balsamic vinegar and maple syrup. Whisk in olive oil until emulsified. Season with salt and pepper and toss with salad. Sprinkle with pomegranate seeds.

ISLE OF MULL OATCAKES

When I tasted these oatcakes from a farm store on Scotland's remote and beautiful Isle of Mull, I knew I had to try to make them myself. This is my remembrance of them. The steel-cut oats add a crunch.

Makes 15 biscuits

1½ cups quick-cooking rolled oats
⅔ cup steel-cut oats
¾ cup all-purpose flour
1 tbsp granulated sugar
1 tsp kosher salt
1 cup unsalted butter, melted
1 tbsp water

Preheat oven to 325°F.

Combine quick-cooking oats, steel-cut oats, flour, sugar and salt in a bowl. Drizzle in the melted butter and water and mix until well combined. Let stand 10 minutes, or until mixture has firmed up and absorbed liquid. If it is still crumbly, add a touch more water.

Press dough into a ball, then pat out on a well-floured surface to about ¼-inch thickness. Cut out 2½-inch rounds with a cookie cutter. Place on a parchment-lined baking sheet. Bake for 25 to 30 minutes or until lightly golden around edges. Cool on baking sheet.

GRAPEFRUIT COMPOTE

This is a good dish for a brunch served either on a platter or in individual serving dishes. Its refreshing flavours complement eggs, frittatas and stratas, as well as rich desserts. It's your choice what to serve it with here, although I like it with the rich millionaire bars (page 319). Cape gooseberries are also known as physalis or groundcherries. Peel back their papery skin to reveal the delicate fruit with a gooseberry quality to it.

Serves 6

¾ cup clementine or mandarin juice
1 tsp grated lime zest
3 tbsp lime juice
2 tbsp honey
1 tsp ground cardamom
3 large red grapefruit
2 large white grapefruit

Garnish:
Cape gooseberries
¼ cup chopped pistachios

Combine clementine juice, lime zest, lime juice, honey and cardamom in a small pot. Bring to a boil, reduce heat and simmer for 2 to 3 minutes to let flavours develop. Cool dressing and strain, discarding zest.

Cut peel and white pith from grapefruit. Working over a bowl, cut segments from between membranes. (Save juice for another use.)

Place grapefruit segments in a glass bowl or in individual glass dishes. Pour over dressing. Garnish with cape gooseberries and pistachios. Serve a millionaire bar on the side.

MOSCATO: RAPPERS' DELIGHT

There are many fitting words for describing wine. Until recently, *hip* was not among them. Or perhaps I should say, not until moscato. A moderately sweet, highly fragrant, often lightly spritzy white, moscato was a fringe category just a few years ago. Now it's one of the bestselling varietals in North America.

The wild sales trajectory owes almost everything to a constituency better known for mixing vodka with Red Bull, namely drinkers in their twenties and early thirties. Why so gaga for moscato? Flavour, for one thing. As a long-time moscato nut, I can understand. But there's more to the appeal: the imprimatur of hip hop royalty.

Superstars Kanye West, T.I. and Lil' Kim are devotees. Kim rhymed it with "yo" in "Lighters Up." But its most influential endorsement came from Canadian rapper Drake, who resourcefully rhymed it with "model" and "bottle" in the 2009 duet "I Invented Sex" with fellow singer Trey Songz.

Moscato is Italian for muscat, a grape with a floral scent and the uncanny flavour of white table grapes. Alsace in France yields superb dry renditions. But the variety also shines well when rendered moderately sweet, nowhere more compellingly than in moscato d'Asti from Italy's northwest Piedmont region. Subtly effervescent and medium-sweet, it's a seductive summer refresher and tends to weigh in at a mere 6 per cent alcohol.

MILLIONAIRE BARS

When I lived in Scotland, we would always have millionaire bars at Christmastime. They were made with homemade shortbread and sweetened condensed milk and were topped with chocolate. Here is an easier version that gives the same taste results. If you cannot find dulce de leche, follow our recipe on page 211. This is a fabulous sticky, gooey dessert. **Makes about 16 bars**

- 2 cups (300 g) shortbread cookie crumbs
- 3 tbsp butter, melted
- 1 cup dulce de leche
- ½ cup mascarpone
- 2 tbsp grated orange zest

Topping:

- ¾ cup chopped chocolate
- ¼ cup unsalted butter

Line an 8-inch square pan with parchment paper.

Combine shortbread crumbs and butter and pat into prepared pan. Warm dulce de leche in a pot. Stir in mascarpone. Add orange zest. Spread over shortbread and refrigerate for 1 hour to set.

Melt chocolate and butter in a heavy pot over low heat, stirring until smooth. Pour over dulce de leche layer and spread evenly with a spatula. Chill until set. Cut into squares.

PAIRING: **Moscato d'Asti**

It's brunch, I know. Wine with dessert can seem like the fast road to ruin (unless you keep the sort of company I do). Let me, then, suggest something on the tame side. How about moscato d'Asti from Italy's Piedmont region? It usually tips the scales at a mere 6 per cent alcohol. Better still, it's lightly effervescent, only moderately sweet and tastes like fresh white table grapes, a fine complement to the fruit as well as the buttery millionaire bars.

APPLE CRANBERRY COMPOTE

For a holiday or winter brunch, this is a perfect dessert served with some cookies. To mellow the tart cranberry taste, the sugar syrup has to be sweet. As the cranberries pop open, their acidity cuts the sweetness. This is also a good dessert after a heavy holiday dinner. You can serve the compote warm or cold. It keeps for about 2 weeks, refrigerated.

Serves 4

- ½ cup butter
- 1 cup granulated sugar
- 2 tart green apples, peeled, cored and sliced
- 1 cup cranberries
- 1 tsp cinnamon
- 2 cups vanilla ice cream

Combine butter and sugar in a skillet. Bring to a boil and boil for 1 minute.

Add apples and cranberries and simmer until apples are tender and cranberries just begin to pop.

Sprinkle cinnamon over ice cream.

Top warm compote with cinnamon ice cream to serve.

APPLES IN CARAMEL CIDER SAUCE

For a quick, fabulous dessert, serve these caramel apples with ice cream. If cider is unavailable, use apple juice mixed with 1 tbsp cider vinegar. For a different presentation, roll out puff pastry and cut into rounds. Place the apples in caramel in individual ramekins and top with pastry rounds. Bake for 20 minutes in a 400°F oven. Turn out so the pastry is on the bottom.

Serves 4 to 6

- 2 cups apple cider
- 1 cup granulated sugar
- 2 tbsp butter
- 4 Spy or Granny Smith apples, peeled, cored and sliced

Boil apple cider in a large skillet over high heat until reduced by half, about 7 minutes. Stir in sugar and boil until mixture turns golden brown, about 5 minutes. Remove from heat and stir in butter until melted. Stir in apples.

Return skillet to medium heat and cook until apples have absorbed some of the caramel and are fairly translucent, 5 to 7 minutes. The sauce will be very thick. Serve warm or cold over ice cream.

PAIRING: **Sweet Vouvray**

Made from chenin blanc, Vouvray can range from dry and sparkling to lusciously sweet. The styles you want to look for here are labelled moelleux (medium sweetness) or liquoreux (very sweet). The wines are delectably honeyed, often with a core that suggests baked apple or fig. They're almost always imbued with good acidity, just like cider.

Reducing Apple Cider: Reducing a bottle of unsweetened apple cider produces a thick, rich caramel that is full of natural pectin. Use a tablespoon in jam making to help low-pectin fruits like strawberries gel. Use as a sauce with apples or peaches, or punch up a sauce for chicken or pork. It keeps for 6 months in the refrigerator.

SCRAMBLED EGGS IN PANCETTA CUPS

I do love eggs, and my favourite recipe has to be the following rich scrambled eggs, which I serve in pancetta cups when I have guests, or over toast with the family. The secret to both the texture and flavour is adding a little uncooked egg to the pan, along with some butter, just before the eggs finish cooking. It makes them totally decadent. Use spicy pancetta if you like heat, and make sure it is thinly sliced. **Serves 6**

12 thin slices pancetta
4 tbsp butter, at room temperature
12 eggs
Salt and freshly ground pepper
3 cups cooked lentils
½ cup kale or other sprouts

Preheat oven to 425°F.
Press a round of pancetta into a mini muffin cup. Repeat to make 12 cups. Bake until pancetta is crisp, 5 to 10 minutes. Remove from pan and drain on paper towels.
Melt 2 tbsp butter in a large skillet over medium-low heat. Whisk eggs in a bowl and season with salt and pepper.
Add all but ¼ cup eggs to skillet. Slowly whisk eggs until softly scrambled, about 4 minutes. They should be quite smooth, with some eggy curds in them. Stir in remaining egg mixture and remaining 2 tbsp butter.
Spoon eggs into pancetta cups. Serve on a bed of lentils and garnish with sprouts.

PAIRING: **Sparkling wine**

I have always considered scrambled eggs the ultimate kitchen crucible. I used to tremble at the prospect of preparing brunch—especially when a new lover sat in judgment—till Lucy taught me the trick of stirring in a bit of uncooked egg at the last minute. These runny, creamy eggs need a zippy palate cleanser, and there's no better choice than dry sparkling wine, such as prosecco from Italy, Cava from Spain or true-blue Champagne from France. The nutty, tangy character of white Burgundy would make a fine alternative, as would a lean, crisp Soave from Italy. All great ways to say "good morning."

UNBREAKABLE BÉARNAISE

Serving poached eggs for brunch? Try this easy béarnaise sauce to go with them. This is similar to hollandaise but much easier to make because it will not curdle (there are no egg yolks in it). It keeps for 3 days refrigerated. The sauce hardens if refrigerated, so remove it from the refrigerator 2 hours before serving.

Makes 1 cup

2 tbsp white wine vinegar
1 tbsp water
2 tsp chopped fresh tarragon
2 tsp minced shallots
6 peppercorns
½ cup unsalted butter
½ cup mayonnaise
2 tbsp whipping cream
Salt

Combine vinegar, water, tarragon, shallots and peppercorns in a small pot. Bring to a boil over medium heat, reduce heat and simmer for 1 to 2 minutes or until reduced to 1 tbsp. Strain, discarding solids. **Melt** butter and stir into vinegar reduction. Place mayonnaise in a medium bowl and whisk butter mixture into it a little at a time until all the butter has been added and the sauce is smooth. Whisk in cream and season with salt.

TART

oranges • grapefruits • mandarins • lemons • limes

tangerines • clementines • tangelos • Ugli fruit • fruit juice

coffee • tomatoes • balsamic vinegar • red wine vinegar

rice vinegar • white wine vinegar • cider vinegar • Sherry vinegar

sumac • cranberries • mirin • Granny Smith apples

yuzu • pomegranates • rhubarb • gooseberries

lemongrass • turmeric

OF ALL THE FRUITY METAPHORS OUT *there—Big Apple, grapes of wrath, going bananas—our favourite involves citrus. Not the one about lemons and cars. The one about tasting the sun. There's money in the metaphor. Marketing wizards tapped it to create such brands as Sunkist oranges and SunnyD fruit drinks as well as that annoyingly memorable 1970s TV slogan for the Florida Citrus Commission delivered by singer Anita Bryant, "A day without orange juice is like a day without sunshine." There's even a British jazz ensemble called Citrus Sun.*

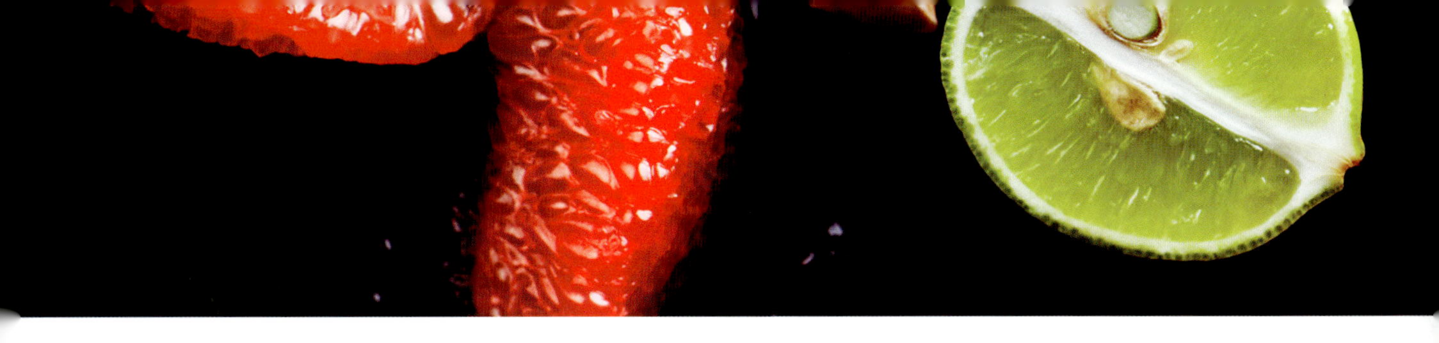

Citrus fruits are the poster ingredients for the category Lucy and I call "tart." The field goes well beyond that, of course, to include such culinary staples as vinegar and tomatoes. But we've made citrus the big star in this chapter. As cooks, we cherish the juice and zest of citrus fruits, especially lemons and limes. They harmonize with virtually all foods, from Thai curries to veal scaloppine, and we think they bring a special bit of magic to poultry, which also features prominently in these pages. They're indispensable to a proper bar, even if your mixology skills extend no further than plugging a lime wedge into the neck of a Corona bottle.

As pervasive as citrus fruits are today, though, their global conquest has been surprisingly recent. Humans first encountered citrus in the form of the citron (a.k.a. Persian apple and, in Hebrew, *etrog*) thousands of years ago, probably in the forests of Malaysia. Millennia would pass before the fragrant but relatively juice-less citron reached Europe, joined by its more popular kin, the orange, grapefruit, lime and lemon.

Then Columbus carried citrus seeds to Hispaniola on his second transatlantic voyage, in 1493. Breakfast in the Americas would never be the same. Today, the planet is home to more than a billion citrus trees, one for every seven mouths. That's a whole lot of sunshine.

Of course, there's no citrusy goodness without acidity, a quality that works its own chemical magic in the kitchen. Lemon and lime juice tenderize meat before it hits the heat, curb bacterial growth, stop trimmed or peeled vegetables such as artichokes from discolouring and act as a sort of "cold cooking" agent to transform the protein of raw fish, yielding, for example, succulent ceviche. On the tongue, acidity plays another vital role, lifting other flavours and acting as a sort of mouthwash to cleanse fats, bringing balance to rich dishes. Think of Tuscan bistecca, a grilled T-bone traditionally served with a wedge of lemon, or fried schnitzel, often served the same way. Or think of lemony cheesecake and Key lime pie. (If you're like us, you never stop thinking about pie.)

In a sense, wine, often rich in acidity, especially in the case of white, plays a similar role at the table. Few are the whites that don't suggest at least a nuance of citrus. But the most conspicuous conduits include sauvignon blanc and super-crisp Australian riesling. You might swear the latter was pressed directly from limes.

MARTINIS

If you really love lemons, go the Lemon Drop Martini route, using lemon-infused vodka and a splash of dry vermouth. But for a more toned-down lemon essence as well as an aromatic enhancement to the entire meal, consider a classic dry martini made with gin, dry vermouth and a twist of lemon peel as a garnish. Some cocktail historians believe lemon zest trumps olives in the authentic-garnish debate.

Every bartender worth his or her salt rimmer has a technique for mixing the "perfect" dry martini. Here's the ingenious method we favour.

Into a shaker of ice, pour 2½ oz gin (or vodka if you're averse to gin's herbal essence) and a quarter cap–full of dry vermouth. Yes, the vermouth first gets poured into the vermouth bottle's cap. This is an intermediate step so you don't accidentally pour too much into the shaker, which can scuttle the drink's de rigueur dryness. Swirl the container for about 30 seconds, till everything's good and cold. Strain the whole thing into a martini glass. Pare a thin strip of peel from a lemon, about 1 inch long, then squeeze it over the drink. Rub the peel around the rim of the glass before tossing it in.

VODKA: IAN FLEMING'S GREATEST VILLAIN?

Blame it on Sean Connery. It's hard to imagine now, but there was a time when gin was more fashionable than vodka. Then came *Dr. No*, the 1962 film debut of author Ian Fleming's James Bond franchise, which featured the Scottish sex symbol in the lead role. In a fateful scene, our debonair secret agent orders a room-service cocktail, a "medium-dry vodka martini," dutifully stirred and not shaken by a waiter. It would become, arguably, the most famous drink in silver-screen history, vodka's Big Moment. Suddenly, cool, bracing gin wasn't so cool anymore, and the martini, once synonymous with that invigorating, flavourful spirit, began its slow and steady decline into adultery.

From there it was a mere hop and skip to the cran-, choco- and appletini corruptions of today. Without gin's inspired juniper essence, neutral vodka opened up a flank for all manner of cloying, candy-store flavourings. A sad state of affairs.

The modern aversion to gin is ironic in a world now awash in vodkas laced with everything from citrus to ginger to—the horror!—root beer and bubble gum. Gin itself starts out as neutral vodka, after all. Then it's steeped in so-called botanicals—mainly juniper but also citrus peel, coriander, cassia bark and orrisroot. Those botanicals are what give the classic martini its bracing appeal. I wouldn't take mine any other way.

But I'm happy to report that gin is fighting the vodka tide. Many of the new premium brands have been taming down the shaving-cream essence of juniper. The resurgence began years ago with such offerings as fruity Tanqueray No. 10 from England and the uncommonly refreshing Hendrick's from Scotland, infused with cucumber and rose petal.

And the classic style known as London Dry is spawning new expressions. You'll find the unapologetic zing of juniper front and centre in award-winning Broker's, an excellent bargain brand. For twice the price, there's the precision-tuned No. 3 from England's Berry Bros. & Rudd, which anchors my home bar and makes the best martini in Christendom. Another winner: The Botanist from Bruichladdich, the single-malt distillery on Scotland's island of Islay. Yes, another Great Scot, just like Sean Connery. Let's call it even, shall we, Mr. Bond?

Menu 1

LOVELY LEMONS

Tuna Ceviche with Endive Watermelon Salad

Chicken from Fez with Preserved Lemon and Olives

Roasted Eggplant Salad

Simple Plum Cardamom Cake

When I lived briefly in Palm Springs, a friend brought me a large bag of lemons she had picked from her lemon tree. These thin-skinned, extra-juicy lemons were a revelation in taste. Determined to use them up, I came up with this lemony, mouth-watering menu.

TUNA CEVICHE WITH ENDIVE WATERMELON SALAD

Use the freshest tuna you can find. Look for a centre-cut piece, as it has less sinew. This should be made an hour before serving. Shape any leftovers into little tuna meatballs and fry them. **Serves 4**

Ceviche:

8 oz (225 g) sushi-grade tuna
3 tbsp chopped shallots
1 tsp chopped green chili
1 tsp capers
¼ tsp grated lemon zest
1 tbsp lemon juice
2 tbsp olive oil
1 tsp soy sauce
2 tbsp chopped fresh cilantro
Salt and freshly ground pepper

Salad:

1 large Belgian endive, thinly sliced into rounds (about 1½ cups)
1½ cups watercress
½ cup thinly sliced watermelon
1 tbsp lemon juice
1 tbsp extra-virgin olive oil
¼ tsp Maldon or other salt

Chop tuna by hand into about ½-inch cubes. Stir in shallots, chili, capers, lemon zest and juice, olive oil and soy sauce. Toss with cilantro and season with salt and pepper. Let sit for 1 hour at room temperature.

Combine endive, watercress and watermelon in a large bowl. Sprinkle with lemon juice and olive oil, season with Maldon salt and gently toss. Divide salad among 4 plates and top with a scoop of tuna ceviche.

PAIRING: **Champagne**

If you've got $40 or more left in your pocket after splurging on sushi-grade tuna, treat this luxurious appetizer with the regal respect it deserves. Pop some Champagne and see why sparkling wine is not just a celebratory froth. You won't regret it. This dish is light in texture and tangy with vinaigrette, so there's lots going on. Crisp bubbly will rise above it all without weighing down the delicate fish. Prosecco or Spanish Cava are good alternatives, as are New Zealand sauvignon blanc, dry riesling and good-quality cold sake.

CHICKEN FROM FEZ WITH PRESERVED LEMON AND OLIVES

Fez is the ancient spiritual centre of Morocco. Its medina, the ancient city centre, is the oldest in existence. Rabbit-warren streets wind through this ancient area—navigating them is a challenge and a guide is a must. Vendors with mounds of brightly coloured exotic spices are everywhere, and this full-flavoured recipe pays homage to them. It is traditionally served with couscous. You can add the Radish and Orange Salad on page 296 as well. The fresher the spices, the better the flavour. You can buy preserved lemons at the grocery store or use our Quick Preserved Lemons recipe on page 335.

Serves 4

2 tsp ground ginger
2 tsp ground cumin
1 tsp turmeric
½ tsp cinnamon
¼ tsp cayenne
2 lb (900 g) bone-in chicken thighs
Salt and freshly ground pepper
2 tbsp olive oil
2 cups chopped onions
1 tbsp chopped garlic
½ tsp saffron threads (optional)
1 tsp honey
¼ cup chopped fresh cilantro
2 tomatoes, chopped
1 cup chicken stock or water
½ preserved lemon, slivered
½ cup cracked green olives, cut in half and pitted
¼ cup chopped fresh parsley

Preheat oven to 375°F.

Combine ginger, cumin, turmeric, cinnamon and cayenne in a bowl. Sprinkle 1 tbsp spice mixture over chicken. Season chicken with salt and pepper.

Heat olive oil in a large skillet over medium-high heat. Add chicken and sauté for 3 minutes per side or until golden. Remove chicken from pan and drain all but 2 tbsp fat from pan. Add onions, reduce heat to medium and sauté for 10 minutes or until softened and slightly golden. Add garlic and cook for another minute. Add saffron (if using), honey, cilantro and remaining spice mixture, then add tomatoes and stock and bring to a boil.

Reduce heat to medium-low. Return chicken to pan skin side up, cover and bake for 15 minutes. Add preserved lemon and olives and bake, uncovered, for another 15 to 25 minutes (depending on size of thighs) or until juices run clear. Sprinkle with parsley before serving.

QUICK PRESERVED LEMONS

There is a long method for preserving lemons that works beautifully, but you need 7 days before you can even consider using them and a month before they are at their peak. I make a lot of marmalade, so I wondered whether using that technique with salt instead of sugar might preserve the lemons well. Here are the perfect and instant results.

Place 3 lemons in a pot and cover with water. Bring to a boil. Cover, reduce heat and simmer for 1 hour.
Transfer lemons to a plate and reserve cooking water. Cut lemons into quarters. Scoop out and discard fruit. Use a sharp knife to remove excess pith from peel. Cut peel quarters in half lengthwise.
Combine 2 cups lemon cooking water and 2 tbsp kosher salt in a medium pot. Bring to a boil. Add lemon peel, reduce heat and simmer gently for 30 minutes or until lemon peel is soft and has absorbed some of the liquid.
Place peel in a container and cover with the lemon brine. To seal, pour a film of olive oil on top and put on the lid. Refrigerate. The lemons will be ready to use in 12 to 24 hours, and will keep for a month.

PAIRING: **Minervois or Corbières**

They make wine in Morocco, some of it based on syrah and inspired by the Mediterranean reds of southern France. Since Moroccan wine is exceedingly hard to come by, I'd suggest the French option, such as Minervois or Corbières. The ripe, sunny fruit will mesh with the preserved lemon and spices, and the wines' herbal characters are magical whenever olives come into play. Alternatives: a luscious Portuguese red from the Douro Valley, jammy primitivo from Puglia or red from the Spanish regions of Jumilla or Almansa (not far from Morocco). Or try a Mediterranean-inspired custom gin and tonic, page 81 in our "Herbal" chapter.

ROASTED EGGPLANT SALAD

Eggplant is an important vegetable in Moroccan cuisine. It grows very well in that climate and is used in everything from salads to stews and tagines. It works well to balance the spices used in Moroccan kitchens and in the chicken dish in this menu.

Serves 4

1 large eggplant
5 tbsp olive oil
Salt and freshly ground pepper
4 tsp chopped garlic
½ tsp ground cumin
½ tsp paprika
¼ tsp cayenne
3 fresh tomatoes, chopped (about 3 cups), or 4 canned tomatoes, chopped
2 tbsp lemon juice, or to taste
2 tbsp chopped fresh parsley

Preheat oven to 450°F.

Peel lengthwise strips from eggplant skin about 1 inch apart. Cut eggplant crosswise in ½-inch slices. Brush both sides lightly with 3 tbsp olive oil. Place eggplant on a parchment-lined baking sheet.

Roast until golden brown, 18 to 20 minutes. Cool on baking sheet. Sprinkle with salt and pepper to taste. Chop eggplant.

Heat remaining 2 tbsp oil in a large skillet over medium heat. Add eggplant, garlic, cumin, paprika and cayenne and sauté for 2 minutes or until garlic starts to soften. Stir in tomatoes. Reduce heat to low and continue to cook, stirring occasionally, until mixture thickens, 20 to 30 minutes. Add lemon juice and stir in parsley. Remove from heat and cool.

Serve at room temperature.

SIMPLE PLUM CARDAMOM CAKE

This is a one-bowl cake that works brilliantly. So quick and easy: beat everything together and bake. It makes a lovely breakfast cake too. Feel free to switch the fruit for a seasonal take. This is an update of one of the most popular recipes from my Globe and Mail *column. Leftovers keep well in an airtight container and are great with a cup of tea.*

Serves 4 (with leftovers)

- 2 large eggs
- ½ cup unsalted butter, softened
- ¼ cup Greek yogurt
- 1½ cups all-purpose flour
- ¾ cup granulated sugar
- 1 tsp baking soda
- ½ tsp kosher salt
- 1 tbsp grated lemon zest
- 1½ tsp ground cardamom
- 1 tsp vanilla
- 1½ cups chopped red or black plums

Preheat oven to 350°F. Grease a loaf pan and line the bottom with parchment paper.

Combine eggs, butter, yogurt, flour, sugar, baking soda, salt, lemon zest, cardamom and vanilla in a large bowl and beat with an electric mixer for 3 minutes or until well combined. Stir in plums.

Spoon batter into prepared pan and bake for 55 to 60 minutes or until a cake tester comes out clean. Cool in pan for 10 minutes, then turn out, peel off parchment and cool completely on a rack.

PAIRING: Late Bottled Vintage Port

Sweet, ripe and plummy, Port is perfect here. Look for the relatively affordable style called Late Bottled Vintage (or LBV). This high-quality Port is made from a single harvest, just like expensive Vintage Port, rather than blended from many years' stock. And unlike tannic, gum-assaulting Vintage Port, it requires no further aging and no decanting to remove sediment.

Cardamom (or cardamon) is an age-old spice that is becoming popular once again. Grown in southern India, it is quite expensive, as the pods have to be hand-picked. The Vikings took the spice back to Sweden, where it is now a staple in Swedish cooking. It is used in Indian cooking and to flavour cakes, side dishes and fruit pies. I much prefer it to cinnamon because it brings a freshness to any recipe.

DIRTY MOJITO

So chic has the Mojito become that it has inspired no shortage of gratuitous variants. Witness the Mojito Italiano, which substitutes basil for mint in the citrusy Cuban long drink. So wrong. There is just one way to improve this classic. More rum!

The drink is built the usual way, with unaged white rum as the base. But then you float a tiny splash of oak-matured rum over top like an oil slick. The dark spirit adds a fetching amber layer, plus a whisper of caramel to every sip without wrecking the underlying balance. It's a revolution we can live with. Use a good-quality dark rum, such as El Dorado 15-year-old from Guyana or Appleton 12-year-old from Jamaica.

4 to 6 mint leaves
Juice of ½ lime
¾ tsp granulated sugar
2 oz white rum
About 5 oz club soda
⅓ oz dark rum

Add mint leaves to a highball glass with lime juice and sugar.
Mash the mint against the side of the glass with a bar spoon, making sure the sugar dissolves in the process.
Fill the glass halfway with crushed ice and pour in white rum. Fill almost to the rim with club soda. Stir gently with the spoon to incorporate the sugar. Then slowly pour in dark rum.

Menu 2

AN EDGY FRANCO-AMERICAN MENU

Roquefort Toasts with Arugula and Dried Pear Salad
Duck Breasts with Blood Orange Salsa
Warm Lemon Poppy Seed Cakes

The first duck breast I had, years ago in Paris, was so thick and juicy I thought they had served me steak by mistake! The waiter did not find it amusing. Duck works beautifully with citrus flavours (think of the classic Duck à l'Orange). I had my first lemon poppy seed cake at a conference in the US and again I fell in love. Here are these two recipes, along with a super salad.

ROQUEFORT TOASTS WITH ARUGULA AND DRIED PEAR SALAD

The toasts on their own make a good hors d'oeuvre for passing.

Serves 4

- ½ cup crumbled Roquefort
- ¼ cup butter, softened
- ¼ tsp chili flakes
- 4 slices baguette, toasted
- 4 cups arugula
- ½ cup pecans, toasted
- 12 slices dried pear (see note, below)

Lemon Dressing:

- 2 tbsp lemon juice
- 1½ tsp maple syrup
- 2 tsp chopped fresh parsley
- ¼ cup olive oil
- Salt and freshly ground pepper

Beat together Roquefort, butter and chili flakes until smooth. Spread on toasts.

Divide arugula among 4 plates. Sprinkle with pecans. Top with pear slices.

Whisk together lemon juice, maple syrup and parsley. Whisk in olive oil until emulsified. Season with salt and pepper. Drizzle over salads. Top with toasts or serve them on the side.

PAIRING: **Alsatian pinot gris**

Were it not for the arugula and the lemon dressing, Port could work nicely here, its ripe fruit a fine match for salty Roquefort and the pear. But you'll need more verve, and you don't want to shut down the palate at the start of a meal with sugary Port. Pinot gris from Alsace has ripe, round, pear-like fruit, opulent mouthfeel and enough acidity to dance with the dressing. Alternative: Oregon pinot gris.

Dried Pear Slices: Using a mandoline or sharp knife, slice pears very thinly. Place pears, without overlapping, on a parchment-lined cookie sheet. Top with another sheet of parchment and another cookie sheet. Bake at 275°F for 35 to 40 minutes or until pears are dry to the touch. They will crisp as they cool. Store in an airtight container for a day or so. A nonstick baking mat can be used instead of parchment paper. Use this method with apples too.

DUCK BREASTS WITH BLOOD ORANGE SALSA

Slowly cooking the duck breasts skin side down releases the fat and crisps the skin. Finish with a fast oven bake. Blood oranges give this dish a beautiful colour, but if they are unavailable use regular oranges or the new Cara Cara oranges with their hint of red. Serve with orzo (page 268) and sugar snap peas or crisp green beans.

Serves 4

Salsa:

½ cup chopped fennel
½ cup chopped blood orange flesh
2 tbsp chopped red onion
2 tsp chopped seeded jalapeño pepper, or to taste
2 tbsp olive oil
2 tbsp blood orange juice
2 tbsp lemon juice
2 tbsp chopped chives
2 tbsp chopped fresh cilantro
¼ tsp granulated sugar
Salt

3 duck breasts (about 12 oz/340 g each)
1 tsp cracked fennel seeds
1 tsp cracked coriander seeds
Salt and freshly ground pepper

Combine fennel, blood orange flesh, red onion, jalapeño, olive oil, blood orange juice, lemon juice, chives, cilantro, sugar and salt to taste. Reserve.

Preheat oven to 450°F.

Score skin of duck breasts at 1-inch intervals (do not cut into meat). Rub with fennel and coriander seeds. Season with salt and pepper. Place skin side down in a cold ovenproof skillet and place over medium heat. Cook for 2 minutes. Reduce heat to low and cook for 15 minutes or until fat is rendered and skin is beginning to crisp. Pour off fat and place skillet in oven. Bake for 10 to 12 minutes or until duck is medium-rare. Remove from skillet and let rest for 5 minutes.

Slice breasts into ½-inch slices. Serve topped with salsa.

PAIRING: **Nero d'Avola**

Blood oranges thrive in Sicily, and the Mediterranean island's signature red, nero d'Avola, happens to suit this dish well. It's full bodied and plummy, with a similar profile to peppery syrah, though with soft tannins and a good acid grip that locks with the citrus in this dish. Alternative: rich, jammy pinot noir from California's Santa Rita Hills.

WARM LEMON POPPY SEED CAKES

These individual cakes are just as spectacular served warm or cold. Reheat them in a 350°F oven for about 10 minutes. One cake is quite a large serving for one person, so I cut them in half, lay them on the plate cut side down and garnish them with a little whipped cream. Mini Bundt cake pans are available at kitchen shops. You can also use a regular muffin pan, but bake only for about 10 to 15 minutes.

Makes 6 cakes, serving 6 to 12

- 1 cup unsalted butter, at room temperature
- 1¼ cups granulated sugar
- 5 large eggs
- ¼ cup sour cream
- ¼ cup chopped candied lemon confit (page 347)
- 2 tbsp grated lemon zest
- 1¾ cups all-purpose flour
- 2 tsp baking powder
- ½ tsp kosher salt
- ⅓ cup poppy seeds
- Lemon syrup (page 346)
- Lemon glaze (page 346)

Preheat the oven to 350°F. Butter and flour 6 mini Bundt moulds.

Beat together butter and sugar in a large bowl with an electric mixer until light and fluffy, about 2 minutes. Beat in eggs, one at a time. Beat in sour cream, lemon confit and lemon zest.

Mix together flour, baking powder and salt in a separate bowl. Fold dry ingredients into wet ingredients. Stir in poppy seeds.

Spoon batter into prepared moulds, leaving ¼-inch space at the top. Bake for 20 minutes or until a cake tester comes out clean. Transfer to a rack and cool in pan for 5 minutes. Invert onto rack and poke holes in the top of each cake. Brush warm cakes with lemon syrup.

Serve half a cake per person topped with a drizzle of lemon glaze.

PAIRING: **Aperol Spritz**

The instinctive pairing here would involve something with a strong taste of lemon, such as limoncello. But that's gilding the lily. Much as I love lemon, too much of a good thing invites fatigue. Besides, you don't want to weigh down Lucy's airy cakes with a heavy liqueur. A frothy Aperol Spritz (page 298 in our "Sweet" chapter), with its sparkling prosecco base and contrasting orange flavour, puts an exclamation mark on this dessert. If you prefer something sweeter, try a late-harvest cabernet franc, a crimson elixir with a complementary taste of red berries.

LEMON SYRUP

¼ cup granulated sugar
2 tbsp lemon juice
2 tbsp water

Bring sugar, lemon juice and water to a boil in a small pot. Cook until sugar is dissolved. Cool slightly before using.

LEMON GLAZE

1¼ cups icing sugar
2 tbsp lemon juice
2 tsp butter, melted

Combine sugar, lemon juice and butter in a medium bowl. Stir until smooth.

CANDIED LEMON CONFIT

These candied lemon slices are a delight to have around the house. Use in cakes, cookies, chicken and fish dishes, as a garnish for dessert or as a flavouring in cream- or custard-based desserts. I like them on toast and in cocktails. You can also candy orange slices. Cut away the flesh and use the peel in recipes.

Cut 2 lemons into ⅓-inch rounds. Remove pits. Place lemon slices in a pot and cover with cold water. Bring to a boil. Boil for 15 minutes or until softened.

Spoon lemon slices into a bowl. Measure 1 cup lemon water and discard remainder. Bring lemon water and 1 cup granulated sugar to a boil. Boil for 2 minutes, then return lemon slices to pot. Reduce heat and simmer gently for 20 to 25 minutes or until lemon rounds have absorbed most of the syrup.

Remove rounds gently and transfer to a parchment-lined baking sheet to cool. Chop them or use whole. Refrigerate until needed. They keep for a month. Save the syrup to brush on cakes or use in fruit salads (or spoon it over oatmeal biscuits, a personal favourite).

Menu 3

VIETNAMESE FLAVOURS

Grapefruit Salad Saigon Style

Vietnamese Fried Chicken

Mandarin Pudding Cake with Lime Leaves

I love Vietnamese flavours because they are citrus based, herbal and very clean. And because of the country's history, there is a French influence as well. I have been experimenting with some recipes that are slotted in my taste memory from such wonderful spots as the Slanted Door in San Francisco. Here are the results.

GRAPEFRUIT SALAD SAIGON STYLE

Vietnamese flavourings infuse this salad with herbal notes. Serve it for lunch, as a light supper or as an unusual first course for a dinner party. Bronze watercress tastes like regular watercress but its colour is beautiful in this dish. Add sautéed small shrimp for a more substantial salad. If lime leaves are not available, add an extra teaspoon of grated lime zest.

Serves 4

Dressing:

2 lime leaves, slivered
½ tsp grated lime zest
2 tbsp lime juice
2 tbsp chopped shallots
2 tbsp rice vinegar
1 tbsp vegetable oil
1 tbsp fish sauce
2 tsp honey
¼ tsp chopped seeded red chili

Salad:

6 cups bronze watercress (about 2 bunches)
1 pink grapefruit, cut into segments and torn into pieces
1 avocado, sliced
2 green onions, slivered
1 tbsp slivered fresh mint
1 tbsp slivered Thai or regular basil
1 tbsp slivered fresh cilantro leaves

Combine lime leaves, lime zest, lime juice, shallots, rice vinegar, vegetable oil, fish sauce, honey and chili in a medium bowl.

Toss watercress leaves with grapefruit, avocado, green onions, mint, basil and cilantro. Toss with dressing.

PAIRING: **New Zealand sauvignon blanc**

There's an uncanny essence of grapefruit in many New Zealand sauvignon blancs, particularly the classic versions of the Marlborough region. But that's not the only reason to dispatch it here. I love the added tropical-fruit notes, especially passion fruit, with vibrant, often spicy Vietnamese food. And the wine's lively acidity and strong grassy-herbal character meet this salad on its terms.

HOW TO FLAME AN ORANGE PEEL

A magic trick involving matches and booze—what could go wrong?! Forget your fear. This will earn you more cocktail cred than any amount of Tom Cruise–style bottle juggling. But it's not just for show. The orange fireworks impart subtle citrusy complexity.

Pare off a thin disc of rind, roughly 1 inch in diameter, from an orange. Hold a lit match or lighter in one hand a little above your drink. With the other hand, clasp the rind, skin side outward, by the outer edges with thumb and two fingers as though turning a dial. Wave the flame against the outer skin for about 2 seconds to warm the surface. Now pull the rind about 1 inch away from the flame and squeeze it so that the citrus oil squirts toward the flame in the direction of the drink. Poof! Big flare.

Wipe the caramelized rind around the glass's rim and drop it into the drink. Suitable for dark cocktails, such as a Sidecar or Negroni.

SIDECAR

How this one slipped through the cracks of the modern cocktail renaissance, I'm at a loss to explain. It easily ranks among the Top 10 classics, the grand drink to emerge from the Prohibition era, yet it's easier today to find a bartender versed in the Slippery Nipple or Screaming Orgasm than one who can stir up this sultry seductress. A shame.

1 oz brandy
4 tsp Cointreau (I prefer Triple Sec)
4 tsp lemon juice

Pour ingredients into a shaker with ice, shake and strain into a martini glass. Garnish with lemon peel. Or try the flamed-orange-peel trick above.

VIETNAMESE FRIED CHICKEN

This is one of those dishes that you can't stop eating. I served it for a street barbecue one year because you don't need forks when the chicken is wrapped up in the lettuce leaves. But my favourite way to serve it is on a large platter where gluttony can take over and you do need a fork.

Serves 4 to 6

Marinade:

- 2 green onions, chopped
- 3 garlic cloves, sliced
- 2 tbsp chopped lemongrass
- 2 tbsp coarsely chopped fresh mint
- 2 tbsp coarsely chopped fresh cilantro
- 2 tbsp fish sauce
- 1 tbsp granulated sugar
- 1 tsp grated lime zest
- 1 tbsp lime juice
- 2 tbsp vegetable oil

- 2 lb (900 g) boneless, skinless chicken thighs or breasts
- ¾ cup all-purpose flour
- ¼ cup cornstarch
- 2 tbsp vegetable oil
- 8 oz (225 g) thin rice noodles, cooked
- Boston lettuce leaves
- 4 green onions, slivered

Combine green onions, garlic, lemongrass, mint, cilantro, fish sauce, sugar, lime zest, lime juice and vegetable oil in a food processor or mini chopper and process to combine.

Trim chicken of all fat. Toss chicken with marinade. Marinate for at least 2 hours or overnight, refrigerated, turning occasionally.

Preheat oven to 400°F.

Combine flour and cornstarch in a medium bowl. Remove chicken from marinade, discarding marinade. Dredge chicken in flour mixture.

Heat oil in a large skillet over medium-high heat. Add chicken and brown, 2 to 3 minutes per side. (You can prepare the dish to this point a few hours ahead.)

Place thighs on a baking sheet and roast for 10 to 15 minutes (depending on thickness) or until juices run clear. Slice chicken into strips. Serve warm or at room temperature.

Pile rice noodles into lettuce leaves. Top with sliced chicken and garnish with green onions. Serve with Fiery Chili Sauce and/or Ginger Lime Dipping Sauce (page 354).

PAIRING: **Australian semillon**

This is a main course, and most people will crave red at this point in the meal (if not sooner). But Asian cuisine more often than not makes an airtight argument for white. Semillon, a regal grape with a subtly oily texture and complex flavours suggesting honey, citrus and candied fruit, supports the vibrant aromatics in this dish.

FIERY CHILI SAUCE

Homemade chili sauce with its sweet, tart, fiery taste makes this meal very special. This sauce keeps for 2 weeks, refrigerated.

Makes about ½ cup

¼ cup granulated sugar
¼ cup water
1 or 2 bird's eye chilies, chopped
3 tbsp fish sauce
1 tsp chopped garlic
1 tsp grated lime zest
2 tsp lime juice
¼ red pepper, thinly sliced

Bring sugar and water to a boil in a small pot. Boil for 2 minutes. Stir in chilies, fish sauce, garlic, lime zest and lime juice. Cool. Pour into a serving bowl and garnish with sliced pepper.

GINGER LIME DIPPING SAUCE

This sauce is similar to the chili sauce but has a real hit of ginger. It keeps for 2 weeks, refrigerated.

Makes about ½ cup

1 red chili, seeded and chopped
Grated zest and juice of 1 lime
¼ cup brown sugar
¼ cup water
2 tbsp finely chopped peeled fresh ginger
2 tbsp fish sauce

Combine all ingredients in a small pot and bring to a boil. Reduce heat and simmer for 2 minutes. Cool.

Gastrique: If Beppi talks about *garrigue* in the "Herbal" chapter, I must discuss gastrique here. It is a sweet-sour sauce base that begins with sugar and vinegar, to which is added stock and often a flavouring such as raspberry purée or herbs. The sauce is boiled down until it becomes quite sticky and is utterly delectable. Use with duck, venison, veal, pork or lamb.

MANDARIN PUDDING CAKE WITH LIME LEAVES

Pudding cake recipes have been around for many years, but using mandarins is a new take on the classic. I have added fresh ginger and lime leaves for an Asian flavour. This pudding is superb warm or cold. You can make one large pudding if you wish; it will need to bake 7 to 10 minutes longer. **Serves 4**

½ cup mandarin juice
4 lime leaves
1 cup table cream or milk
3 large eggs, separated
Pinch kosher salt
½ cup + 2 tbsp granulated sugar
2 tbsp unsalted butter, softened
1 tbsp grated mandarin zest
2 tsp grated fresh ginger
¼ cup all-purpose flour
1 tbsp icing sugar

Preheat oven to 350°F. Butter four 1-cup ramekins.

Combine mandarin juice and lime leaves in a small pot. Bring to a boil over medium heat and reduce to ¼ cup, about 8 to 10 minutes. Cool. Remove lime leaves and stir in cream. Reserve.

Beat egg whites with a pinch of salt in a medium bowl with an electric mixer. When whites are frothy, gradually beat in ½ cup sugar and continue beating until soft peaks form. Reserve.

Beat butter and remaining 2 tbsp sugar with unwashed beaters in a large bowl until light and fluffy. Beat in egg yolks, one at a time, then beat in mandarin zest and ginger. Beat in flour just until combined. In a slow, steady stream, beat in reserved cream mixture.

Stir one-third of egg whites into yolk mixture. Fold in remaining whites in two additions.

Divide batter among ramekins. Place ramekins in a baking pan and pour in hot water until it comes halfway up the sides of the ramekins.

Bake for 18 to 20 minutes or until top is set (the centre of the cake will still be liquid). Remove ramekins from water bath and cool for 10 minutes. Sift icing sugar over top and serve hot.

PAIRING: **Late-harvest gewürztraminer or late-harvest riesling**

Lucy has pulled me in two directions with her nifty Asian tweak. Sweet gewürztraminer comes with a gingery aroma, while sweet riesling toys with lime. They both like to play with mandarin.

VINEGAR

Vinegar is both a luxurious ingredient (aged balsamic and Sherry vinegars can command high prices) and a practical one, with uses varying from adding flavour to salads, tenderizing meats, preserving pickles, making sauces and cleaning coffee pots. It is among the world's oldest prepared foods. In essence, it is wine that has been exposed to airborne bacteria that turn alcohol into acetic acid. The name itself comes from the French *vinaigre*, or "sour wine."

Not all vinegars are made from wine. Rice vinegar (which the Chinese have been making for 3000 years) and cider vinegar each have a different base.

Experimenting with various vinegars will change the taste of many recipes.

Rice Vinegar: Rice vinegar is most commonly associated with Asian cooking, but it adds a nice touch to many Western dishes too. Made from fermented rice, it is less acidic (about 4 per cent) and has a sweeter, milder flavour than other vinegars. There are several types of rice vinegar. Japanese rice vinegar is a subtle, very low acidity golden vinegar; seasoned Japanese rice vinegar has been seasoned with sugar and salt and is often used to flavour sushi rice. There are three Chinese vinegars: red (a curious mix of sweet and sour flavours, often used in sauces and noodle dishes), white (the most acidic of the three, used for sweet-and-sour dishes and pickling) and black (a rich vinegar that works well with braised dishes and can be substituted for balsamic vinegar). Although traditionally each of these is preferred for particular recipes, you can choose the one you like the best and use it where you like. If you don't have rice vinegar on hand, dilute white wine vinegar or cider vinegar with a little water.

Balsamic Vinegar: Balsamic vinegar originated in Modena, Italy, and the best balsamics continue to be made there. Artisans reduce white grapes to syrup and then keep the resulting "must" in wooden barrels (with a small quantity of older balsamic vinegar added to encourage acetification) for a minimum of 12 years. Each year, the vinegar is moved to a smaller barrel made of a different kind of wood. As you can imagine, all this adds up to a very high price for authentic balsamic vinegar. (To confirm authenticity, look on the bottle for the codes API MO or API RE, indicating that the vinegar was made in the provinces of Modena or Reggio Emilia.) If you can afford it, it is money well spent, as there is no comparison between the real thing and those of lesser quality.

Authentic balsamics are not used for cooking. They are used as a flavour inducer on meat, poultry and fish, and the really expensive ones are often sipped as a digestif after dinner. However, the moderately priced balsamics are just fine for everyday cooking. Many of them are essentially wine vinegar sweetened with sugars, but their sweeter taste still makes this vinegar an excellent choice for dishes that might be overwhelmed by too much acid.

Sherry Vinegar: The Spanish have been making Sherry vinegar for at least 500 years, and they've honed the process to a fine art. Originally appearing by accident in wineries—to the great distress of the winery owners—Sherry vinegar today results from painstaking efforts and a highly refined process, and is regarded by many as the finest of vinegars. Sherry vinegars traditionally age for 30 to 75 years, and high-quality Sherry vinegar is costlier than Sherry itself. It is a sweet vinegar with a sharp, sour aftertaste that is excellent in sauces and salads.

Wine Vinegar: Red wine vinegar and its lighter, less commonly used counterpart, white wine vinegar, are among the most basic and versatile of vinegars. They also have the highest levels of acidity—the pucker power when you taste vinegar. Commercial brands are usually around 5 per cent acidity, and traditionally prepared wine vinegar can be as high as 7 per cent. Mix it into other ingredients with caution, as you will not want to overwhelm the dish. This vinegar, used judiciously, will intensify all the flavours in a dish, rather than overpowering them. You should also keep its acidity in mind when selecting a wine to pair with your dish. I don't like red wine vinegar in salad dressing, except for grain salads—it's too sharp. For lettuce or vegetables, use white wine vinegar or lemon juice instead.

MORE TART

CHICKEN ADOBO

A classic dish using unseasoned rice vinegar, adobo is the national dish of the Philippines. It can be made with chicken or pork or a combination of both. Make it a day ahead for the best flavour. Have the butcher cut up the chicken for you or buy breasts and legs on the bone. Serve with rice.

Serves 4

- 1 chicken (3 lb/1.35 kg), cut in 8 pieces
- ¼ cup finely chopped garlic
- 2 tsp cracked peppercorns
- ½ cup rice vinegar
- 3 tbsp soy sauce
- ½ tsp hot Asian chili sauce, such as sriracha
- 2 bay leaves
- 1 cup water
- 2 tbsp olive oil
- 1 onion, sliced
- 2 cups baby spinach

Cut each chicken breast in half lengthwise. Combine garlic, peppercorns, vinegar, soy sauce, chili sauce and bay leaves in a sauté pan or high-sided skillet. Add chicken and marinate for 30 minutes.

Add water and arrange chicken so that it is mostly submerged in cooking liquid. Bring to a boil over medium heat. Reduce heat and simmer, uncovered, until chicken is just tender, about 25 minutes, turning once halfway through cooking time.

Transfer chicken to a plate and pat dry with paper towels. Pour sauce into a bowl and skim excess fat from top.

Return skillet to stovetop and heat oil over medium heat. Add chicken and cook until golden brown, about 2 minutes per side. Transfer to a plate. Add onion to skillet and sauté until tender, 5 to 6 minutes. Add chicken along with sauce and spinach. Simmer for 5 minutes or until chicken is fully cooked, scraping bottom of pan with a spoon to dissolve any brown bits.

Cool, then skim fat. Refrigerate until needed. Reheat over medium heat for 10 to 15 minutes or until everything is hot.

PAIRING: **South African chenin blanc**

Usually dry but with a suggestion of sweetness balanced by racy acidity, South African chenin blanc softens the soft chili kick and frolics with the vinegar and soy. Alternative: Austrian grüner veltliner.

WILD SALMON WITH BALSAMIC GLAZE AND FENNEL CONFIT

If wild salmon is not available, the dish is still excellent with farmed. Use the glaze to decorate plates or for adding to sauces; it keeps for 3 months, refrigerated.

Serves 4

Glaze:
1 cup balsamic vinegar
½ cup red wine
1 tsp granulated sugar

Fennel Confit:
2 tbsp butter
1 small fennel bulb, core removed and thinly sliced crosswise
1 cup sliced red onions
¼ cup orange juice
½ tsp granulated sugar
Salt and freshly ground pepper

Fish:
1 tbsp olive oil
4 wild salmon fillets (6 oz/170 g each)

Combine balsamic vinegar, wine and sugar in a small pot. Bring to a boil, then boil for 12 minutes or until you just begin to see the bottom of the pot as you stir. Remove from heat. The glaze will thicken considerably as it cools. You will have about ⅓ cup. Reserve.

Melt butter in a large skillet over medium heat while the glaze is cooling. When butter sizzles, add fennel, onions, orange juice and sugar and toss to distribute. Bring to a boil, then reduce heat to low. Cover and cook for 10 minutes or until fennel is softened.

Uncover, increase heat to medium and cook, stirring occasionally, for 8 minutes or until fennel is caramelized. Season with salt and pepper. Keep warm.

Heat a large nonstick skillet over high heat until hot. Season salmon flesh with salt and pepper. Add oil and then salmon, skin side up. Season skin with salt and pepper. Cook for 2 minutes or until golden, then turn fish over and cook 2 minutes longer. Cover and cook for 3 to 5 minutes or until fish is just cooked through.

Place fish on 4 plates. Serve with fennel confit and drizzle with balsamic glaze.

PAIRING: **New World pinot noir**

The best red for salmon is pinot noir. Its medium body matches the fish's weight, and the wine's earthy undertones are the oenological equivalent of setting the salmon on a bed of lentils, a classic culinary combination. Here I'd specifically choose a fruitier New World pinot rather than a red Burgundy because the jammy quality resonates with the vaguely sweet fennel confit.

ZESTY PORK WITH HONEY AND SHERRY VINEGAR SAUCE

To keep pork juicy and tender, cook it until slightly pink. Pork medallions are cut from the tenderloin. The cinnamon and coriander dusting is scrumptious. Serve with saffron rice and buttered spinach. **Serves 4**

8 pork medallions (3 oz/85 g each)
Salt and freshly ground pepper
2 tsp ground coriander
2 tsp cinnamon
2 tbsp olive oil
½ cup red wine
¼ cup Sherry vinegar
1 tsp honey
1 cup chicken stock

Preheat oven to 425°F.

Season pork with salt and pepper. Dust with coriander and cinnamon.

Heat olive oil in a large ovenproof skillet over medium-high heat. Fry pork for 3 minutes, turning frequently, or until browned on all sides. Place skillet in oven and roast pork for 5 to 8 minutes (thinner end pieces take less time than middle pieces) or until pork is cooked through but still slightly pink in the centre. Reduce heat to 200°F.

Transfer pork to a plate. Keep warm in oven.

Return skillet to medium-high heat and add wine, vinegar and honey. Bring to a boil and cook for 5 minutes or until syrupy, stirring to scrape any brown bits from the bottom of the pan. Add chicken stock and boil until it has just begun to thicken, about 4 minutes. Serve over pork.

PAIRING: **Beaujolais**

Pork almost always loves a bright, cherry-like Beaujolais, and the vinegar sauce pretty much excludes reds imbued with less than Beaujolais's mouth-watering acidity. Alternative: crisp, dry riesling from New York's Finger Lakes region.

RED RICE SALAD WITH RED WINE VINEGAR

Aromatic red rice has a mahogany colour and is minimally milled to keep most of its bran husk intact. Its flavour is nutty and sometimes popcorn-like. The rice is perfect for a rice salad because it is slightly chewy and does not get mushy. If you like goat cheese, sprinkle it over the finished salad. **Makes 2½ cups**

3 cups water
2 cups red rice
½ cup olive oil
¼ cup red wine vinegar
Salt and freshly ground pepper
1 cup chopped green onions
1 cup diced cucumber
½ cup slivered pitted black olives
¼ cup pine nuts, toasted
¼ cup chopped fresh dill
2 tbsp chopped fresh parsley

Bring water to a boil in a medium pot. Sprinkle in rice and return to a boil. Cover, reduce heat to low and steam for 35 minutes or until rice is tender but slightly chewy and water is absorbed. Remove from heat but keep covered for 5 minutes.

Whisk together oil and vinegar. Season with salt and pepper. Toss half of dressing with rice and cool.

Combine rice with green onions, cucumber, olives, pine nuts, dill and parsley. Toss with remaining dressing.

chilies • sambal oelek • sriracha sauce

Indian curry pastes • Thai curry pastes • horseradish

wasabi • hot mustard • chutney • radishes • arugula • habaneros

ginger • garlic • Hungarian paprika • cayenne • bird's eye chilies

cinnamon • cloves • mace • star anise • Chinese 5 spice powder

garam masala • cardamom • fennel seeds

nutmeg • allspice

SPICES HAVE BEEN ENHANCING FOOD

*for 50,000 years, long before Bobby Flay and Emeril, long before Tabasco and Taco Bell. They usually improved flavour, but often their purpose had as much to do with hygiene and health, adding preservative or purported medicinal qualities. Distinct from the leafy greens we call herbs, spices span the gamut from dried seeds to roots to bark to the flesh of such fruits as peppers. That one word—*spice*—covers everything from the tongue-searing heat of Thai and habanero chilies to the less incendiary but arrestingly fragrant ingredients responsible for Cantonese stir-fries and the complex curries of India and Pakistan. Where there's spice there's not always fire.*

Chinese cooks employ ginger, star anise and garlic largely for aromatic punch. Indian chefs counterbalance as many as a dozen spices—cardamom, green chilies and mace, among others—with such cooling agents as coconut milk, yogurt and lime juice. Southwestern dishes incorporate the subtle sweetness of corn and squash to temper the burn. In Spain and North Africa, cooks may deploy their spices by way of a Trojan horse—fatty proteins in the form of chorizo and merguez sausages. I'm fond of floating a whole fresh chili pepper in a tumbler of sweet-and-mellow bourbon on the rocks, the pepper slowly releasing subtle spice. Balance, as always in cooking and cocktail mixology, is everything.

It's curious that so many of us love spice, especially scorching-hot chilies. Are we fools for finding ecstasy in the agony? Not quite. Capsaicin, the compound that gives chilies their kick, releases endorphins into the bloodstream, the closest thing to morphine produced by the body. It's a natural high, and more fun than jogging.

We know what you're thinking: beer will figure prominently in this chapter. Sorry to disappoint. Beer, counterintuitively, only fans the flames. The dry liquid, usually consumed in large gulps, carries the heat to every receptor in the mouth. It's cold, but once the chill vanishes, every taste bud feels the pain. Rich, mouth-coating texture and cooling sugar are your best defences at a time like this. Think of the mango and yogurt lassis of the Indian subcontinent.

There are choice options from wine's arsenal too. Alsace, the northern region of France that specializes in seductively aromatic whites such as gewürztraminer, riesling, pinot gris and muscat (a.k.a. moscato), should have been annexed by Thailand or India long ago. Its wines, essentially dry but usually opulent and rounded, work beautifully with spicy foods of all kinds. And viognier, an oily-textured white grape nuanced with orange blossom and honey, which rises to its zenith in France's northern Rhone Valley, unquestionably is our best match for curry. Keep a bottle handy in the fridge if you enjoy Indian takeout.

We'll buy the next round of beer if you disagree.

Menu 1

A MODERN INDIAN MENU

Sweet Potato Mulligatawny Soup

Baked Goan Black Cod

Shaved Cauliflower and Swiss Chard Curry

Basmati Rice Pilau

Jewel in the Crown Ice Cream Cake

I love Indian food. I grew up with it, as my father had developed a taste for it while serving in the British Army in India during the war. He used to take the family to Indian restaurants in Glasgow. This menu is the opposite of what we ate then, which were usually brown saucy dishes quite indistinguishable from each other. This menu has clean flavours, uses modern techniques and produces a dinner to savour.

CURRY

Although curry is of Indian origin, it is made all over Southeast Asia and the Caribbean, and there is even a "British" curry style left over from the time of the Raj. Curry need not be lavished with chilies; it is the balance of the spices in it that gives curry its distinctive flavour.

Make your own curry dinner for friends. I usually make one of the following curries and serve it with rice, mango chutney, lime pickle (for those who like it a whole lot hotter), and a tomato and onion salad. I purchase Indian naan bread.

Indian Curry: In India, curry is never made with curry powder or curry paste. Different mixes of spices are ground for each type of curry made, and each home has its own particular blend of spice too. Today, as we get more pressed for time, commercial curry pastes in various heats and for different uses are making large inroads into the market, making Indian cooking at home much easier. It will always be a better curry if you toast and grind your own spices, but these pastes are a good substitute.

Thai Red, Green and Yellow Curry: Thai curry is fragrant and well balanced with sweetness and heat. To make the best Thai curry, you should grind your own spice paste, but as that can be a long and involved process, buy a good-quality Thai curry paste. I prefer Mae Ploy brand.

Malaysian Curry: Malaysian curry is very hot. It features coconut, both shredded and as coconut milk, along with lemongrass, galangal, ginger and lime leaves, as well as Indian spices. It can be either wet or dry. A spice paste called rempah is the basic building block.

West Indian Curry: A combination of sweeter spices such as cinnamon and star anise give Caribbean curry its distinctive flavour. It is not too hot on its own, but it can be heated up with hot sauce.

SWEET POTATO MULLIGATAWNY SOUP

The soothing combination of lentils and sweet potatoes makes this a great soup before any meal. Mulligatawny was a British Raj soup—the English in India adapted Indian ingredients to make a soup that was less spicy and more familiar to them. They liked it so much, it has since become an English classic! This version has a little spicy curry paste that gently lifts the soup to new heights. Though not always necessary, I like to purée mulligatawny soups.

Serves 4 to 6

- 2 tbsp vegetable oil
- 1 cup chopped onions
- 3 cups chopped sweet potatoes
- 1 cup chopped carrots
- 1 tsp chopped fresh ginger
- 1 tsp ground cumin
- 1 tsp ground coriander
- 1 tsp mild Indian curry paste or curry powder
- ¼ cup red lentils
- 4 cups chicken stock
- ½ cup coconut milk
- Salt and freshly ground pepper
- 2 tbsp chopped fresh cilantro
- 2 tsp lemon juice

Heat oil in a large pot over medium heat. Add onions and sauté for 2 minutes or until they begin to soften. Add sweet potatoes and carrots and sauté for 5 minutes.

Add ginger, cumin, coriander and curry paste and sauté for 1 minute or until fragrant. Add lentils and stir to coat with spices.

Add stock and coconut milk and bring to a boil. Reduce heat to medium-low and simmer for 15 to 20 minutes or until vegetables are very soft and lentils have exploded.

Purée soup and season with salt and pepper. Stir in cilantro and lemon juice just before serving.

PAIRING: **Gewürztraminer**

It's worth learning to pronounce geh-VURTS-tra-meener if only for soups like this, and, in fact, for Indian dishes more generally. The aromatic spices beg for a wine with strong fruit and heady aromas of its own, in this case an uncanny essence of rose petal and ginger. Usually dry, gewürztraminers can be richly concentrated, especially those of the grape's homeland of Alsace, a textural requisite for the rich soup.

BAKED GOAN BLACK COD

Goan food is usually very spicy and often contains vinegar in the marinade. The vinegar mellows the spice. Although Goan food is often grilled, I like this fish better when baked in a hot oven—it is easier to handle and tastes better. Black cod is more buttery and forgiving than some other fish. Halibut or other firm-fleshed fish work too.

Serves 4

Sauce:
¼ cup plain yogurt
1 tbsp finely chopped cucumber
1 tbsp finely chopped red onion
2 tsp finely chopped fresh mint
Salt and freshly ground pepper

Goan Marinade:
2 tbsp vegetable oil
1 tbsp white vinegar
1 tbsp grated fresh ginger
1 tbsp chopped garlic
1 tbsp medium Indian curry paste

4 skin-on black cod fillets (6 to 8 oz/170 to 225 g each)
Mint sprigs for garnish

Combine yogurt with cucumber, onion and mint in a small bowl. Season with salt and pepper. Reserve.
Preheat oven to 450°F.
Stir together oil, vinegar, ginger, garlic and curry paste. Season with salt and pepper. Place cod skin side down in a baking dish and pour over marinade. Marinate for 15 minutes.
Place cod in oven and bake for 12 to 15 minutes (depending on thickness) or until white juices begin to appear and fish starts to split. Arrange cod on serving plates and garnish with mint sprigs.
Serve with yogurt sauce and Shaved Cauliflower and Swiss Chard Curry (page 371).

Cheater's Hot Pickle: If you cannot find lime or any other kind of hot pickle, then use chutney and add ¼ tsp cayenne and 1 tsp lime juice.

SHAVED CAULIFLOWER AND SWISS CHARD CURRY

Shaving vegetables as opposed to just cutting them up gives a whole new look to dishes, and the vegetables seem to taste better.

Serves 4

- 2 tbsp vegetable oil
- 1 cup finely chopped onions
- 1 tbsp finely chopped garlic
- 1 tbsp finely chopped fresh ginger
- 1 tsp mustard seeds
- ¼ tsp chopped red chili
- 6 cups shaved cauliflower (½ large head)
- 4 cups shredded Swiss chard
- ¼ cup water or chicken stock
- 2 tsp garam masala
- Salt and freshly ground pepper
- 2 tbsp chopped fresh mint

Heat vegetable oil in a large skillet over medium-low heat. Add onions and sauté for 7 minutes or until turning gold. Add garlic and ginger and cook for 3 more minutes or until onions are very soft.

Add mustard seeds and red chili and sauté 1 minute longer. Increase heat to medium. Add cauliflower and continue to cook until cauliflower is a bit limp, 2 to 3 minutes. Stir in Swiss chard. Add water and garam masala and cook 3 minutes longer or until cauliflower is tender. Season with salt and pepper.

Serve garnished with mint.

PAIRING: **Viognier**

The British like to drink lager with their beloved curries. Pity, really. Despite its cold temperature, beer is a heat conductor where spice is concerned. The blissful pairing for this menu is viognier (vee-OH-nyay), an oily-textured white grape that coats the palate, matching the curry in texture while also adding complementary overtones of citrus and flowers.

To shave cauliflower, cut in half and remove the stalk. Lay flat side down on a mandoline (cut into quarters if necessary) and shave back and forth. You will get lots of little pieces but it works beautifully. All root vegetables shave well, as do firm zucchini and cucumber. Avoid broccoli.

BASMATI RICE PILAU

A pilau is a spiced rice dish made with basmati rice, a nutty-flavoured Indian long-grain rice. Newer methods of picking and cleaning basmati mean it no longer has to be soaked to get rid of any impurities. **Serves 4**

- 2 cups basmati rice
- 2 cups water
- 6 cloves
- 2 bay leaves
- 2 (1-inch) pieces cinnamon stick
- 1 tsp cumin seeds
- 1 tsp turmeric
- Salt
- 1 cup fresh or frozen green peas

Rinse rice with cold water and drain. Add to a heavy pot along with water, cloves, bay leaves, cinnamon sticks, cumin seeds, turmeric and salt to taste. Bring to a boil over high heat. Cover, reduce heat to low and cook for 12 to 15 minutes or until rice is tender.

Remove from heat, remove bay leaves and cinnamon sticks, and stir in peas. Cover and let sit for 5 minutes before serving.

JEWEL IN THE CROWN ICE CREAM CAKE

One of my favourite TV series was the 1984 Jewel in the Crown, *set in India during the last days of the Raj. Featuring lush landscapes, great stories and passionate love affairs, it was a classic. This is my dessert to celebrate those times. It's British in style, but with some Indian spicing. Use a bowl that will give a good shape to the cake when you turn it out. The brownies should sit across the top of the cake. When it is turned out, they will be the bottom layer. The number of brownies you need will depend on the width of your bowl. Cut them in half horizontally if necessary.*

Serves 4

- 4 small passion fruit
- 4 cups vanilla frozen yogurt or ice cream, softened
- ½ tsp ground cardamom
- ½ tsp ground ginger
- ½ tsp cinnamon
- Pinch ground cloves
- 8-inch square of chocolate brownies
- 2 tbsp brandy

Line a 6-inch-wide, deep freezer-proof bowl with plastic wrap.

Remove pulp from passion fruits and purée with a hand blender. Reserve.

Mix ice cream with cardamom, ginger, cinnamon and cloves in a large bowl until well combined. Drop spoonfuls of passion fruit purée over ice cream and swirl through. Scrape into lined bowl.

Cut brownies and fit over the ice cream to cover. Brush brownies with brandy. Cover with parchment and foil and freeze for at least 4 hours.

Remove from freezer and soften at room temperature for 15 minutes. Turn out onto a serving dish. Cut with a warm knife.

PAIRING: **Pedro Ximénez Sherry**

England loves Sherry, an affection dating back to 1587, when Sir Francis Drake raided the seaport of Cadiz to thwart an invasion by the Spanish Armada. Among the booty Sir Francis returned with were thousands of barrels of Spain's delectable fortified wine, giving birth to a British love affair with the elixir. Dark as molasses and just as sweet, the syrupy style known as Pedro Ximénez, intensely redolent of raisin, works like fruit syrup on a sundae when matched with this decadent ice-cream treasure.

CAPITAL

RYE'S RENAISSANCE

Before Cal-Ital cuisine and before Chicago-style pizza, there was the Manhattan, the first great—and still finest—example of Italian-American fusion. A simple mix of two parts American whisky to one part Italian vermouth with a dash of bitters, it's the only cocktail that can call itself a fair rival to the iconic martini.

As with many classics, its origins are sketchy. Some say it was born at New York's Manhattan Club in 1874. Others attribute it to a Broadway saloon keeper remembered simply as Black. No matter. What's critical is the spirit. The classic base is rye, not bourbon or Canadian, though these two whiskies, more than rye, helped popularize the velvety, bracing Manhattan after Prohibition.

Contrary to widespread belief, spicy rye grain is not an ingredient in most Canadian brands, which tend to be built around corn and wheat. Rye had been used in small quantities as a subtle seasoning, giving rise to the impression that Canadian spirits were made entirely from the grain. American, on the other hand, relied mainly on rye for more than a century following Independence. George Washington became a rye distiller in retirement (always my favourite president).

The spirit beat a retreat with the decline of distilling in the US Northeast. Corn-based Kentucky bourbon filled the void, as did Canadian whisky, thanks to a cross-border marketing opportunity called Prohibition. Happily, rye has staged a renaissance. Long-established US brands such as Old Overholt and Rittenhouse are growing along with many smaller-batch gems, including Old Potrero and Sazerac. Wiser's Legacy, my top new Canadian choice, is made mainly from rye.

Not that any whisky can botch the marvellous Manhattan. It's just that corn is smoother and sweeter, overlapping the vermouth. Rye, on the other hand, delivers a jolt of musky spice, like crushed chilies in marinara sauce.

Menu 2

AN ECLECTIC ASIAN MENU

Thai Clam Chowder

Spicy Fish Cakes with Zesty Citrus Sauce

Coconut Curry Shrimp

Fruit in Spiced Syrup

When I was in Australia I fell in love with the food there. The variety of fish and shellfish that were new to me and the strong Asian influences blew my palate away. It all made me think about flavours a little differently. The chefs weren't doing "fusion" so much as trying to get at the essence of local ingredients while using global cooking techniques. This all-fish menu, with its herbal and clean flavours, comes from that mindset.

THAI CLAM CHOWDER

This Thai-influenced clam chowder, with its clean, slightly spicy flavour, is much more exciting than the original tomato-based Manhattan version.

Serves 4 to 6

- 1 tbsp vegetable oil
- ½ cup diced bacon
- 1½ cups diced red potatoes
- 1 cup diced onions
- 1 cup diced fennel
- 1 tsp Thai red curry paste
- 2 cups water or fish stock
- ½ cup white wine
- 1 tsp fresh thyme (or ¼ tsp dried)
- 2 cups canned tomatoes
- 18 littleneck or cherrystone clams
- 2 tbsp chopped fresh parsley
- 2 tbsp lime juice
- Salt and freshly ground pepper

Heat oil in a soup pot over medium heat. Add bacon and sauté until beginning to crisp, about 2 minutes. Add potatoes, onions and fennel and sauté for 2 minutes or until beginning to soften. Add curry paste and sauté another minute. Add water, wine and thyme and bring to a boil. Add tomatoes, cover, reduce heat to low and simmer for 12 minutes or until potatoes are just cooked through.

Increase heat to high and add clams. Boil until shells open, about 6 minutes, removing clams as they open. Discard any that don't open. Reduce heat again. Reserve 4 or 6 clams for garnish, and remove clam meat from remaining shells. Return clam meat to soup, add parsley and lime juice and simmer for 1 minute. Season with salt and pepper. Garnish each serving with a clam in its shell.

PAIRING: **Chenin blanc**

Aromatic and fruity enough to survive the curry sauce, chenin blanc comes with solid acid backbone to stand up to the tomatoes and zippy lime. South Africa is the white grape's leading producer in volume terms and makes excellent, affordable examples, though dry Vouvray, crafted from the same French variety, is equally good here. Alternative: Argentine torrontes, a floral, grapey—and attractively affordable—dry white growing in popularity.

SPICY FISH CAKES WITH ZESTY CITRUS SAUCE

Use cod, whiting or haddock for these cakes. In Thailand they are usually deep-fried, but shallow frying gives just as good a result.

Makes 12 fish cakes

- 1 lb (450 g) skinless haddock fillets
- ¼ cup chopped green onions
- 2 tbsp chopped lemongrass
- 2 tbsp coarsely chopped fresh cilantro
- 2 tbsp cornstarch
- 2 tbsp fish sauce
- 2 tsp Thai red curry paste
- 1½ tsp grated lime zest
- 1 tsp lime juice
- ¼ tsp granulated sugar
- 1 egg
- 1 cup thinly sliced long beans (or green beans)
- 2 tbsp vegetable oil

Cut fish into cubes. Place in a food processor or mini chopper with green onions, lemongrass, cilantro, cornstarch, fish sauce, curry paste, lime zest and juice, sugar and egg. Pulse in short bursts until mixture is a smooth paste. Stir in long beans. Cover and refrigerate for 1 hour.

Roll mixture into 12 balls. Press each ball flat to form a cake.

Heat oil in a large skillet over medium-high heat. Fry cakes in batches for 1 to 2 minutes on each side or until brown. Add more oil to pan as needed. Drain cakes on paper towels.

Serve as finger food with Zesty Citrus Sauce (page 381) or with a watercress salad as a first course.

PAIRING: **Sparkling wine**

I want Lucy to start an upscale gastropub so I can eat these cakes once a week without having to invite myself to her house for dinner. The logic behind fish cakes and bubbly is the logic behind one of the world's classic food-and-drink pairings, fish and chips with beer. The beverage is crisp and frothy, dancing through the oil while refreshing the palate. I like a simple Spanish Cava or Italian prosecco in this context because the spices would erase some of the delicate nuances in pricy, bona fide Champagne. Alternative: New Zealand sauvignon blanc.

To use lemongrass, discard the woody upper stalk and peel away any tough outer layers. If you are using the lemongrass to flavour a liquid, smash it with the side of a knife and add it to the liquid; remove after cooking. For flavouring a dish, finely chop the pale tender inner leaves about 1 inch up from the base. Lemongrass keeps in the refrigerator for 2 weeks.

ZESTY CITRUS SAUCE

This sauce enhances the flavour of the spicy fish cakes.

Makes about ½ cup

- ¼ cup water
- 2 tbsp chopped fresh mint
- 1 tsp grated lime zest
- 2 tbsp lime juice
- 2 tbsp lemon juice
- 1 tbsp fish sauce
- 4 tsp brown sugar
- 1 tsp grated fresh ginger
- 1 tsp sambal oelek

Combine all ingredients in a bowl. Let sit for 1 hour before serving.

Sambal oelek is made from chilies, with a little vinegar and salt. It is the purest form of Asian chili paste you can buy.

COCONUT CURRY SHRIMP

I love Thai red curries in all their forms—with chicken or shrimp or vegetarian. Thai red curry is a bit milder than the green, and I usually combine it with lots of fragrant herbs. You can make the sauce base ahead of time and keep it refrigerated for a week, or double the quantity and freeze some. Serve with Thai jasmine rice.

Serves 4

- 1 tbsp vegetable oil
- 1 cup chopped red onions
- 2 tbsp chopped fresh ginger
- 1 tbsp chopped garlic
- 1 can (14 oz/400 mL) coconut milk
- 1 tbsp red curry paste (or more to taste)
- 1 large Japanese eggplant, cut in ½-inch pieces
- 1 cup canned chopped tomatoes, drained and crushed
- 1 cup water
- 2 tbsp fish sauce
- 1 tsp grated lime zest
- 2 lime leaves (optional)
- 1 tsp granulated sugar
- 1 lb (450 g) shrimp, peeled and deveined
- 2 cups packed spinach
- ¼ cup chopped fresh Thai or regular basil
- 2 tbsp chopped fresh cilantro
- Salt and freshly ground pepper
- 1 tbsp lime juice

Heat oil in a large skillet over medium-high heat. Add onions and sauté until softened, about 2 to 3 minutes. Add ginger and garlic and toss together. Add coconut milk and curry paste. Increase heat to high and boil for 5 minutes or until thick enough to coat a spoon. Add eggplant, tomatoes, water, fish sauce, lime zest, lime leaves (if using) and sugar. Simmer for 5 minutes or until eggplant is just tender. Reduce heat to medium-low.

Stir in shrimp and spinach. Cook until shrimp are pink and slightly curled. Stir in basil and cilantro. Taste for seasoning, adding salt, pepper or lime juice as needed.

PAIRING: **Alsatian or New Zealand pinot gris**

There is a slightly sweet, highly fruity quality to most pinot gris from Alsace and New Zealand, which is why I tend to prefer them with spicy dishes more than, say, those of Oregon or British Columbia. Sweetness softens spice without muting its aromatic verve, whereas drier wines can develop a sour taste. And they've got body to support the rich curry.

FRUIT IN SPICED SYRUP

I keep this syrup in my refrigerator and use it to douse most cut-up fruit or even a cake that is a little dry. It will keep for 1 month.

Makes ⅔ cup syrup

Syrup:
1 cup water
1 cup granulated sugar
1 lime, sliced in ⅓-inch rounds
3 thin slices fresh ginger, smashed
3 star anise
1-inch piece cinnamon stick
1 whole dried chili

Fruit:
8 cups mixed cut-up fruit such as kiwis, mangoes, papaya, figs, strawberries, and melon

Combine all syrup ingredients in a heavy pot over high heat. Bring to a boil and boil for 2 minutes. Reduce heat to medium-low and simmer for 10 more minutes or until very flavourful. Cool completely in pot. Strain.

Combine fruit and syrup and marinate, refrigerated, for 4 hours before serving.

PAIRING: **Lemon bubbles**

Add 1 oz limoncello to a champagne flute. Top with inexpensive sparkling wine such as prosecco and garnish with a sliver of lemon zest. Asia meets Italia.

Menu 3

MULTICULTURAL SENEGALESE DINNER

Senegalese Soup

Chicken Yassa

Fresh Chili Mangoes with Mango Ice Cream

This menu is from Senegal in West Africa, a country that is known for its sophisticated and interesting food. Influences range from Portuguese to French with a dollop of Asian. Peanuts are used as a protein, as they are a staple crop there. Millet and couscous are favourite starches. The food is spicy and loaded with flavour.

SENEGALESE SOUP

In her cooking school in the 1960s, my mother used flour to thicken this soup and a combination of eggs and cream to enrich it at the end. Certainly you could use the eggs and cream, but I like the flavour of the coconut milk with the garam masala. You can buy garam masala or make your own. Use any tart apple, such as Pink Lady.

Serves 4 to 6

2 tbsp butter
2 cups chopped cored peeled tart apples
1 cup chopped onions
1 cup chopped celery
2 fresh small Thai red chilies, seeded
½ cup red lentils
1 tbsp garam masala
4 cups chicken stock
Salt and freshly ground pepper
½ cup coconut milk

Garnish:
¼ cup coconut milk
¼ cup thinly sliced chives

Melt butter in a soup pot over medium heat. Add apples, onions, celery and chilies. Sauté for about 3 minutes or until vegetables start to soften.
Add lentils and garam masala and sauté until you can smell the spices. Add stock and bring to a boil. Reduce heat to medium-low and simmer for 20 minutes or until vegetables and apples are tender.
Purée in a food processor. Return to pot and season with salt and pepper. Stir in coconut milk and simmer for 5 minutes. Cool soup.
Refrigerate overnight. Drizzle some coconut milk over top and sprinkle with chives before serving.

PAIRING: **Tokaji furmint**

Hibiscus tea ranks as a national beverage in Senegal, a largely Muslim country. That's not to say the nation is one big dry zone; there's locally made beer, such as Flag and Bière La Gazelle. I'd be more inclined toward a so-called aromatic white, such as tokaji furmint from Hungary, part of a new wave of whites riding on the storied reputation of the country's sumptuously sweet tokaji aszú dessert wines, also mainly based on the furmint grape. Dry furmint has the floral, fruity intensity to surf the spicy waves of this soup. Alternative: any of the new breed of aromatic white blends—either dry or off-dry and often made from one or more of chenin blanc, moscato, viognier, pinot gris and gewürztraminer—such as Ménage à Trois or Big House White from California.

CHICKEN YASSA

Yassa is a term for spicy marinated chicken from Senegal. The heat in this mouth-watering dish comes from chilies, and you can use less or more as you prefer. You can make this with any parts of the chicken, but legs on the bone have extra juiciness when cooked this way. In Senegal they would serve this with rice, couscous or a bean called niébé, or cowpeas, similar to black-eyed peas. **Serves 4 to 6**

Marinade:
1 tsp grated lemon zest
¼ cup lemon juice
2 tbsp vegetable oil
1 tsp minced Thai red chilies, seeded
3 lb (1.35 kg) chicken legs, cut in half
Salt and freshly ground pepper

Sauce:
2 tbsp vegetable oil
5 cups sliced red onions (about 3)
2 tbsp Dijon mustard
1 tsp grated lemon zest
1½ cups chicken stock or water
1½ cups diced sweet potatoes
½ cup pimiento-stuffed olives, cut in thirds
¼ cup chopped fresh parsley

Combine lemon zest, lemon juice, vegetable oil and chilies in a medium bowl. Add chicken pieces and onions and toss together. Cover and marinate, refrigerated, for at least 2 hours or overnight.

Preheat oven to 425°F.

Remove chicken from marinade and pat dry. Season with salt and pepper.

Heat 2 tbsp vegetable oil in a large skillet over medium-high heat. Add chicken in batches and brown well, 2 to 3 minutes per side. Transfer to a rack in a roasting pan. Roast chicken for 20 to 30 minutes or until juices run clear.

Drain all but 1 tbsp oil from skillet while chicken is roasting. Return skillet to medium-high heat. Add onions and season with salt to bring out juices. Cook, stirring occasionally, for 7 to 10 minutes or until onions are soft and browned. Add mustard, lemon zest and stock and stir until combined. Stir in sweet potatoes and olives. Bring to a boil and boil for 1 minute. Reduce heat to medium-low, cover and simmer for 16 to 18 minutes or until crisp-tender. Uncover and continue cooking until vegetables are tender, 5 to 10 minutes.

Serve chicken coated with vegetables and sauce. Sprinkle with parsley.

PAIRING: **Chenin blanc**

Honeyed and floral, chenin blanc is a star in South Africa, a country that shares a continent with Senegal. Sometimes vaguely sweet yet always tight and crisp, the Cape's signature white is as mouth-watering as the chicken itself.

FRESH CHILI MANGOES WITH MANGO ICE CREAM

Look for mangoes from May through July, when the luscious Ataulfo variety is available. These sweet fruits should be eaten over the sink, as they are so juicy. They need little embellishment, but chilies temper the sweetness and add a background note that elevates this dessert.

Serves 4

3 mangoes
¼ tsp grated lime zest
2 tbsp lime juice
¼ tsp chili flakes
½ cup chopped flaked coconut
1 pint mango ice cream

Peel mangoes and cut into thick slices. Sprinkle with lime zest, lime juice, chili flakes and coconut. Stir together gently.

Divide among 4 plates and top with mango ice cream.

PAIRING: **Moscato d'Asti**

Fresh fruit is a tough cookie where wine matching is concerned. When you add spice and ice cream, things get tougher still. The solution is moscato d'Asti from Italy, gently sparkling and aromatic, with a floral scent and a flavour of table grapes.

BITTERS: SPICES IN A BOTTLE

Let's get the slightly misleading nomenclature out of the way first. Bitters are not always bitter. Think of them as liquid flavourings designed to impart aromatic verve to cocktails, the bartender's answer to the spice rack in your kitchen. In fact, there's usually plenty of spice in the bottle in the form of such ingredients as celery seed, cinnamon, cassia bark and various roots, which are often found in combination with herbs and citrus peels.

Until recently, the category was pretty much synonymous with Angostura, the iconic brand with the oversized label, available in most supermarkets for less than $10. It's the not so secret ingredient in a variety of classic potations, including the Manhattan and the Champagne Cocktail. No bar is complete without it.

Founded in the 1820s, amber-hued Angostura escaped the fate of hundreds of other nineteenth-century bitters that either dried up during Prohibition or ran afoul of health-claims laws (most got their start as purported medicinal tonics). The other venerable survivor is Peychaud's, an anise-scented nectar essential to New Orleans's signature cocktail, the Sazerac, a marvellous classic based on rye, sugar and absinthe.

Though cocktail bitters usually contain 40 to 55 per cent alcohol—a handy solvent for extracting flavours from those spices, roots, herbs and peels—they are legally defined as "non-potable" flavourings, intended to be dashed like Tabasco sauce from small bottles rather than consumed on their own. That's why they can be sold in supermarkets. Desperate Prohibition-era Americans sometimes feigned ill health and began to ingest the potent elixirs straight, leading to an inevitable crackdown.

Bitters may have languished in Prohibition's wake, but they've resurfaced with a vengeance. Credit the revival to a new generation of young mixologists, who began crafting custom extracts behind the bar to recapture the cocktail's pre-Prohibition Golden Age.

I wouldn't suggest making your own at home unless you have a zeal for chemistry and too much time on your hands. It's hard to achieve the right flavour balance, a proposition that involves steeping hard-to-source ingredients in neutral alcohol for weeks in more mason jars than my Italian mother used for a year's supply of marinara sauce. Besides, there's no need, thanks to the recent boom in ready-made brands.

The new offerings include such excellent examples as smoky-peppery Moondog and Asian spice–infused Denman, from Vancouver's Kale & Nori Culinary Arts. Both bring a welcome bass note of spice to just about any brown-spirit cocktail. I'd also highly recommend Bittermens' aptly named Hellfire Habanero Shrub, from Brooklyn, NY (excellent with Tequila); Fee Brothers West Indian Orange, from Rochester, NY (essential for the classic Bronx cocktail); and The Bitter Truth Original Celery, from Germany (delicious with many gin and vodka drinks). These and dozens of others can be found at select gourmet food and pri-

POK POK WINGS

These wings are inspired by the ones made by Chef Andy Ricker of Pok Pok Restaurant in Portland, Oregon. Their sweet, salty, spicy flavour has stayed with me, and this is my own inauthentic but decadent version. The Vietnamese make a caramel sauce base for some of their savoury dishes, and this is what I have used here.

Serves 6

Sauce:
1 cup granulated sugar
1½ cups water
½ cup fish sauce
2 tbsp chopped garlic
2 tbsp sambal oelek

Chicken Wings:
¼ cup warm water
2 lb (900 g) chicken wings
1 tbsp vegetable oil
2 tbsp coarsely chopped garlic
Vegetable oil for deep-frying
¾ cup rice flour
Fresh cilantro leaves for garnish

Combine sugar and 1 cup water in a large skillet. Heat over medium-high heat until sugar is melted and begins to caramelize, 8 to 10 minutes. When caramel is medium brown, carefully stir in remaining ½ cup water, fish sauce, garlic and sambal oelek. The mixture may seize, but continue stirring and it will come back together. Reduce heat to medium and cook for 5 minutes or until sauce is thickened. Remove from heat.
Stir one-quarter of caramel sauce with ¼ cup warm water in a large bowl. Add chicken wings and toss to coat. Marinate, refrigerated, for 2 to 3 hours.
Heat 1 tbsp vegetable oil in a small skillet over medium heat. Add coarsely chopped garlic and cook, stirring constantly, until golden brown, about 3 minutes. Remove from heat.
Heat 2 inches oil in a high-sided skillet or wok to about 350°F. Remove wings from marinade (discarding marinade). Toss wings with rice flour. Add wings to oil in batches and fry for 5 minutes or until golden and cooked through. Drain on a rack. Reheat remaining caramel sauce and toss with wings. Scatter with fried garlic and garnish with cilantro.

PAIRING: **West Coast Pale Ale**

This is upscale street food. The advantage of preparing it at home is that you can enjoy it with wine or beer—at least better wine or beer than you might find on a Bangkok street corner. A robust craft brew from Oregon, such as a West Coast Pale Ale, would be choice. The heavy-hop bitterness counterbalances the sweet caramel sauce while offering mouth-watering citrusy tang. If you prefer wine, try a bittersweet, but ultimately dry, grüner veltliner, Austria's signature white. Prefer red? A jammy primitivo from Puglia will wrap its cuddly arms around the wings' spice.

RUM MANGO LASSI

I crave chilies. I grow a half-dozen varieties in the garden, including hellfire habaneros and a little green-and-white-striped devil called Fish Hot. But I went down for the count one night at a Thai restaurant, convinced the cook had accidentally overturned into my chicken curry a beaker of mutant-strain pepper sauce developed by the Pentagon's chemical-warfare unit.

I tried water. I tried gewürztraminer (my Thai restaurant standby). I tried prayer. No relief. Luckily, my convulsions drew the attention of the good proprietor, an acquaintance, who swiftly materialized with a mango lassi, a sort of fruit milkshake. Instant salvation—on the house.

Be not afraid of the alcohol in this personal recipe. The modest dose of rum adds body and an aromatic kick rather than heat.

Makes 2 drinks

¾ cup plain yogurt
3 oz milk
3 oz canned mango pulp
2 oz white rum (or dark if you prefer a hint of sweetness)

Place yogurt, milk and mango pulp in a blender or food processor and blend for 30 seconds. Divide between 2 highball glasses containing ice and 1 oz each of the rum. Stir. Top with a couple of ground pistachios or garnish with a mint sprig.

SOUTH AFRICAN BOBOTIE

A fusion—like much of South Africa's cooking—of spices and styles, bobotie is the country's signature dish, fiery, sweet and tart all at once. It is always served with yellow rice (page 395) and is often made with lamb rather than beef.

Serves 6

- 2 tbsp vegetable oil
- 2 cups chopped onions
- 1 tbsp ground ginger
- 1 tbsp curry powder or Indian curry paste
- 1 tbsp turmeric
- 1 tbsp brown sugar
- 1½ lb (675 g) ground beef
- 2 slices white bread, soaked in milk, squeezed dry and torn
- ½ cup raisins
- 2 tbsp white vinegar
- 2 tbsp tomato paste
- 2 tbsp mango chutney
- 1 tbsp apricot jam or orange marmalade
- Salt and freshly ground pepper

Topping:

- 2 eggs
- 1½ cups milk
- Pinch kosher salt
- 1 tsp grated lemon zest

Preheat oven to 350°F.

Heat oil in a large skillet over medium heat. Add onions and sauté until softened, about 3 minutes. Add ginger, curry powder, turmeric and sugar and cook until fragrant, about 1 minute. Add ground beef and sauté for 2 minutes or until it starts to lose its pinkness. Add bread, raisins, vinegar, tomato paste, chutney and apricot jam and season with salt and pepper. Cook, stirring, for 5 to 7 minutes or until flavours have come together. Taste for seasoning, adding salt, pepper or more spice, if needed. Transfer to a greased casserole dish.

Beat together eggs, milk, salt and lemon zest and pour over meat mixture. Bake for 45 minutes or until top is set.

YELLOW RICE

The main ingredient in yellow rice is turmeric. Turmeric is one of the healthiest spices, with digestive, painkilling, anti-inflammatory and even anti-cancer properties.

Serves 6

3 cups water
2 cups long-grain rice, preferably Thai scented or basmati
2 tsp turmeric
3 (1-inch) pieces cinnamon stick
1 cup raisins
Salt

Combine water, rice, turmeric and cinnamon sticks in a pot and bring to a boil over high heat. Reduce heat to low, stir in raisins, cover and simmer for 12 to 15 minutes or until rice is tender. Season with salt.

PAIRING: **Shiraz**

The bold, spicy flavours of this curried ground-beef dish beg for a dauntless, fruity red. Fortunately for fans of South African wine, there's plenty of choice at attractive prices among the Cape's offerings. I'd go with shiraz, full bodied and round, with a hint of cracked pepper to sing—and zing—with the spices and shimmy with the chutney. Alternative: pinotage, the bracing and pungent South African cross between pinot noir and cinsault, its signature hint of smoke a complement to the sweet sauce.

ROOSTER BRAND
Marque Rooster
Superior
500 ml
TOMATO PASTE
CONCENTRATED 28/30%
DOUBLE CONCENTRE
DE TOMATES 28/30%
POMODORO ITALIANO

UMAMI

aged meats • cured meats • red meats • poultry
potatoes • sweet potatoes • tuna • shrimp • scallops
dried sardines • mackerel • prawns • cod • oysters • squid
shellfish • kombu • anchovies • ripe tomatoes • celery • spinach
napa cabbage • tofu • edamame • soybeans • soy sauce
broccoli • green tea • shiitake and enokitake mushrooms
cabbage • carrots • Parmesan • fish sauce
Worcestershire sauce

REMEMBER THAT RUDIMENTARY MAP

of the tongue from biology class, the one depicting four basic taste regions, sour, bitter, salty and sweet? Turns out science was wrong. There's a fifth taste, umami, and it's been changing the way smart cooks think about food. For this vital breakthrough we can thank the late Japanese chemist Kikunae Ikeda, patron saint of tasty goodness. Toiling in relative obscurity in 1908 (his name would go uncelebrated in the West until recently), Ikeda drew inspiration from nothing as iconic as Newton's falling apple but from a bowl of seaweed soup. Enchanted by the broth's flavour, he wondered whether the subaquatic plant contained a special ingredient that could be isolated and added to other foods. He found his answer in glutamate, an amino acid with a savoury, meaty taste distinct from sour, bitter, salty and sweet.

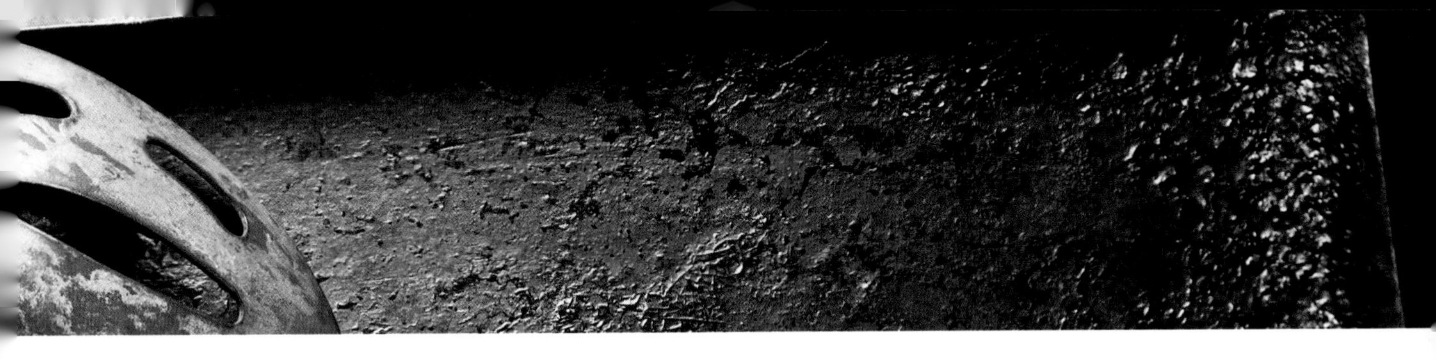

The baby was christened umami, a hybrid of the Japanese words *umai*, for "delicious," and *mi*, meaning "essence." Physiological vindication would come in the 1990s, when researchers at the University of Miami identified separate umami taste receptors on the tongue. Time to reprint all those Biology 101 textbooks!

There's been controversy along the way. Ikeda acquired something of a sketchy reputation for patenting the manufacture of monosodium glutamate, a salty, crystalline form of the amino acid whose virtue lay in the fact that it could be sprinkled as a seasoning—his holy grail. Eschewed by Western cooks, MSG is believed to cause such ills as headaches, mouth numbness and sweating, the culprit behind "Chinese restaurant syndrome."

But MSG is not pure glutamate, a building block of life found in virtually all bodily tissue. Human breast milk is rich in glutamate. And many foods that taste bland may in fact possess umami potential. That's because glutamate is often bonded to other molecules, hiding like Waldo from our taste buds. Enzymatic action such as fermentation, aging and curing can light it up. In the kitchen, it's chiefly found in such foods as Parmesan cheese, prosciutto, soy sauce and a host of other condiments.

Another boost comes from molecules known as nucleotides—also found in living tissue—which amplify glutamate, turning an unplugged experience into a high-watt umami rock show. You'll find nucleotides in ripe tomatoes, for example, and in especially high concentrations in anchovies, one reason anchovies go so well with Parmesan in Caesar salad.

Cooking can unlock the deliciousness too. Eat a fresh mushroom and it can taste boring; sauté it for 10 minutes and bingo, liberated glutamate. When you prepare stocks, sauces and soups, you're practising glutamate chemistry, drawing out umami compounds into the savoury solution.

Anchovies, soy sauce, MSG—it all might sound like a wine or beer lover's nightmare. But guess what? There's umami in your glass, a fact explored with laudable enthusiasm by US-based Master of Wine and food-and-wine-pairing expert Tim Hanni, who has been dubbed the Swami of Umami. Alcoholic beverages rely on fermentation, glutamate's old friend.

Kikunae Ikeda, we toast you.

Menu 1

THE PLEASURE OF PORCINI

Spicy Chilled Pea Soup with Crisp Mint

Porcini-Dusted Veal Chops

Anchovy-Roasted Fingerlings

Lemon and Orange Olive Oil Cake

The first porcini mushroom I tasted was sautéed and loaded with garlic and olive oil. After I recovered I immediately had a second one. They grow all over eastern Europe and are in season in the fall. Dried is the way to go in North America because, although we do grow some porcini, they have not reached the flavour heights of the European varieties. The upside of using dried porcini is that they are available year round, so you could do this menu in the spring with fresh peas in the soup and lovely new potatoes alongside the veal, or use frozen peas in the winter, when the citrus fruits in the dessert are at their peak.

SPICY CHILLED PEA SOUP WITH CRISP MINT

Once you taste the perfect blend of ingredients with umami-loaded chicken stock, you will make this soup again and again. Green curry sauce gives it a spicy lift, and arugula balances the sweetness of the peas with its subtle peppery flavour. Homemade stock is best, or buy chicken broth at the butcher shop or a low-salt supermarket brand. A blender works best here because it breaks down the pea skins, making a smooth purée, but a food mill is another good option. If you use a food processor, make sure that you keep processing until the soup is as smooth as possible. Serve in chilled mugs. **Serves 6**

2 tbsp vegetable oil
1 cup chopped onions
½ cup chopped floury potatoes
1 tsp chopped fresh ginger
1½ tsp Thai green curry paste
4 cups chicken stock
3 cups fresh or frozen peas
2 cups arugula
⅓ cup whipping cream
Salt and freshly ground pepper

Garnish:
1 tbsp vegetable oil
20 fresh mint leaves

Heat vegetable oil in a large pot over medium heat. Add onions and sauté for 2 minutes or until softened. Add potatoes and ginger and sauté for another 2 minutes or until potatoes are coated with oil. Stir in green curry paste.

Add chicken stock and bring to a boil. Reduce heat and simmer for 5 to 7 minutes, until potatoes are softened. Add peas and arugula and cook until peas are softened, about 3 minutes. Add cream and bring to a boil.

Purée in batches in a blender or food processor and season with salt and pepper. Chill.

Heat oil in a skillet over medium heat. Add mint leaves and fry until crisp. Drain on paper towels.

Serve soup garnished with fried mint leaves.

PAIRING: **Sauvignon blanc**

They really should rename sauvignon blanc. I think of it as sauvignon green. Its grassy flavour and zesty bite make it an ideal choice for Lucy's refreshing and complex soup. My vote goes to the especially fruity styles of Chile and New Zealand, though I wouldn't turn my nose up at a French Sancerre or South African sauvignon blanc.

PORCINI-DUSTED VEAL CHOPS

This is a superb way to prepare veal chops. The earthiness of the mushrooms brings out the sweetness in the veal, creating that Umami flavour. Dried porcini are sometimes sold under their French name, cèpes. Serve with Creamy Spinach (page 186) and the fingerling potatoes (page 404). **Serves 4**

1¼ cups dried porcini mushrooms
½ tsp peppercorns
Salt
4 veal chops (about 1 inch thick), bones scraped clean
3 tbsp extra-virgin olive oil

Sauce:
½ cup red wine
2 cups chicken stock
1 tbsp balsamic vinegar
2 tbsp butter, cubed

Grind ¼ cup dried porcini and peppercorns in a coffee grinder or spice mill until fine. Mix with salt to taste.

Brush both sides of veal chops with some oil, then pat a layer of ground porcini mixture onto both sides. Marinate for 30 minutes.

Soak remaining 1 cup dried porcini in 2 cups hot water for 30 minutes while veal marinates.

Drain soaked porcini, reserving liquid. Thinly slice mushrooms.

Preheat oven to 450°F.

Heat a large ovenproof nonstick skillet over high heat and add remaining oil. Sear chops for about 2 minutes a side or until browned. Place skillet in oven and roast chops for 10 to 12 minutes or until slightly pink in centre. Remove chops from skillet and let sit for 5 minutes.

Add sliced porcini to skillet along with red wine, stock and porcini soaking liquid. Bring to a boil and boil until reduced by half. Add vinegar and boil until reduced by half and thickened. Remove from heat and swirl in butter. Serve next to chops.

PAIRING: **Chianti**

I instinctively descended into my cellar for a Chianti when Lucy invited me over to sample these chops. It's medium weight and earthy, the ideal partner for delicate veal adorned with porcini. She declared the wine a success. After tucking into two portions of veal, I declared her my honorary Italian sister.

ANCHOVY-ROASTED FINGERLINGS

Gilding the veal chop in this menu calls for these outrageous potatoes. Anchovies are appearing in all sorts of dishes right now, either front and centre or as a background taste. I love them. But if you want less anchovy flavour, soak them in milk for 30 minutes before using. This is one ingredient where price matters: usually, the more expensive anchovies are of a higher quality, and Spanish are, to my taste, the best.

Serves 4

2 lb (900 g) fingerling potatoes
4 tbsp olive oil
Salt and freshly ground pepper
6 anchovy fillets, chopped
¼ cup chopped fresh parsley
1 tbsp chopped garlic

Preheat oven to 450°F.
Toss fingerlings with 2 tbsp olive oil in a baking dish. Season lightly with salt and pepper.
Combine anchovies, parsley, garlic and remaining 2 tbsp olive oil.
Roast potatoes for 25 minutes. Sprinkle in anchovy mixture and toss with potatoes. Bake for another 5 minutes or until potatoes are tender.

Truffled Pecorino: You can buy sensational truffled Pecorino cheese from Italy. Beppi likes it grated over pasta with a touch of whipping cream. I like it shaved over hot slices of roasted filet. We both love it with poached eggs, where it adds an earthy richness. It does not melt well, making it a poor but still tasty choice for grilled cheese.

LEMON AND ORANGE OLIVE OIL CAKE

For a party at my friend Nathan Fong's house, one of his friends made this superb olive oil cake. It is so easy and so good. I whip it up when friends are coming for dinner and serve it with rosemary-scented seasonal berries (see note below). The umami flavour comes from using an excellent green extra-virgin olive oil.

Serves 6

- 2 eggs
- Grated zest of 1 lemon and 1 orange
- 1¼ cups granulated sugar
- ¾ cup milk
- ¾ cup extra-virgin olive oil
- 1¼ cups all-purpose flour
- ½ tsp baking powder
- ½ tsp baking soda
- Pinch salt

Preheat oven to 350°F. Line a 9-inch round cake pan with parchment paper. Oil the sides with a little olive oil and dust with flour.

Stir together eggs, lemon and orange zests, sugar, milk and olive oil in a medium bowl.

Mix together flour, baking powder, baking soda and salt in a large bowl.

Stir wet ingredients into dry ingredients until combined. Pour batter into cake pan and bake for 40 to 50 minutes or until a cake tester comes out clean. Cool in pan for 10 minutes, then turn out on a rack to cool completely.

PAIRING: **Passito di Pantelleria**

The island of Pantelleria, off Sicily's coast and near Tunisia, produces an exotically perfumed and ancient dessert wine from the muscat of Alexandria grape (known locally as zibibbo). The grapes are left to dry after harvest to concentrate sugars in a process known as *passito*, yielding an ambrosial amber nectar that can suggest apricot, peach, orange, dried fig and honey. The excellent producer Donnafugata makes a splendid one called Ben Ryé, but there are others. Don't pass on the perfect excuse to try this *passito*.

Rosemary-Scented Berries: Make a syrup with ½ cup water, ½ cup granulated sugar and 1 large sprig of rosemary. Boil for 2 minutes, then cool. Remove rosemary. Toss syrup with berries of your choice.

Menu 1

A BEPPI-INFLUENCED MENU

Crostini with Prosciutto and Fig Marmalade

Tagliatelle with Anchovies, Olive Oil, Ripe Tomatoes, Garlic and Parmesan

Fritto Misto with Italian Tartar Sauce

Cherry Almond Biscotti

Is it that I spend so much time in Italy or that Beppi has influenced me so thoroughly that I have included an Italian menu in this chapter? All I know is that the flavours in this meal are sensational. The menu is inspired by a trip to Venice, where I found the food to be fair to middling; that is, until I stumbled upon a little trattoria along a dark, damp street. With the freshest seafood, local wine and a humming atmosphere, it was a memorable meal.

CROSTINI WITH PROSCIUTTO AND FIG MARMALADE

Thin baguettes are the best size for crostini. Cut into ¼-inch-thick slices and toast. You will have fig marmalade left over, but it is wonderful with curries and as a condiment with cold ham or turkey.

Makes 24 crostini

1½ cups fig marmalade (page 409)
24 rounds of bread, toasted
12 thin slices of prosciutto, cut in half
Parsley sprigs for garnish

Spread fig marmalade on each toast. Top with a slice of prosciutto gently rolled to look like a flower. Nestle a sprig of parsley inside each roll of prosciutto.

PAIRING: **Lillet**

With apologies to Italy, here's a French pairing for an Italian-inspired appetizer. Lillet is a marvellous Bordeaux aperitif made from white wine and liqueur steeped in citrus. Medium-sweet, it comes in white, rosé and red versions and is designed to be served chilled, either straight from the fridge or over ice, in a white-wine glass. I like the white and rosé versions for these crostini, just sweet enough to keep up with the marmalade and counterbalance the meaty, salty prosciutto. Alternative: the Campari Kir cocktail, page 38 in our "Bitter" chapter.

FIG MARMALADE

You can buy this kind of preparation, but I like to make my own so I can control the sweet/spicy flavour. I use Mission figs for this. It keeps for 2 months, refrigerated. **Makes 1½ cups**

8 oz (225 g) dried figs, chopped
½ cup golden raisins
2 tbsp granulated sugar
2 tbsp cider vinegar
2 tbsp orange marmalade
¼ tsp chili flakes
1 cup orange juice
¾ cup water
Salt and freshly ground pepper

Combine all ingredients in a medium pot. Bring to a boil, reduce heat and simmer, stirring occasionally to make sure mixture does not stick, for 35 to 45 minutes or until mixture is thickened.
Purée half of mixture in a food processor or with a hand blender. Stir back into marmalade. If mixture is too thick, add a couple of tablespoons more water.

TAGLIATELLE WITH ANCHOVIES, OLIVE OIL, RIPE TOMATOES, GARLIC AND PARMESAN

This is a pasta dish with assertive umami flavours. It is my favourite pasta, easy to make and perfect to eat.

Serves 2 as a main dish, 4 as an appetizer

- ⅓ cup olive oil
- 2 tbsp thinly sliced garlic
- 2 tbsp chopped anchovies
- 1 tsp chili flakes
- 2 cups cherry tomatoes, halved and seeded
- 8 oz (225 g) tagliatelle
- ½ cup grated Parmesan
- 2 tbsp chopped fresh parsley
- Salt and freshly ground pepper

Heat olive oil in a large skillet over medium-low heat. Add garlic and anchovies and cook gently for 6 minutes or until anchovies are melted into the oil. Increase heat to medium-high. Add chili flakes and cherry tomatoes. Toss together until tomatoes begin to soften.

Bring a large pot of salted water to a boil. Add tagliatelle and boil until al dente. Drain, reserving ½ cup pasta cooking water.

Toss pasta with sauce, adding ¼ cup pasta cooking water to keep pasta moist. Add more water by the spoonful if needed. Stir in Parmesan and parsley. Season with salt and pepper.

PAIRING: **Crisp Italian whites**

You want a lean white here, one that will lurk wisely in the background rather than leap forward with too much fruit only to be cut down to size by the assertive ingredients. Just about any herbaceous Italian white should succeed, and fortunately there are many to choose from. My top choices include greco di Tufo, Orvieto, verdicchio and vernaccia di San Gimignano. Alternative: dry Spanish rosé.

FRITTO MISTO WITH ITALIAN TARTAR SAUCE

Venice is surrounded by water full of a wide variety of fish and other aquatic life. One of my favourite dishes there is fritto misto, served at many seafood restaurants. Originally it was a dish to use up the little fish that were caught in the nets, but today it has become far more sophisticated. Shrimp, scallops, squid and other seafood are part of the mix, along with the more typical sardines (usually with the bones). Depending on the restaurant, sometimes fritto misto is floured and fried. Other restaurants use a batter, which I prefer. This is a very light batter, so the taste of the seafood zings in your mouth. Fry it just before needed. **Serves 4**

About 4 cups vegetable oil for deep-frying

Batter:
1¼ cups all-purpose flour
¼ cup cornstarch
1 tsp baking powder
1 tsp kosher salt
Freshly ground pepper
1½ cups very cold water
2 tbsp vegetable oil

Seafood:
4 extra-large scallops
4 fresh sardines, cleaned, heads removed if desired
8 extra-large shrimp, peeled and deveined
3 squid, cut in ¼-inch rings with tentacles
Salt and freshly ground pepper
1 cup all-purpose flour

To finish:
1 lemon, cut in wedges
Italian Tartar Sauce (page 413)

Preheat oven to 200°F.

Heat 3 inches oil in a wok or deep-fryer to 350°F or until a cube of bread turns brown in 15 seconds.

Combine flour, cornstarch, baking powder, salt and pepper to taste in a bowl.

Pour water and 2 tbsp oil into a large bowl, and whisk in flour mixture to make a smooth batter.

Season all the seafood with salt and pepper. Place 1 cup flour on a plate for dredging. Dredge scallops in flour and dip in batter to coat. Fry for 2 to 3 minutes or until lightly browned and just cooked through. Drain on paper towels, then transfer to a baking sheet and keep warm in oven.

Repeat with sardines, frying for 2 to 3 minutes or until lightly browned and just cooked through. Repeat with shrimp, frying for 2 minutes or until pink and lightly curled. Repeat with squid, frying for 1 minute or until opaque.

Place seafood on a platter and garnish with lemon wedges. Serve with Italian Tartar Sauce.

ITALIAN TARTAR SAUCE

This zesty sauce is flavoured with basil and incorporates both anchovies and capers, all ingredients used extensively in Italian cooking.

Makes about 1¼ cups

1 cup mayonnaise
2 anchovy fillets, finely chopped
2 tbsp chopped flat-leaf parsley
2 tbsp chopped fresh basil
1 tbsp chopped gherkins
1 tbsp chopped capers
1 tbsp lemon juice
½ tsp chopped garlic
½ tsp chili flakes
Salt to taste

Combine all ingredients in a bowl.

PAIRING: **Soave**

Stick with the Venetian theme and serve Soave, a crisp white of the surrounding Veneto area—acidity for the batter and delicate weight to match the seafood. If you prefer red, go with one of Hemingway's favourites, Valpolicella, about which he enthused while on an extended stay at the Gritti Palace hotel on the Grand Canal to convalesce following injuries suffered in Africa. Scampi and Valpolicella—it's known as "the Hemingway cure."

CHERRY ALMOND BISCOTTI

These biscotti are slightly softer and more umami than regular biscotti because of the olive oil. Biscotti made with butter have a slightly harder texture. You can change the almonds for hazelnuts or pecans. Biscotti keep for about a month stored in cookie tins in a cool place.

Makes 24 biscotti

2 cups all-purpose flour
¾ cup granulated sugar
1 tbsp baking powder
Pinch salt
1 cup coarsely chopped almonds
½ cup dried cherries
1 tbsp grated orange zest

3 large eggs
½ cup olive oil
¼ cup fresh orange juice or amaretto

Egg Wash:
1 egg beaten with a pinch salt
¼ cup granulated sugar

Preheat oven to 325°F. Butter and flour a cookie sheet or line with parchment paper.

Combine flour, sugar, baking powder, salt, almonds, cherries and orange zest in a large bowl.

Whisk together eggs and olive oil in a separate bowl. Stir in orange juice. Make a well in middle of dry ingredients, add wet ingredients and slowly stir to form a dough.

Divide dough in half and place on cookie sheet. Shape into 2 loaves, each about 9 inches long and 5 inches wide. Brush with egg wash and sprinkle with sugar. Bake for 30 minutes or until dough is golden with cracks on top. It will not be firm to the touch. Cool on racks for 20 minutes.

Cut each log into ½-inch slices. Return to cookie sheet and bake for 15 minutes on each side or until golden brown and dried out. Cool on racks.

PAIRING: **Amarone**

This one may land me in trouble with the wine-pairing police. Amarone is virtually dry. The cookies are sweet. A lopsided faceoff like that usually ends in bitter defeat for the wine. But I like to dunk my biscotti, which have a crumbly, dry texture. (Instruct your guests to give the heretical, decadent ritual a whirl.) Sweet Italian wines like the traditional Marsala and Vin Santo work, but I find that dry reds, especially Amarone, work better (think doughnuts dunked into unsweetened black coffee). Amarone, a broad-shouldered Italian red made from dried grapes, tends to taste of cherry and raisin—it's technically dry but usually comes with a vague hint of sweetness. Alternative: the Champagne Cocktail, page 191 in our "Nutty" chapter.

Biscotti are hard Italian cookies that are dipped into coffee or Marsala. They first appeared in Roman times, when hard biscuits of almonds and honey were made for celebrations. Later, sailors discovered that if they twice-baked their bread (think rusks), it would last longer on sea voyages. *Biscotti* itself means "twice baked." The first baking is to set the shape of the dough, the second one to dry out the individual biscotti.

Menu 3

ESSENCE OF SOUL

Chicken Soup with Vegetables and Parmesan Dumplings

Lemon-Scented Roast Chicken

Perfect Roast Potatoes

Frenched Green Beans and Snow Peas

Umami Apple Pie

Chicken soup is the best example of umami taste. Made from real chicken, lots of fresh vegetables and some love, it bubbles away contentedly on the stove, filling the house with mouth-watering smells. It is a pick-me-up when I feel low and practically penicillin for a sore throat. Paired with chicken soup in this menu are the finest of dishes: perfect roast chicken and, for dessert, iconic apple pie. This is my best family dinner.

CHICKEN SOUP WITH VEGETABLES AND PARMESAN DUMPLINGS

Make the dumplings a few hours ahead of time and reheat them in the soup. Making your own stock is best; otherwise, buy chicken broth at the butcher shop or a low-salt supermarket version. **Serves 4 to 6**

Parmesan Dumplings:
1 large egg
¾ cup grated Parmesan
¼ cup chopped chives
½ tsp grated lemon zest
¼ tsp chili flakes
¼ cup all-purpose flour
¼ tsp kosher salt
Freshly ground pepper

Soup:
6 cups chicken stock
½ cup finely diced carrots
½ cup finely diced parsnips
2 cups shredded spinach
Salt and freshly ground pepper
¼ cup chopped chives

Whisk egg in a bowl until frothy. Stir in Parmesan, chives, lemon zest and chili flakes. Blend in flour. Season with salt and pepper.

Bring a large pot of salted water to a simmer. Form 1 heaping teaspoon of dough at a time into oval dumplings with wet hands. Drop into simmering water and cook for 3 to 4 minutes or until dumplings float and are cooked through. Remove with a slotted spoon to a bowl.

Heat chicken stock in a large pot over medium-high heat. Add carrots and parsnips and simmer gently for 5 to 8 minutes or until just cooked through. Add spinach and simmer 1 minute longer or until wilted. Season with salt and pepper.

Reheat dumplings in soup just before serving. Garnish with chives.

PAIRING: **Dry Sherry**

There's lots of umami flavour in dry Sherry, whether light fino, manzanilla or richer Amontillado. It's got the bracing tang and fortified depth to stay afloat where other wines would drown in this soupy sea.

LEMON-SCENTED ROAST CHICKEN

I've tried every which way to roast a chicken: I have slow roasted it for 5 hours, butterflied and roasted it flat, and roasted it at very high heat, but I still go back to my tried-and-true French method. This chicken is always a favourite with its crispy skin, juicy meat and simple but delicious lemony sauce. The roasted garlic is a real treat as an accompaniment. If you prefer flattened chicken, this recipe still works. Simply cut the back off the chicken, flatten it and roast for 45 minutes. **Serves 4**

1 chicken (4 to 5 lb/1.8 to 2.25 kg)
3 tbsp butter, softened
1 tsp grated lemon zest
2 tsp chopped fresh rosemary (or 1 tsp dried)
1 lemon, cut in chunks
Kosher salt and freshly ground pepper
4 shallots, peeled, cut in half if large
2 heads garlic, cut in half horizontally
1 tbsp olive oil

Sauce:
2 tbsp lemon juice
1 tsp granulated sugar
1 cup chicken stock
2 tbsp butter

Preheat oven to 400°F.
Bend wing tips under wings to give the chicken a good shape.
Combine butter and lemon zest. Loosen breast skin slightly with your fingertips and carefully smear some lemon butter underneath skin, being careful not to tear skin. Rub remaining lemon butter over chicken. Sprinkle with 1 tsp rosemary. Toss remaining rosemary in the cavity and add cut-up lemon. Season skin liberally with salt and less liberally with pepper. Place on rack in a roasting pan.
Toss shallots and garlic with olive oil. Place in roasting pan, the garlic cut side down.
Roast for 1 hour 15 minutes to 1 hour 30 minutes or until juices run clear. Baste occasionally if you remember. Transfer chicken to a carving board and let sit for 10 minutes. Remove garlic and shallots from pan and reserve. Skim fat from roasting pan, leaving any pan juices.
Place pan over high heat and add lemon juice and sugar. Bring to a boil and boil for 1 minute. Immediately add stock, scraping up any bits on bottom of pan, and bring to a boil. Add any chicken juices from carving board and boil until reduced by half. Remove from heat and whisk in butter.
Carve chicken, coat with sauce and serve ½ head of garlic and 1 shallot with each portion. Squeeze out the garlic and eat with chicken.

PAIRING: **Chablis**

I love crisp chardonnay with this zesty chicken, and the best example is Chablis. There's weighty substance to the wine and plenty of complexity, and roast chicken provides the ideal canvas to show off the wine's true colours while the mineral tingle of Chablis meshes with the lemon.

PERFECT ROAST POTATOES

I've tested a lot of different roast potatoes, but this old-fashioned British method yields the most perfect results. The potatoes are fluffy inside with a crisp, mouth-watering exterior. These can be roasted in the same oven as the chicken. Use similarly sized potatoes so they roast evenly. **Serves 6**

3 lb (1.35 kg) medium Yukon Gold potatoes, peeled
⅓ cup olive oil or duck or beef fat
2 tsp crumbled dried rosemary
Salt and freshly ground pepper

Preheat oven to 400°F.
Place potatoes in a pot with enough cold water to cover them. Bring to a boil and boil for 7 minutes. Drain well and return to pot. Shake pot over turned-off burner to rough potatoes up a bit. This will give the crunchy exterior. Cut potatoes in half lengthwise and each half into quarters or thirds.
Pour oil into a roasting pan large enough to hold potatoes in one layer (or use 2 pans). Heat pan in oven or on top of stove until hot.
Add potatoes and turn to coat with oil. Sprinkle with rosemary and season with salt and pepper. Roast, turning occasionally, for 1 hour or until potatoes are crisp and golden.

Potato Textures: Roasted red potatoes are creamier than Yukon Golds, which when roasted become quite fluffy on the inside. Fluffy wins for me.

FRENCHED GREEN BEANS AND SNOW PEAS

Green vegetables are always good with chicken. Here, the roasted portobello mushroom gives extra umami flavour.

Serves 4

- 1 portobello mushroom, stem removed
- 1 tsp olive oil
- Salt and freshly ground pepper
- 4 oz (115 g) green beans
- 4 oz (115 g) snow peas
- 2 tbsp butter
- ¼ cup thinly sliced red onion
- 2 tsp chopped fresh tarragon

Preheat oven to 450°F.

Place portobello mushroom gill side up on a small baking sheet. Drizzle with olive oil and season with salt and pepper.

Roast for 10 to 12 minutes or until tender and juicy. Cool and finely dice. Reserve.

French green beans and snow peas (see note, below).

Melt butter in a large skillet over medium-high heat. Add red onion and sauté for 1 minute or until softened. Add beans and snow peas and sauté for another 1 to 2 minutes or until vegetables are crisp-tender.

Sprinkle with reserved mushroom and tarragon and sauté for 1 minute longer to combine flavours. Season with salt and pepper.

How to French Beans: When beans are a little fatter than you want, French-cutting them makes a beautiful presentation and takes away any toughness. First, top and tail the beans. Next, you have three options:

- You can buy a tool called a "bean frencher" that strips each bean lengthwise into three long strips.
- If you have good knife skills, you can cut the beans on the diagonal into thin strips.
- If your knife skills are not too advanced, hold the knife at a 45-degree angle to the bean and cut on the diagonal starting at the stem end.

These techniques work well with snow peas too.

UMAMI APPLE PIE

One issue I have with apple pies is that the apples are not soft and juicy enough. To avoid that, I use several different kinds of apples, some hard and some soft, and precook them for a few minutes to just soften.

Serves 6 to 8

Cheddar Pastry:
2½ cups all-purpose flour
½ tsp kosher salt
1 cup cold unsalted butter, cut in cubes
1 cup shredded white cheddar
6 to 8 tbsp cold water

Egg Wash:
1 egg yolk beaten with 1 tbsp milk

Filling:
10 cups sliced cored peeled mixed apples (about 6 to 7 large apples such as Honeycrisp, Gala, McIntosh, Pink Lady)
2 tbsp lemon juice
1 cup granulated sugar
1 tsp cinnamon
½ tsp ground allspice
3 tbsp tapioca flour
2 tbsp unsalted butter, cut in small pieces

Combine flour, salt, butter and cheese in a food processor. Pulse until butter is the size of small peas. Transfer to a bowl, drizzle with cold water and toss with your fingertips or a rubber spatula, adding more water if needed until pastry holds its shape when squeezed between the fingers. Gather pastry together and divide into two balls, one slightly larger than the other. Flatten each into a disc, wrap in plastic wrap and chill for 30 minutes.

Preheat oven to 425°F.

Roll out larger portion of pastry on a lightly floured surface to fit an 8-inch pie plate, leaving a ½-inch overhang. Chill until needed. Roll out second piece for the top. Chill.

Combine apples, lemon juice, sugar, cinnamon and allspice in a large skillet. Cook over medium heat, stirring gently, for 5 minutes or until apples just begin to soften. Remove from heat and let stand for 5 minutes to absorb more of the syrup.

Stir in tapioca flour and heap into pie shell, mounding apples in the middle. Dot with butter. Cover with top layer of pastry, seal edges and crimp. Brush with egg wash. Cut small steam vents in top of pastry.

Bake for 15 minutes. Reduce heat to 350°F and bake for another 30 to 40 minutes or until crust is golden, apples are tender and juice is bubbling. If pastry begins to brown too quickly, cover with a sheet of parchment paper.

PAIRING: **Coteaux du Layon**

How about honey, apricot and lemon to go with your pie? The sweet wines of Coteaux du Layon in the Loire Valley, based on chenin blanc, add a splash of magic to baked apple desserts.

BACON-WASHED BOURBON

Back in the early years of the millennium, if you could fry bacon, your career as a trendy-restaurant sous chef was pretty much guaranteed. Pork belly, a back-pocket flavouring agent of cooks through the ages, declared victory over all, including the ice-cream course. Today, that same skill could land you a job behind the bar.

Bacon-washed bourbon might sound like a Monty Python joke, or a fast route to trichinosis. But suspend your disbelief (or disgust). It's not just a dumb novelty, it's compelling, the smoky bacon bringing depth to the sweet corn liquor. It's also the best way I know to work pork into your diet without much in the way of added calories (assuming you've counted the bourbon calories). Substitute rye or Canadian corn whisky if you like. Serve it in a variety of drinks—as the base for a hoggy Manhattan (bourbon and sweet vermouth), on the rocks with a red chili pepper tossed in as a garnish, or with a splash each of vermouth and kirsch.

1 bottle decent bourbon, such as Maker's Mark or Jim Beam Black
6 thick strips very smoky bacon

Fry the bacon until most of the fat is rendered. Remove bacon strips and consume in another context. When the fat in the pan has cooled but is still liquid, pour it into a large mason jar and follow with the whole bottle of bourbon. Let the mixture steep at room temperature for 8 hours. Place the jar in the freezer overnight. Remove the congealed fat by straining the liquid through a coffee filter into another vessel. Presto: clear-brown, potable porky goodness.

BUFFAL

MEDITERRANEAN RELISH

This relish is full of uses. Serve it with meat or chicken or toss with pasta and some pasta cooking water. Spread it on crackers. Add a spoonful to brighten up a sauce. Relish keeps for 2 weeks, refrigerated.

Makes about 1½ cups

1 tbsp olive oil
¼ cup chopped pancetta
½ cup chopped onion
1 cup puréed canned tomatoes
¼ cup pitted black olives, chopped
1 tbsp chopped fresh parsley
Salt and freshly ground pepper

Heat oil in a medium skillet over medium heat. Add pancetta and onion and sauté until pancetta is slightly crisped. Stir in tomatoes and bring to a boil.

Reduce heat and simmer for 5 minutes or until slightly thickened. Stir in olives and parsley. Season with salt and pepper.

PLUM GALETTE

I tweeted whether I should include an apple or a plum pie in this book, and the vote was 50–50. I chose the apple because I think apple pies are iconic, but because I have always loved plum pies, here is a plum galette. A galette is a free-form country tart. The rich flavour of plums and their juices is marvellous with a sweet, crisp pastry. I use a little cornmeal to thicken the juices, but instant tapioca or tapioca flour is fine too. You can make this with peaches, but because they are juicier, use an extra tablespoon of cornmeal in the filling.

Serves 6 to 8

Pastry:
2 cups all-purpose flour
1 tsp ground cardamom (optional)
½ tsp kosher salt
¾ cup unsalted butter, cut in chunks
3 tbsp cold water
2 tbsp lemon juice or white vinegar

Filling:
2 tbsp + ¼ cup granulated sugar
2 tbsp fine cornmeal
2 lb (900 g) black plums, pitted and each cut in 8 wedges

Glaze:
1 egg yolk beaten with ¼ tsp salt
2 tsp granulated sugar

Combine flour, cardamom and salt in a large bowl or food processor. Cut in butter until the size of small peas.
Combine 2 tbsp water and lemon juice and sprinkle over flour mixture, gathering pastry together with your fingertips until it holds together and does not feel sticky. Add a little more water if mixture is too dry. Gather pastry into a ball, flatten into a disc, wrap in plastic wrap and chill for 45 minutes.
Preheat oven to 425°F.
Place pastry on a large sheet of parchment paper and roll into a 14-inch circle. Slide parchment with pastry onto a baking sheet. Combine 2 tbsp sugar with cornmeal and sprinkle over pastry, leaving a 2-inch border all around. Arrange plums over cornmeal mixture. Sprinkle with remaining ¼ cup sugar.
Fold edge of pastry up over plums, pleating pastry as necessary so that fruit is enclosed at the edges but the centre is open. Brush pastry with egg glaze and sprinkle with 2 tsp sugar.
Bake for 15 minutes. Reduce heat to 350°F and bake for another 30 minutes or until juices are bubbling and pastry is golden. If pastry begins to brown too quickly, cover with a sheet of parchment. Cool on a rack until juices have thickened and cooled.

PAIRING: **Port**

I love the way prune-like Port adds a dimension of ripeness to this free-form pie and complements baking spices such as cardamom. Look for the styles labelled Ruby or Late Bottled Vintage.

CHILLIN' SAKE

Just who is to blame for warm sake I cannot say. Japan's sublime rice brew is by definition a beer, not a tea, and therefore best served cold. You don't see people drinking mulled beer, do you?

The cheap sake destined for heating typically is made with Uncle Ben's–style white rice, often stretched with lots of distilled alcohol, the beverage equivalent of processed Spam. Cold sake, on the other hand, is more like prime steak, made with high-starch, brown-skinned grains grown specifically for the purpose.

Chill tightens acidity and focuses complex aromas that range from melon and fig to cucumber, mineral and honey. It shines in a white-wine glass and pairs with just about anything.

李白

ULTIMATE UMAMI PASTE

I always have this on hand. Use it on pasta, to add flavour to a dull sauce or dotted over vegetables. I even garnish soup with it. Poached eggs are a delight when scattered with umami paste. This will keep for 3 weeks, refrigerated.

Makes 1 cup

1½ cups grated Parmesan
⅓ cup chopped, oil-packed anchovies
¼ cup tomato paste
2 tbsp chopped garlic
2 tbsp soy sauce
⅔ cup olive oil

Add Parmesan, anchovies, tomato paste, garlic and soy sauce to a food processor. Process till slightly chunky.

Add olive oil and pulse until well combined and quite smooth.

Taste for seasoning, adding pepper if needed.

QUICK UMAMI MISO SOUP

I buy dashi in powdered form at the Asian grocery. Follow the package directions for a perfect stock.

Makes 5 cups

- 5 cups dashi stock
- 4 shiitake mushrooms, slivered
- 1 cup diced firm tofu
- 3 tbsp white or red miso
- 2 cups packed baby spinach
- 3 green onions, chopped

Bring stock to a simmer and add mushrooms and tofu. Simmer for 5 minutes. Combine miso with a little stock, then stir back into soup. Add spinach. Simmer for a minute or two, until hot.
Garnish soup with green onions.

PAIRING: **Amontillado Sherry**

Frankly, this delectable soup is a full package of umami deliciousness and needs no help from outside. But if you can't bear to leave your guests' glasses empty, serve Amontillado Sherry. Its yeasty flavour will cozy up to the fermented miso. Alternative: sake.

ACKNOWLEDGEMENTS

FROM BOTH OF US

Working again with Kirsten Hanson, our book editor, has been a pleasure and privilege. The material flowed easily, and our concerns were always met with genuine enthusiasm, grand vision and formidable patience.

Our agent at Westwood Creative Artists, Hilary McMahon, was invaluable for her commitment to us and the book — for testing recipes, sending comments and generally being there to advocate and listen at every twist and turn. The champagne's on us.

Ryan Szulc, our superb photographer, can coax awesome light and design into every glorious frame. We will never forget his virtuosity with the smoke shots. Artistry aside, he also happens to be wonderfully low-key and good-natured, which made for a perfect working atmosphere.

Ryan's wife, Madeleine Johari, has matchless taste, and her propping gave the photographs fresh style and vitality.

Eshun Mott worked for Lucy for 12 years before she left to do an outstanding job as food editor at *Today's Parent*. She came back to do the food styling, pulling together the art and design with her natural and elegant approach.

Lucy met Colleen Nicholson in Italy on a media trip, and they became fast friends. Colleen has acted as ex officio art director, graphic designer and layout artist. Her taste is always impressive.

Anya Oberdorf was our book co-ordinator. She merged text from both of us, calmly pulled together the chapters and made our lives so much easier.

We are immensely grateful to our support group at HarperCollins: Alan Jones, who produced the brilliant design and layout, a visual feast; and Noelle Zitzer, our production co-ordinator, who kept us on our deadline toes.

To Kathryn Hayward, Lori Fazari, Danny Sinopoli, Melanie Morassutti and Danielle Adams—our editors at *The Globe and Mail*—thank you for helping us look professional and smart, day in and day out.

Kristina Gutkauskas worked as Lucy's assistant throughout the book production, organizing everything and fixing recipes, and she was always there to devour the desserts.

Kristen Eppich, Lucy's current recipe tester, stepped in midway through the project and helped to finalize recipes and assist at the photography shoot.

Thank you to Shaun Oakey, copy editor extraordinaire, for working wonders with the manuscript. Though it pains us to admit it, you were always right.

To Phillip Crawley, *The Globe and Mail*'s publisher and chief executive officer, thank you for supporting our vision.

And lastly to David Kent, president and CEO of HarperCollins Canada, thank you for being David Kent.

FROM LUCY

Thanks to Jody Dunn and the staff at *Food & Drink* for always listening to my ideas, even when they are off centre, and for elegantly making them look beautiful in the pages of the magazine.

Sharing food is a special time in my family. Friday night dinners, holidays and birthdays all take place around our table. I want to thank my daughters, Emma and Katie, who always suggest that I cook for special occasions and who support all my endeavours, even though they make me unavailable at times; Bruce, my husband, who is always committed and caring, and is the best dishwasher around; and all our grandchildren, for whom I cook at least three separate meals whenever they come for dinner — it keeps me on my toes.

Alison Fryer and Julia Aitken are my frequent dining companions, with whom I discuss most things food. They have heard my concerns throughout the process of creating this book. I thank them both for standing by me with help, ideas and support.

FROM BEPPI

My thanks to Jill Borra, *The Globe and Mail*'s executive editor, and Kevin Siu, deputy executive editor, for lifting me on their shoulders and championing food-and-drinks coverage at the paper. I owe them more drinks than could safely be consumed in a lifetime.

To Kathryn Hayward, *The Globe and Mail*'s Life editor, whose graceful editing and guidance always makes me sound wiser than I am.

To Cathrin Bradbury, former features editor at *The Globe and Mail*, for taking a crusty news journalist under her wing and gifting him with the welcome words: "How would you like to be my wine columnist?"

To Dan Driver, steward of *The Globe and Mail*'s mailroom, for guarding a steady stream of incoming wine and spirit samples with an intrusion-detection system worthy of the Pentagon.

To Zosia Bielski for her sage advice, constant encouragement, moral support and, not least, the gift of a purple Sharpie marker and white sketch board, without which most of my contributions would still be spinning their wheels in the quicksand of my brain.

And to John Crosariol for his bottomless generosity, technical support, wise counsel and dear brotherly love.

INDEX

A

aglianico, 254
Aïoli, 157
akvavit, 283
albariño, 42, 174
ales. *See under* beers
Almasa, 335
amari, 21
Amarone, 47, 145, 415
anchovies
  wine choices with, 174
  Anchovy and Tomato Tapas, 42
  Anchovy Goat Cheese Biscuits, 144
  Anchovy-Roasted Fingerlings, 404
  Italian Tartar Sauce, 413
  Kale and White Anchovy Salad, 177
  Marmalade of Greens, 49
  Mint Salsa Verde, 89
  Tagliatelle with Anchovies, Olive Oil, Ripe Tomatoes, Garlic and Parmesan, 410
  Ultimate Umami Paste, 430
  Veal Scaloppine with Tomato Caper Sauce, 259
Antipasto, 254
Aperol Spritz, 298, 345
appetizers/first courses
  tapas, 173–9
  Anchovy and Tomato Tapas, 42
  Antipasto, 254
  Apple and Avocado Soup, 70
  Asian Shrimp Cocktail, 98
  Beet and Blue Potato Salad with Local Blue Cheese, 216
  Buffalo Mozzarella and Pickled Fennel, 257
  Chicken Liver Pâté in a Foie Gras Style, 303
  Crushed Chickpeas with Jalapeños, 175
  Dandelion Pesto on Naan, 27
  Gougères with Green Salad, 182
  Grapefruit Salad Saigon Style, 350
  Grilled Bread and Vegetable Salad, 106
  Herring Tartar, 283
  Homemade Ricotta with Rhubarb Compote and Grilled Bread, 154–5
  Kale and White Anchovy Salad, 177
  Oysters with Horseradish Gelée, 265
  Pok Pok Wings, 392
  Roasted Asparagus Salad with Green Mayonnaise, 148
  Roquefort Toasts with Arugula and Dried Pear Salad, 342
  Saffron Risotto with Scallops, 132
  Savoury Apple and Thyme Tart, 90
  Seared Beef Filet with Brown Butter Mayonnaise, 176
  Shrimp Catalan, 179
  Sweet Potato and Black Bean Empanadas, 202–3
  Tagliatelle with Anchovies, Olive Oil, Ripe Tomatoes, Garlic and Parmesan, 410
  Tuna Ceviche with Endive Watermelon Salad, 332
  Vegetarian Charcuterie, 60
  See also hors d'oeuvres
apple cider
  to reduce, 320
  Apples in Caramel Cider Sauce, 321
  Savoury Apple and Thyme Tart, 90
apples
  to dry, 342
  Apple Amaretti Parfait, 231
  Apple and Avocado Soup, 70
  Apple Cranberry Compote, 320
  Apples in Caramel Cider Sauce, 321
  Caramelized Onion and Cheese Fondue, 192
  Cream of Lentil Soup with Horseradish, 224
  Herring Tartar, 283
  Honey Marmalade Cake, 297
  Japanese Chicken Curry, 247–8
  Pear, Apple and Cornmeal Crunch, 221
  Savoury Apple and Thyme Tart, 90
  Senegalese Soup, 386
  Sorrel Soup with Chive Oil, 24
  Umami Apple Pie, 423
apricots
  Mustard Fruit Compote, 143
Arctic Char, Slow-Baked, with Crisp Potatoes, 61
Argentinian Short Ribs, 204
  Grilled, 235
arugula
  Arugula Salad with Stilton and Redcurrant Vinaigrette, 304
  Roasted Asparagus Salad with Green Mayonnaise, 148
  Roquefort Toasts with Arugula and Dried Pear Salad, 342
  Savoury Apple and Thyme Tart, 90
  Spicy Chilled Pea Soup with Crisp Mint, 402
  Spicy Green Herb Mayonnaise, 88
Asian Shrimp Cocktail, 98
asparagus
  to peel, 148
  Roasted Asparagus Salad with Green Mayonnaise, 148
assyrtiko, 174

avocados
  Apple and Avocado Soup, 70
  Grapefruit Salad Saigon Style, 350

B

bacon
  Bacon-Washed Bourbon, 424
  Braised Escarole, 45
  Candied Bacon, 123
  Irish Cheddar, Bacon and Chard Tart, 36
  Slow-Baked Arctic Char with Crisp Potatoes, 61
  Smoked Caesar, 122
  Sticky Toffee Bacon, 314
  Thai Clam Chowder, 378
  See also pork
Baked Goan Black Cod, 370
balsamic vinegar, 356–7
  Wild Salmon with Balsamic Glaze and Fennel Confit, 359
Banana Bread, 111
Bandol red, 79
Bannock, 220
Banyuls, 271, 306
Barbaresco, 141
Barbecue Sauce, 115
barbera, 60
Barley Pilaf, 230
basil, fresh, 83
  Lime Basil Éclairs, 85–6
  Lime Basil Icing, 86
  Lime Basil Pastry Cream, 85
Basmati Rice Pilau, 372
beans, black
  Sweet Potato and Black Bean Empanadas, 202–3
beans, fava
  Saffron Risotto with Scallops, 132
beans, green
  to French, 421
  Frenched Green Beans and Snow Peas, 421
  Green Beans with Red Onions, 64
beans, long
  Spicy Fish Cakes with Zesty Citrus Sauce, 380–1
beans, white
  Kale and Bean Soup, 53
Béarnaise, Unbreakable, 323
Beaujolais, 60, 87, 266, 360
beef
  alternative steak cuts, 107
  to braise, 208
  Argentinian Short Ribs, 204
  Bistecca Fiorentina, 121
  Grilled Argentinian Short Ribs, 235
  Grilled Hanger Steak with Smoky Corn and Tomato Salsa, 108
  Korean Beef Noodle Stir-Fry, 168
  Miami Ribs Miami Style, 116
  Seared Beef Filet with Brown Butter Mayonnaise, 176
  South African Bobotie, 394
beers
  honey beer, 295
  hops, 21, 50
  India Pale Ale, 50, 115
  Irish ale, 36
  pilsner, 9, 60, 118, 192
  Rauchbier, 117
  Senegalese beer, 386
  spiced harvest ale, 231
  stout, 37, 111, 127
  West Coast Pale Ale, 392
  Beer Toasts, 51
  Caramelized Onion and Cheese Fondue, 192
  Cheddar Ale Bread, 52
  Irish Cheddar, Bacon and Chard Tart, 36
  Stout Cake, 37
beet greens
  Braised Escarole, 45
  Braised Winter Greens, 268
beets
  Beet and Blue Potato Salad with Local Blue Cheese, 216
  Maple-Glazed Salmon with Beets, Ricotta and Dill, 305
  Shaved Root Vegetable Salad, 34
Belgian Baked Fries, 280
beverages, alcoholic, 8–16
  bargain bottles, 16
  bar pantry, 9
  with brunch dishes, 311, 322
  glassware for, 12–13
  wine pantry, 10
  See also beers; cocktails and mixed drinks; wines
beverages, non-alcoholic
  coffee or espresso with dessert, 47, 111
  green tea, 251
  hibiscus tea, 386
  soda with fruit ice cubes, 311
biscuits
  Anchovy Goat Cheese Biscuits, 144
  Isle of Mull Oatcakes, 316
Bison Burger with Homemade Ketchup, The Just-Right, 218
Bistecca Fiorentina, 121
bitter flavours, 19–21
  hops, 50
  and salt, 21, 44, 269
  for supertasters, 31
  tannins, 269
bitters, 9, 191, 390–1
blackberries
  Fruit Ice Cubes, 311
  Peach and Blackberry Compote, 65
blueberries
  Fruit Ice Cubes, 311

Bok Choy Stir-Fry, 102
Bordeaux, white, 130
bourbon. *See under* whisk(e)y
Bourride from Marseille, 156
Braised Escarole, 45
Braised Winter Greens, 268
braising, 208
brandy and Cognac
  Champagne Cocktail, 191, 415
  Chicken Liver Pâté in a Foie Gras Style, 303
  Sidecar, 351
breads, quick
  Banana Bread, 111
  Bannock, 220
  Cheddar Ale Bread, 52
  Sopaipillas, 75
breads and toasts
  Beer Toasts, 51
  Crostini with Prosciutto and Fig Marmalade, 408–9
  Homemade Ricotta with Rhubarb Compote and Grilled Bread, 154–5
  Roquefort Toasts, 342
brining, 267
  for pork, 266
  for Quick Preserved Lemons, 335
Brown Butter Mayonnaise, 176
Brûléed Rice Pudding with Icewine-Soaked Raisins, 306
brunch dishes
  sparkling wines with, 311, 322
  Apple Cranberry Compote, 320
  Double-Baked Soufflés with English Cheddar, 310–11
  Grapefruit Compote, 317
  Isle of Mull Oatcakes, 316
  Millionaire Bars, 319
  Scrambled Eggs in Pancetta Cups, 322
  Sticky Toffee Bacon, 314
  Unbreakable Béarnaise, poached eggs with, 323
  Walnut and Endive Salad, 315
Brussels sprouts
  Roasted Brussels Sprout Leaves, 175
  Shallot and Brussels Sprout Compote, 229
Buffalo Mozzarella and Pickled Fennel, 257
burgers and rolls
  The Just-Right Bison Burger with Homemade Ketchup, 218
  Lobster Rolls, 278
Burgundy, white, 141, 185, 226, 244, 322
  red, 225
butter
  to brown, 176
  Herb Butter, 61

C

cabbage
  Bok Choy Stir-Fry, 102
  Chilean Pulmay, 73
  Napa Pickles, 250
  Silky Tofu Soup, 166
  Spicy Mango Slaw, 281
cabernet franc
  icewine, 271, 303, 304
  late-harvest, 345
cabernet sauvignon, 16, 79, 121
Caffè Latte Panna Cotta with Decadent Chocolate Cookies, 47–8
cakes
  Honey Marmalade Cake, 297
  Lemon and Orange Olive Oil Cake, 405
  Mandarin Pudding Cake with Lime Leaves, 355
  Simple Plum Cardamom Cake, 337
  Stout Cake, 37
  Triple Ginger Cake, 251
  Warm Chocolate Caramel Cakes, 271–2
  Warm Lemon Poppy Seed Cakes, 345–7
  See also desserts
Campari Kir, 38, 408
Campari Royale, 38
Canadian icewines. *See under* icewines
Canadian whisky. *See under* whisk(e)y
Candied Bacon, 123
Candied Lemon Confit, 347
candies
  Caramel Pecan Popcorn, 282
  Salted Caramels, 272
Cape gooseberries (physalis)
  Grapefruit Compote, 317
capers
  Herb Butter, 61
  Italian Tartar Sauce, 413
  Marmalade of Greens, 49
  Mint Salsa Verde, 89
  Roasted Asparagus Salad with Green Mayonnaise, 148
  Tomato Caper Sauce, 259
Caramel Cakes, Warm Chocolate, 271–2
Caramelized Onion and Cheese Fondue, 192
Caramelized Walnuts, 144
Caramel-Pecan-Dusted Sea Bass with Cranberry Wine Sauce, 185–6
Caramel Pecan Popcorn, 282
Caramels, Salted, 272
cardamom, 337
  Simple Plum Cardamom Cake, 337
carmenère, 16, 73
carrots
  Carrot, Ginger and Coriander Soup, 292
  Korean Beef Noodle Stir-Fry, 168
  Shaved Root Vegetable Salad, 34
  Sweet Potato Mulligatawny Soup, 369
Cassata Parfait, 260

cauliflower
Caramelized Onion and Cheese Fondue, 192
Shaved Cauliflower and Swiss Chard Curry, 371
Cava, 10, 16, 138, 255, 322, 332, 380
Chablis, 10, 87, 265, 419
Champagne, 244, 255, 265, 322, 332
Champagne Cocktail, 191, 415
chard, Swiss
Braised Escarole, 45
Braised Winter Greens, 268
Irish Cheddar, Bacon and Chard Tart, 36
Marmalade of Greens, 49
Shaved Cauliflower and Swiss Chard Curry, 371
chardonnay, 10
late-harvest, 282
New World oaked, 292, 305
unoaked, 24, 87
Cheddar Ale Bread, 52
Cheddar Pastry, 423
cheese
for antipasto, 254
for fondue, 192
wines to serve with, 145
Anchovy Goat Cheese Biscuits, 144
Arugula Salad with Stilton and Redcurrant Vinaigrette, 304
Beet and Blue Potato Salad with Local Blue Cheese, 216
Buffalo Mozzarella and Pickled Fennel, 257
Caramelized Onion and Cheese Fondue, 192
Cheddar Ale Bread, 52
Cheddar Pastry, 423
Chicken Soup with Vegetables and Parmesan Dumplings, 418
The Composed Cheese Plate, 142–4
Dandelion Pesto on Naan, 27
Double-Baked Soufflés with English Cheddar, 310–11
Garganelli with Prosciutto and Peas, 258
Gougères with Green Salad, 182
Irish Cheddar, Bacon and Chard Tart, 36
Kale and Bean Soup, 53
Marmalade of Greens, 49
Roquefort Toasts with Arugula and Dried Pear Salad, 342
Savoury Apple and Thyme Tart, 90
Shaved Root Vegetable Salad, 34
Sweet Potato and Black Bean Empanadas, 202–3
Tagliatelle with Anchovies, Olive Oil, Ripe Tomatoes, Garlic and Parmesan, 410
truffled, 404
Ultimate Umami Paste, 430
Umami Apple Pie, 423
Vegetarian Charcuterie, 60
Yogurt Cheese, 158
See also mascarpone; ricotta
chenin blanc
Quarts de Chaume, 231
South Africa, 16, 130, 358, 379, 387
cherries
Cherry Almond Biscotti, 414
Chicken Liver Pâté in a Foie Gras Style, 303
Chestnut-Stuffed Portobello Mushrooms, 226–7
Chianti, 10, 141, 226, 403
chicken
to brine, 267
Chicken Adobo, 358
Chicken from Fez with Preserved Lemon and Olives, 334–5
Chicken Soup with Vegetables and Parmesan Dumplings, 418
Chicken Yassa, 387
Japanese Chicken Curry, 247–8
Kickass Chicken Wings, 118
Pok Pok Wings, 392
Sweet-Spicy Garlic Chicken, 294
Vietnamese Fried Chicken, 353–4
Chicken Liver Pâté in a Foie Gras Style, 303
Chickpeas, Crushed, with Jalapeños, 175
Chilean Pulmay, 73
Chimichurri Sauce, 236
chives
Chicken Soup with Vegetables and Parmesan Dumplings, 418
Chive Oil, 25
Roasted Asparagus Salad with Green Mayonnaise, 148
Senegalese Soup, 386
Six-Minute Eggs on Fresh Field Greens, 138
chives, Chinese (garlic)
Korean Beef Noodle Stir-Fry, 168
chocolate
Caffé Latte Panna Cotta with Decadent Chocolate Cookies, 47–8
Cassata Parfait, 260
Chocolate Cajeta, 153
Decadent Chocolate Cookies, 48
Dulce de Leche Tartlets, 237
Jewel in the Crown Ice Cream Cake, 373
Millionaire Bars, 319
Smoky Dark Chocolate Bars, 103
Stout Cake, 37
Warm Chocolate Caramel Cakes, 271–2
chorizo sausages
Chilean Pulmay, 73
Speedy Spanish Halibut, 43
Choux Pastry, 85
cilantro, fresh, 63
Carrot, Ginger and Coriander Soup, 292
Chicken from Fez with Preserved Lemon and Olives, 334–5

Mango Cilantro Salsa, 70
Pebre, 74
Smoky Corn and Tomato Salsa, 110
Spicy Mango Slaw, 281
Clammy Sammy, 138, 265, 275
clams
Chilean Pulmay, 73
Thai Clam Chowder, 378
Classic Poached Salmon with Spicy Green Herb Mayonnaise, 87–8
cocktails and mixed drinks
bitters in, 390–1
flamed orange peel with, 351
Aperol Spritz, 298
Campari Kir, 38, 408
Campari Royale, 38
Champagne Cocktail, 191, 415
Clammy Sammy, 138, 265, 275
Custom Gin and Tonic, 81, 335
Dirty Mojito, 339
Kir, 38
Manhattans, 375, 424
martinis, 174, 328, 329
Red and Green, 101, 198
Reverse Saketini, 98
Rum Mango Lassi, 393
Rumpuccino, 149
Sidecar, 351
Smoked Caesar, 43, 122
Spiced Rum with Coke, 282
coconut and coconut milk
Asian Shrimp Cocktail, 98
Coconut Curry Shrimp, 382
Fresh Chili Mangoes with Mango Ice Cream, 388
Senegalese Soup, 386
Sweet Potato Mulligatawny Soup, 369
cod
Baked Goan Black Cod, 370
Bourride from Marseille, 156
Spicy Fish Cakes with Zesty Citrus Sauce, 380–1
coffee
served with dessert, 47, 111
Caffè Latte Panna Cotta with Decadent Chocolate Cookies, 47–8
Honey Marmalade Cake, 297
Rumpuccino, 149
Cognac. *See* brandy and Cognac
collard greens
Braised Escarole, 45
Braised Winter Greens, 268
Colli Piacentini, 258
Composed Cheese Plate, The, 142–4
conserves and condiments
Apple Cranberry Compote, 320
Cheaters Hot Pickle, 370
Chimichurri Sauce, 236
Chive Oil, 25
Cranberry Ginger Chutney, 233
Cucumber Pickles, 249
Fiery Chili Sauce, 354
Fig Marmalade, 409
Ginger Lime Dipping Sauce, 354
Mediterranean Relish, 426
Napa Pickles, 250
Pickled Fennel, 257
Rhubarb Compote, 154–5
Spiced Syrup, 303
Tomato Ketchup, 219
Ultimate Umami Paste, 430
See also sauces and spreads, savoury
cookies and bars
biscotti, 415
Cherry Almond Biscotti, 414
Decadent Chocolate Cookies, 48
Lemon Balm Shortbread, 66
Millionaire Bars, 319
Smoky Dark Chocolate Bars, 103
See also desserts
Corbières, 16, 115, 335
corn
Caramel Pecan Popcorn, 282
Grilled Hanger Steak with Smoky Corn and Tomato Salsa, 108
Smoky Corn and Tomato Salsa, 110
cornmeal
Mushroom Ragu with Polenta, 140–1
Pear, Apple and Cornmeal Crunch, 221
Polenta, 140
Coteaux du Layon, 231, 423
Côtes du Rhône, 115
Court Bouillon, 88
cranberries
Apple Cranberry Compote, 320
Cranberry Ginger Chutney, 233
Mustard Fruit Compote, 143
cranberry juice
Cranberry Wine Sauce, 186
Cream of Lentil Soup with Horseradish, 224
Creamy Spinach, 186
creamy textures, 125–7
Crémant d'Alsace, 255
Crème Fraîche, 158
Crostini with Prosciutto and Fig Marmalade, 408–9
Crushed Chickpeas with Jalapeños, 175
cucumbers
to shave, 371
Cucumber Pickles, 249
Red Rice Salad with Red Wine Vinegar, 361

cucumbers (*cont.*)
Vegetarian Charcuterie, 60
Watermelon Gazpacho, 78
curries, 368
Baked Goan Black Cod, 370
Coconut Curry Shrimp, 382
Goan Marinade, 370
Japanese Chicken Curry, 247–8
Shaved Cauliflower and Swiss Chard Curry, 371
Sweet Potato Mulligatawny Soup, 369
Custom Gin and Tonic, 81, 335

D

dandelion greens
Dandelion Pesto on Naan, 27
dashi
Napa Pickles, 250
Quick Umami Miso Soup, 431
Decadent Chocolate Cookies, 48
Definitive Stockyards Spareribs, The, 115
desserts
wines to serve with, 211
Apple Amaretti Parfait, 231
Apple Cranberry Compote, 320
Apples in Caramel Cider Sauce, 321
Brûléed Rice Pudding with Icewine-Soaked Raisins, 306
Caffè Latte Panna Cotta with Decadent Chocolate Cookies, 47–8
Caramel Pecan Popcorn, 282
Cassata Parfait, 260
Chocolate Cajeta, 153
Dulce de Leche Flan, 210–11
Eton Mess, 134
Fresh Chili Mangoes with Mango Ice Cream, 388
Fruit in Spiced Syrup, 383
Grapefruit Compote, 317
Grilled Peanut Butter and Banana Bread Sandwiches, 111
Hazelnut Meringue Roulade, 189
Jewel in the Crown Ice Cream Cake, 373
Mandarin Pudding Cake with Lime Leaves, 355
Millionaire Bars, 319
Peach and Blackberry Compote, 65
Pear, Apple and Cornmeal Crunch, 221
Rhubarb Sponge Pudding, 30
Sopaipillas, 75
See also cakes; cookies and bars; pies, pastries and tarts, sweet
dill, fresh, 63
Beet and Blue Potato Salad with Local Blue Cheese, 216
Herring Tartar, 283
Maple-Glazed Salmon with Beets, Ricotta and Dill, 305
Red Rice Salad with Red Wine Vinegar, 361
Dirty Mojito, 339
Double-Baked Soufflés with English Cheddar, 310–11
Douro Valley wines, 335
Duck Breasts with Blood Orange Salsa, 343
Dulce de Leche, 211
Dulce de Leche Flan, 210–11
Dulce de Leche Tartlets, 237
Millionaire Bars, 319
Dumplings, Parmesan, 418

E

earthy flavours, 195–7
edamame
Quinoa Spinach Risotto, 80
Saffron Risotto with Scallops, 132
eggplant
Coconut Curry Shrimp, 382
Grilled Bread and Vegetable Salad, 106
Roasted Eggplant Salad, 336
eggs
to thicken stew, 150
Double-Baked Soufflés with English Cheddar, 310–11
Meringues, 134
Meringue topping, 152
poached, with Unbreakable Béarnaise, 323
Scrambled Eggs in Pancetta Cups, 322
Silky Tofu Soup, 166
Six-Minute Eggs on Fresh Field Greens, 138
endive, Belgian
Braised Escarole, 45
Braised Winter Greens, 268
Caramelized Onion and Cheese Fondue, 192
Tuna Ceviche with Endive Watermelon Salad, 332
Walnut and Endive Salad, 315
equipment
glassware, 12–13
hand blender, 26
for home bar, 10
smoking gun, 116
escarole
Braised Escarole, 45
Braised Winter Greens, 268
Buffalo Mozzarella and Pickled Fennel, 257
Eton Mess, 134

F

Falanghina, 257
fennel
Bourride from Marseille, 156
Buffalo Mozzarella and Pickled Fennel, 257
Duck Breasts with Blood Orange Salsa, 343
Fennel and Turnip Soup, 130
Lobster Rolls, 278
Thai Clam Chowder, 378
Wild Salmon with Balsamic Glaze and Fennel Confit, 359
fennel seeds
Chestnut-Stuffed Portobello Mushrooms, 226–7

Duck Breasts with Blood Orange Salsa, 343
Herb and Spice Roast Rack of Pork, 266
Sweet-Spicy Garlic Chicken, 294
Fiery Chili Sauce, 354
figs
Crostini with Prosciutto and Fig Marmalade, 408–9
Fruit in Spiced Syrup, 383
fish
Court Bouillon for poaching, 88
See also specific varieties
flour, self-raising, 30
Frenched Green Beans and Snow Peas, 421
Fresh Chili Mangoes with Mango Ice Cream, 388
frisée
Braised Escarole, 45
Braised Winter Greens, 268
Fritto Misto with Italian Tartar Sauce, 412–13
fruit
to dry, 342
Fruit Ice Cubes, 311
Fruit in Spiced Syrup, 383
Mustard Fruit Compote, 143
See also specific varieties (apples, blueberries, cherries, etc.)

G

Garganelli with Prosciutto and Peas, 258
garlic
Aïoli, 157
Chicken Adobo, 358
Chimichurri Sauce, 236
Lemon-Scented Roast Chicken, 419
garlic (Chinese) chives
Korean Beef Noodle Stir-Fry, 168
garnacha, 295
garrigue, 57, 83
gastrique, 354
gewürztraminer, 145, 292, 295, 369
late-harvest, 75, 221, 297, 355
gin, 9
Custom Gin and Tonic, 81, 335
martinis, 174, 328–9
Reverse Saketini, 98
ginger
Apple Amaretti Parfait, 231
Carrot, Ginger and Coriander Soup, 292
Cranberry Ginger Chutney, 233
Fruit in Spiced Syrup, 383
Ginger Lime Dipping Sauce, 354
Miso Ginger Vinaigrette, 245
Triple Ginger Cake, 251
glassware, 12–13
Glazed Orange Slices, 171
glazes
Balsamic Glaze, 359
Lemon Glaze, 346
Goan Marinade, 370
golden syrup (Lyle's), 288
Rhubarb Sponge Pudding, 30
Salted Caramels, 272
Gougères with Green Salad, 182
grapefruit
Grapefruit Compote, 317
Grapefruit Salad Saigon Style, 350
greco di Tufo, 29, 410
Green Beans with Red Onions, 64
greens, bitter
Braised Escarole, 45
Marmalade of Greens, 49
greens, salad. *See* lettuces and salad greens
Grilled Argentinian Short Ribs, 235
Grilled Bread and Vegetable Salad, 106
Grilled Hanger Steak with Smoky Corn and Tomato Salsa, 108
Grilled Peanut Butter and Banana Bread Sandwiches, 111
Grilled Pork Skewers, 29
grüner veltliner, 16, 166, 192, 247, 358, 392

H

haddock
Spicy Fish Cakes with Zesty Citrus Sauce, 380–1
halibut
Baked Goan Black Cod, 370
Caramel-Pecan-Dusted Sea Bass with Cranberry Wine Sauce, 185–6
Speedy Spanish Halibut, 43
Herbalicious Rack of Lamb, 79
Herb and Spice Roast Rack of Pork, 266
Herb Butter, 61
herbs
for garnishes, 56–7
in Global Store Cupboard, 5–6
herbal flavours, 55–7, 67, 82–3
as leafy greens, 63
Herring Tartar, 283
hibiscus tea, 386
Homemade Ricotta with Rhubarb Compote and Grilled Bread, 154–5
honey, 288
Honey Marmalade Cake, 297
hops, 21, 50
hors d'oeuvres
Anchovy and Tomato Tapas, 42
Asian Shrimp Cocktail, 98
Crostini with Prosciutto and Fig Marmalade, 408–9
Crushed Chickpeas with Jalapeños, 175
Homemade Ricotta with Rhubarb Compote and Grilled Bread, 154–5
Marmalade of Greens, 49
Roasted Brussels Sprout Leaves, 175

hors d'oeuvres (*cont.*)
Roquefort Toasts, 342
Sweet Potato and Black Bean Empanadas, 202–3
horseradish
Cream of Lentil Soup with Horseradish, 224
Oysters with Horseradish Gelée, 265

I

ice cream
Apple Cranberry Compote, 320
Apples in Caramel Cider Sauce, 321
Fresh Chili Mangoes with Mango Ice Cream, 388
Jewel in the Crown Ice Cream Cake, 373
icewines, 307
cabernet franc, 271, 303, 304
Canadian, 307
sparkling, 152
Brûléed Rice Pudding with Icewine-Soaked Raisins, 306
Icewine Extravaganza, 301–7
Indian curries, 368
inzolia, 174
Irish Cheddar, Bacon and Chard Tart, 36
Irish whiskey. *See under* whisk(e)y
Isle of Mull Oatcakes, 316
Italian Tartar Sauce, 413

J

Japanese Chicken Curry, 247–8
Jerusalem Artichoke and Potato Purée, 207
Jewel in the Crown Ice Cream Cake, 373
Jumilla wines, 108, 335
Just-Right Bison Burger with Homemade Ketchup, The, 218

K

kale
Kale and Bean Soup, 53
Kale and White Anchovy Salad, 177
Marmalade of Greens, 49
kale sprouts
Scrambled Eggs in Pancetta Cups, 322
Kickass Chicken Wings, 118
kimchi
Korean Beef Noodle Stir-Fry, 168
Silky Tofu Soup, 166
kiwi
Fruit in Spiced Syrup, 383
Korean Beef Noodle Stir-Fry, 168
Korean chili paste (gochujang), 166, 167
Silky Tofu Soup, 166

L

lamb
to braise, 208
Herbalicious Rack of Lamb, 79
Lamb from Puglia, 150
South African Bobotie, 394
20-Hour Lamb Shoulder Roast, 232
lambrusco, 258
Languedoc-Roussillon wines, 16, 295, 306
late-harvest wines
chardonnay, 282
gewürztraminer, 75, 221, 297, 355
riesling, 65, 221, 282, 306, 355
torrentes, 211
trockenbeerenauslese, 152
vidal, 282, 306, 307
lavender, fresh
Lemon Balm Shortbread, 66
leeks
Bourride from Marseille, 156
Braised Winter Greens, 268
Double-Baked Soufflés with English Cheddar, 310–11
legumes. *See* beans, black; beans, white; chickpeas; lentils
lemon balm, 67
Lemon Balm Shortbread, 66
Peach and Blackberry Compote, 65
Lemon Drop Martini, 328
lemongrass
to cut and use, 379
Spicy Fish Cakes with Zesty Citrus Sauce, 380–1
Vietnamese Fried Chicken, 353–4
lemons and lemon juice
Candied Lemon Confit, 347
Chicken from Fez with Preserved Lemon and Olives, 334–5
Chicken Yassa, 387
Lemon and Orange Olive Oil Cake, 405
Lemon Curd, 152
Lemon Dijon Vinaigrette, 106
Lemon Dressing, 342
Lemon Glaze, 346
Lemon Meringue Tart, 152
Lemon-Scented Roast Chicken, 419
Lemon Syrup, 346
Quick Preserved Lemons, 335
Sidecar, 351
Warm Lemon Poppy Seed Cakes, 345–7
Zesty Citrus Sauce, 381
lemon thyme, 91
Herb Butter, 61
See also thyme, fresh
lemon verbena, 67
lentils
Cream of Lentil Soup with Horseradish, 224
Scrambled Eggs in Pancetta Cups, 322
Senegalese Soup, 386
Sweet Potato Mulligatawny Soup, 369
lettuces and salad greens
herbs as, 63
Beet and Blue Potato Salad with Local Blue Cheese, 216
Gougères with Green Salad, 182

Lobster Rolls, 278
Shaved Root Vegetable Salad, 34
Six-Minute Eggs on Fresh Field Greens, 138
Vegetarian Charcuterie, 60
Vietnamese Fried Chicken, 353–4
Lillet, 408
lime leaves
Asian Shrimp Cocktail, 98
Coconut Curry Shrimp, 382
Cranberry Ginger Chutney, 233
Grapefruit Salad Saigon Style, 350
Lime Basil Éclairs, 85–6
Lime Basil Pastry Cream, 85
Mandarin Pudding Cake with Lime Leaves, 355
limes and lime juice
Asian Shrimp Cocktail, 98
Cranberry Ginger Chutney, 233
Fresh Chili Mangoes with Mango Ice Cream, 388
Fruit in Spiced Syrup, 383
Ginger Lime Dipping Sauce, 354
Grapefruit Compote, 317
Grapefruit Salad Saigon Style, 350
Lime Basil Éclairs, 85–6
Lime Basil Icing, 86
Lime Basil Pastry Cream, 85
Pebre, 74
Spicy Mango Slaw, 281
Watermelon Gazpacho, 78
Zesty Citrus Sauce, 381
liqueurs
amaretto, 171
Cointreau, 351
elderflower, 251
Irish cream, 111
St-Germain, 251
Triple Sec, 351
Lobster Rolls, 278

M

Madeira, 260
main courses
Baked Goan Black Cod, 370
Bistecca Fiorentina, 121
Caramelized Onion and Cheese Fondue, 192
Caramel-Pecan-Dusted Sea Bass with Cranberry Wine Sauce, 185–6
Chestnut-Stuffed Portobello Mushrooms, 226–7
Chicken Adobo, 358
Chicken from Fez with Preserved Lemon and Olives, 334–5
Chicken Yassa, 387
Chilean Pulmay, 73
Classic Poached Salmon with Spicy Green Herb Mayonnaise, 87–8
Coconut Curry Shrimp, 382
The Definitive Stockyards Spareribs, 115
Duck Breasts with Blood Orange Salsa, 343
Fritto Misto with Italian Tartar Sauce, 412–13
Grilled Hanger Steak with Smoky Corn and Tomato Salsa, 108
Grilled Pork Skewers, 29
Herb and Spice Roast Rack of Pork, 266
Irish Cheddar, Bacon and Chard Tart, 36
The Just-Right Bison Burger with Homemade Ketchup, 218
Kickass Chicken Wings, 118
Korean Beef Noodle Stir-Fry, 168
Lamb from Puglia, 150
Lemon-Scented Roast Chicken, 419
Maple-Glazed Salmon with Beets, Ricotta and Dill, 305
Miami Ribs Miami Style, 116
Mushroom Ragu with Polenta, 140–1
Porcini-Dusted Veal Chops, 403
Saffron Risotto with Scallops, 132
Six-Minute Eggs on Fresh Field Greens, 138
Slow-Baked Arctic Char with Crisp Potatoes, 61
South African Bobotie, 394
Speedy Spanish Halibut, 43
Spicy Fish Cakes with Zesty Citrus Sauce, 380–1
Sweet-Spicy Garlic Chicken, 294
Tagliatelle with Anchovies, Olive Oil, Ripe Tomatoes, Garlic and Parmesan, 410
Veal Scaloppine with Tomato Caper Sauce, 259
Vietnamese Fried Chicken, 353–4
Wild Salmon with Balsamic Glaze and Fennel Confit, 359
Zesty Pork with Honey and Sherry Vinegar Sauce, 360
Malaysian curries, 368
malbec, 16, 204
Mandarin Pudding Cake with Lime Leaves, 355
mango chutney
South African Bobotie, 394
mangoes
Fresh Chili Mangoes with Mango Ice Cream, 388
Fruit in Spiced Syrup, 383
Mango Cilantro Salsa, 70
Rum Mango Lassi, 393
Spicy Mango Slaw, 281
Manhattan, 375, 424
maple syrup
as a sweetener, 288
Caramel Pecan Popcorn, 282
Maple-Glazed Salmon with Beets, Ricotta and Dill, 305
Rhubarb Sponge Pudding, 30
Sticky Toffee Bacon, 314
Triple Ginger Cake, 251
marinades
for chicken, 244, 353, 387
for chicken wings, 392
for fish, 370
for meats, 89, 108, 168
for ribs, 204

Marmalade of Greens, 49
Marsala, 30, 260, 415
martinis, 174, 328, 329
mascarpone
  Apple Amaretti Parfait, 231
  Creamy Spinach, 186
  Grilled Peanut Butter and Banana Bread Sandwiches, 111
  Hazelnut Meringue Roulade, 189
  Millionaire Bars, 319
  Peach and Blackberry Compote, 65
  See also cheese
mayonnaise
  Aïoli, 157
  Brown Butter Mayonnaise, 176
  Green Mayonnaise, 148
  Spicy Green Herb Mayonnaise, 88
meats
  for antipasto, 254
  the asado, 206
  to braise, 208
  to brine, 267
  cooked on the bone, 113
  to smoke, 99
  See also specific varieties
Mediterranean Relish, 426
melons
  Fruit in Spiced Syrup, 383
  Tuna Ceviche with Endive Watermelon Salad, 332
mencia, 43
menus
  An Argentinian Odyssey, 201–11
  A Beppi-Influenced Menu, 407–14
  Bitter British, 33–7
  Bones, 113–21
  Brining: A Celebratory Menu, 263–72
  Casual Chic, 59–66
  C is for Chile, 69–75
  Cruising the Mediterranean, 77–86
  Easy-peasy Brunch, 309–19
  An Eclectic Asian Menu, 377–83
  An Edgy Franco-American Menu, 341–7
  An End of Summer Dinner, 181–9
  Essence of Soul, 417–23
  European Unity, 129–34
  A Family Meal Right Off the Grill, 105–11
  A First Nations Dinner, 215–21
  From Tapas to Table, 41–7
  Icewine Extravaganza, 301–7
  Italian Simplicity, 253–60
  Lovely Lemons, 331–7
  A Modern Indian Menu, 367–73
  Modern Korean, 165–71
  Multicultural Sengalaese Dinner, 385–8
  The Pleasure of Porcini, 401–5
  A Rosh Hashanah Dinner, 291–7
  Salmon with a Cup of Tea, 97–103
  Sophisticated Vegetarian Dinner, 137–44
  Spring Has Sprung, 147–52
  A Sushi-free Japanese Meal, 243–51
  A Tapas Menu, 173–9
  A Trouble-free Spring Dinner, 23–30
  Truck-stop Treats, 277–82
  A Vegetarian Holiday Dinner, 223–31
  Vietnamese Flavours, 349–55
Meringue(s), 134, 189
merlot, 16, 29, 121, 218
Miami Ribs Miami Style, 116
Millionaire Bars, 319
Minervois, 16, 115, 335
mint, fresh, 82
  Dirty Mojito, 339
  Lemon Balm Shortbread, 66
  Mint Salsa Verde, 89
  Spicy Chilled Pea Soup with Crisp Mint, 402
  Spicy Mango Slaw, 281
mirin
  Cucumber Pickles, 249
miso
  Miso Ginger Vinaigrette, 245
  Mushroom Miso Salad, 244
  Quick Umami Miso Soup, 431
Monbazillac, 143
monkfish
  Bourride from Marseille, 156
montepulciano d'Abruzzo, 16, 259
Mop Sauce, 115
mourvèdre/monastrell, 57, 79, 108
muscadet, 265
muscat/moscato, 318
  black muscat (California), 47, 134
  dry muscat (Alsace), 98, 318
  moscatel (Portugal and Spain), 189
  moscato d'Asti, 85, 221, 297, 318, 319, 388
  muscat de Beaumes de Venise, 171, 297
  muscat de Rivesaltes, 271
mushrooms
  Chestnut-Stuffed Portobello Mushrooms, 226–7
  Frenched Green Beans and Snow Peas, 421
  Korean Beef Noodle Stir-Fry, 168
  Mushroom Miso Salad, 244
  Mushroom Ragu with Polenta, 140–1
  Porcini-Dusted Veal Chops, 403
  Quick Umami Miso Soup, 431
  Slow-Baked Arctic Char with Crisp Potatoes, 61
mussels
  Chilean Pulmay, 73
Mustard Barbecue Sauce, 116

N

Naan, Dandelion Pesto on, 27
Napa Pickles, 250
negromaro, 10, 16, 150

nero d'Avola, 16, 343
nuts
Caramel-Pecan-Dusted Sea Bass with Cranberry Wine Sauce, 185–6
Caramel Pecan Popcorn, 282
Cherry Almond Biscotti, 414
Hazelnut Meringue Roulade, 189
Orange Almond Tart with White Chocolate Cream, 170–1
Peanut Butter and Banana Bread Sandwiches, Grilled, 111
Pear, Apple and Cornmeal Crunch, 221
Roquefort Toasts with Arugula and Dried Pear Salad, 342
Shrimp Catalan, 179
nutty flavours, 161–3

O

Oatcakes, Isle of Mull, 316
oils, 6
olives
for Antipasto, 254
Chicken from Fez with Preserved Lemon and Olives, 334–5
Chicken Yassa, 387
Marmalade of Greens, 49
Mediterranean Relish, 426
Red Rice Salad with Red Wine Vinegar, 361
onions, green
Grapefruit Salad Saigon Style, 350
Korean Beef Noodle Stir-Fry, 168
Mint Salsa Verde, 89
Pebre, 74
Quick Umami Miso Soup, 431
Red Rice Salad with Red Wine Vinegar, 361
Spicy Fish Cakes with Zesty Citrus Sauce, 380–1
Spicy Green Herb Mayonnaise, 88
Vietnamese Fried Chicken, 353–4
onions, red
Argentinian Short Ribs, 204
Beet and Blue Potato Salad with Local Blue Cheese, 216
Chicken Yassa, 387
Coconut Curry Shrimp, 382
Green Beans with Red Onions, 64
Grilled Bread and Vegetable Salad, 106
Herring Tartar, 283
Smoky Corn and Tomato Salsa, 110
Spicy Mango Slaw, 281
Vegetarian Charcuterie, 60
Watermelon Gazpacho, 78
Wild Salmon with Balsamic Glaze and Fennel Confit, 359
onions, sweetness of, 288
orange marmalade
Fig Marmalade, 409
Honey Marmalade Cake, 297
orange peel, candied
Cassata Parfait, 260
oranges and orange juice
to flame orange peel, 351
Cranberry Ginger Chutney, 233
Duck Breasts with Blood Orange Salsa, 343
Fig Marmalade, 409
Glazed Orange Slices, 171
Grapefruit Compote, 317
Herb and Spice Roast Rack of Pork, 266
Lemon and Orange Olive Oil Cake, 405
Mandarin Pudding Cake with Lime Leaves, 355
Orange Almond Tart with White Chocolate Cream, 170–1
Radish and Orange Salad, 296
Sopaipillas, 75
Sweet-Spicy Garlic Chicken, 294
oregano, fresh
Argentinian Short Ribs, 204
Chimichurri Sauce, 236
Grilled Bread and Vegetable Salad, 106
Orvieto, 410
Orzo, 268
Oysters with Horseradish Gelée, 265

P

pancetta
Braised Escarole, 45
Lamb from Puglia, 150
Mediterranean Relish, 426
Scrambled Eggs in Pancetta Cups, 322
Shaved Root Vegetable Salad, 34
Slow-Baked Arctic Char with Crisp Potatoes, 61
See also pork
papaya
Fruit in Spiced Syrup, 383
paprika, smoked Spanish, 110
parsley, flat-leaf fresh, 82
Chimichurri Sauce, 236
Pebre, 74
parsnips
Chicken Soup with Vegetables and Parmesan Dumplings, 418
passion fruit
Jewel in the Crown Ice Cream Cake, 373
passito di Pantelleria, 405
pasta and noodles
to cook al dente, 258
Garganelli with Prosciutto and Peas, 258
Korean Beef Noodle Stir-Fry, 168
Orzo, 268
Tagliatelle with Anchovies, Olive Oil, Ripe Tomatoes, Garlic and Parmesan, 410
Vietnamese Fried Chicken, 353–4
pastry
with ale, 36

pastry (*cont.*)
with cardamom, 427
for empanadas, 202–3
with lemon juice, 170
Cheddar Pastry, 423
Choux Pastry, 85
Shortcrust Pastry, 90
peaches
Peach and Blackberry Compote, 65
Plum Galette, 427
Peanut Butter and Banana Bread Sandwiches, Grilled, 111
pears
to dry, 342
Caramelized Onion and Cheese Fondue, 192
Mustard Fruit Compote, 143
Pear, Apple and Cornmeal Crunch, 221
Roquefort Toasts with Arugula and Dried Pear Salad, 342
peas
Basmati Rice Pilau, 372
Frenched Green Beans and Snow Peas, 421
Garganelli with Prosciutto and Peas, 258
Lamb from Puglia, 150
Saffron Risotto with Scallops, 132
Spicy Chilled Pea Soup with Crisp Mint, 402
Pebre, 74
Pedro Ximénez Sherry, 373
peppers, hot chili
Apple and Avocado Soup, 70
Chicken Yassa, 387
Crushed Chickpeas with Jalapeños, 175
Fiery Chili Sauce, 354
Fruit in Spiced Syrup, 383
Pebre, 74
Senegalese Soup, 386
Spicy Mango Slaw, 281
Sweet Potato and Black Bean Empanadas, 202–3
Tomato Ketchup, 219
peppers, sweet red or yellow
Grilled Bread and Vegetable Salad, 106
Smoky Corn and Tomato Salsa, 110
Speedy Spanish Halibut, 43
Watermelon Gazpacho, 78
Perfect Roast Potatoes, 420
pickles
for Antipasto, 254
Cheaters Hot Pickle, 370
Cucumber Pickles, 249
Japanese style, 249
Napa Pickles, 250
Pickled Fennel, 257
pies, pastries and tarts, savoury
Gougères with Green Salad, 182
Irish Cheddar, Bacon and Chard Tart, 36
Savoury Apple and Thyme Tart, 90
Sweet Potato and Black Bean Empanadas, 202–3
pies, pastries and tarts, sweet
Dulce de Leche Tartlets, 237
Lemon Meringue Tart, 152
Lime Basil Éclairs, 85–6
Orange Almond Tart with White Chocolate Cream, 170–1
Plum Galette, 427
Umami Apple Pie, 423
See also desserts
pine nuts
Red Rice Salad with Red Wine Vinegar, 361
Shrimp Catalan, 179
pinotage, 395
pinot gris/grigio, 63, 216, 342, 382
Campari Kir, 38
pinot noir, 141, 225, 359
California, 216, 225, 305, 343
New Zealand, 225, 305
Oregon, 185
pistachios
Grapefruit Compote, 317
plum jam
Smoky Dark Chocolate Bars, 103
plums
Plum Galette, 427
Simple Plum Cardamom Cake, 337
Pok Pok Wings, 392
Polenta, 140
pomegranate juice
Rich Red Wine Sauce, 227
pomegranate seeds
Sopaipillas, 75
Walnut and Endive Salad, 315
Popcorn, Caramel Pecan, 282
poppy seeds
Warm Lemon Poppy Seed Cakes, 345–7
Porcini-Dusted Veal Chops, 403
pork
to braise, 208
Chilean Pulmay, 73
The Definitive Stockyards Spareribs, 115
Grilled Pork Skewers, 29
Herb and Spice Roast Rack of Pork, 266
Zesty Pork with Honey and Sherry Vinegar Sauce, 360
See also specific types (bacon, chorizo sausages, pancetta, prosciutto)
Port, 271
with cheese, 145
Late Bottled Vintage, 271, 337, 427
Ruby, 427
tawny, 37
potatoes
texture, 420
Anchovy-Roasted Fingerlings, 404
Beet and Blue Potato Salad with Local Blue Cheese, 216
Belgian Baked Fries, 280

Caramelized Onion and Cheese Fondue, 192
Chilean Pulmay, 73
Jerusalem Artichoke and Potato Purée, 207
Perfect Roast Potatoes, 420
Slow-Baked Arctic Char with Crisp Potatoes, 61
Sorrel Soup with Chive Oil, 24
Thai Clam Chowder, 378
potatoes, sweet. *See* sweet potatoes
poultry. *See* chicken; duck
primitivo, 16, 150, 335, 392
prosciutto
Crostini with Prosciutto and Fig Marmalade, 408–9
Garganelli with Prosciutto and Peas, 258
See also pork
prosecco, 255, 322, 332, 380
with limoncello, 383
with St-Germain, 251
Aperol Spritz, 298, 345
Campari Royale, 38
prunes
Mustard Fruit Compote, 143
pumpkin
Sopaipillas, 75

Q

Quarts de Chaume, 231
Quick Preserved Lemons, 335
Quick Umami Miso Soup, 431
Quinoa Spinach Risotto, 80

R

Radish and Orange Salad, 296
raisins
Brûléed Rice Pudding with Icewine-Soaked Raisins, 306
Fig Marmalade, 409
Marmalade of Greens, 49
South African Bobotie, 394
Triple Ginger Cake, 251
Yellow Rice, 395
rapini
Marmalade of Greens, 49
raspberries
Eton Mess, 134
Fruit Ice Cubes, 311
recioto, 47, 260
Red and Green, 101, 198
redcurrant jelly
Chicken Liver Pâté in a Foie Gras Style, 303
Redcurrant Vinaigrette, 304
Red Rice Salad with Red Wine Vinegar, 361
Reverse Saketini, 98
rhubarb
Homemade Ricotta with Rhubarb Compote and Grilled Bread, 154–5
Rhubarb Sponge Pudding, 30
rice
to make risotto, 131
Basmati Rice Pilau, 372
Brûléed Rice Pudding with Icewine-Soaked Raisins, 306
Red Rice Salad with Red Wine Vinegar, 361
Saffron Rice, 44
Saffron Risotto with Scallops, 132
Yellow Rice, 395
rice flour
Pear, Apple and Cornmeal Crunch, 221
Pok Pok Wings, 392
rice vinegar, 356
Chicken Adobo, 358
Cucumber Pickles, 249
Grapefruit Salad Saigon Style, 350
Miso Ginger Vinaigrette, 245
Rich Red Wine Sauce, 227
ricotta
Cassata Parfait, 260
Homemade Ricotta, 154
Homemade Ricotta with Rhubarb Compote and Grilled Bread, 154–5
Maple-Glazed Salmon with Beets, Ricotta and Dill, 305
See also cheese
riesling
dry, 101, 247, 278, 332, 360
icewines, 85, 152
late-harvest (auslese), 65, 221, 282, 306, 355
off-dry (halbtrocken), 101, 155, 216
Rivesaltes, 271
Roasted Asparagus Salad with Green Mayonnaise, 148
Roasted Brussels Sprout Leaves, 175
Roasted Eggplant Salad, 336
Roquefort Toasts with Arugula and Dried Pear Salad, 342
rosado, 174
rosemary, fresh, 82
Buffalo Mozzarella and Pickled Fennel, 257
Grilled Pork Skewers, 29
Herbalicious Rack of Lamb, 79
Lemon Balm Shortbread, 66
Mustard Barbecue Sauce, 116
Rosemary Syrup, 405
Speedy Spanish Halibut, 43
20-Hour Lamb Shoulder Roast, 232
rosé wines, 43, 156, 174, 410
sparkling, 304
Rueda, 16, 42
rum
dark oak-aged, 221
with dessert, 221
spiced, with Coke, 282
Dirty Mojito, 339
Rum Mango Lassi, 393
Rumpuccino, 149
rye. *See under* whisk(e)y

S

saffron
Chicken from Fez with Preserved Lemon and Olives, 334–5
Saffron Rice, 44
Saffron Risotto with Scallops, 132
sage, fresh, 83
Herb and Spice Roast Rack of Pork, 266
sake, 98, 247, 332, 428, 431
Reverse Saketini, 98
salad dressings
with dill, 216
Lemon Dijon Vinaigrette, 106
Lemon Dressing, 342
Miso Ginger Vinaigrette, 245
Redcurrant Vinaigrette, 304
Shallot Vinaigrette, 34
Tarragon Dressing, 60
salads
Arugula Salad with Stilton and Redcurrant Vinaigrette, 304
Beet and Blue Potato Salad with Local Blue Cheese, 216
Buffalo Mozzarella and Pickled Fennel, 257
Gougères with Green Salad, 182
Grapefruit Salad Saigon Style, 350
Grilled Bread and Vegetable Salad, 106
Kale and White Anchovy Salad, 177
Mushroom Miso Salad, 244
Radish and Orange Salad, 296
Red Rice Salad with Red Wine Vinegar, 361
Roasted Eggplant Salad, 336
Roquefort Toasts with Arugula and Dried Pear Salad, 342
Shaved Root Vegetable Salad, 34
Six-Minute Eggs on Fresh Field Greens, 138
Spicy Mango Slaw, 281
Tuna Ceviche with Endive Watermelon Salad, 332
Vegetarian Charcuterie, 60
Walnut and Endive Salad, 315
salmon
Classic Poached Salmon with Spicy Green Herb Mayonnaise, 87–8
Maple-Glazed Salmon with Beets, Ricotta and Dill, 305
Tea-smoked Salmon, 101
Wild Salmon with Balsamic Glaze and Fennel Confit, 359
salsas
Blood Orange Salsa, 343
Mint Salsa Verde, 89
Smoky Corn and Tomato Salsa, 110
Salted Caramels, 272
salt(s), 6
and bitter flavours, 21, 44, 269
for brining, 267
kosher, 267
salty flavours, 239–41
and tannins, 269
sambal oolek, 381
Kickass Chicken Wings, 118
Pok Pok Wings, 392
Zesty Citrus Sauce, 381
Sancerre, 34, 402
sandwiches. *See* burgers and rolls
sangiovese di Romagna, 258, 259
sardines
Fritto Misto with Italian Tartar Sauce, 412–13
sauces, syrups and spreads, sweet
Candied Lemon Confit, 347
Lemon Curd, 152
Lemon Glaze, 346
Lemon Syrup, 346
Lime Basil Icing, 86
Lime Basil Pastry Cream, 85
Peach Syrup, 65
Raspberry Sauce, 134
Rosemary Syrup, 405
Spiced Syrup, 383
sauces and spreads, savoury
gastrique base for, 354
Aïoli, 157
Barbecue Sauce, 115
Brown Butter Mayonnaise, 176
Chimichurri Sauce, 236
Cranberry Wine Sauce, 186
Fiery Chili Sauce, 354
Fig Marmalade, 409
Ginger Lime Dipping Sauce, 354
Green Mayonnaise, 148
Herb Butter, 61
Italian Tartar Sauce, 413
for Kickass Chicken Wings, 118
Mango Cilantro Salsa, 70
Marmalade of Greens, 49
Mediterranean Relish, 426
Mint Salsa Verde, 89
Mop Sauce, 115
Mustard Barbecue Sauce, 116
Mustard Fruit Compote, 143
Pebre, 74
Rich Red Wine Sauce, 227
Sherry Vinegar sauce, 360
Smoky Corn and Tomato Salsa, 110
Spicy Green Herb Mayonnaise, 88
Tomato Caper Sauce, 259
Ultimate Umami Paste, 430
Unbreakable Béarnaise, 323
Zesty Citrus Sauce, 381
See also conserves and condiments
Sauternes, 103, 143, 303
sauvignon blanc, 60, 145, 148
Bordeaux, 130

Chile, 16, 70, 278, 402
Loire (Sauvignon de Touraine), 183
New Zealand, 16, 78, 98, 166, 278, 332, 350, 380, 402
South Africa, 16, 130, 278, 402
Savoury Apple and Thyme Tart, 90
Sazerac, 9, 390
scallops
Fritto Misto with Italian Tartar Sauce, 412–13
Saffron Risotto with Scallops, 132
Scotch. *See under* whisk(e)y
Scrambled Eggs in Pancetta Cups, 322
Sea Bass, Caramel-Pecan-Dusted, with Cranberry Wine Sauce, 185–6
Seared Beef Filet with Brown Butter Mayonnaise, 176
semillon, 130, 295, 353
botrytized, 103
Senegalese Soup, 386
shallots, 229
Herb Butter, 61
Lemon-Scented Roast Chicken, 419
Lobster Rolls, 278
Mushroom Ragu with Polenta, 140–1
Saffron Risotto with Scallops, 132
Shallot and Brussels Sprout Compote, 229
Shallot Vinaigrette, 34
Shaved Cauliflower and Swiss Chard Curry, 371
Shaved Root Vegetable Salad, 34
shellfish. *See specific varieties*
Sherry, 174, 261, 418
for martinis, 174
Amontillado, 418, 431
manzanilla, 174, 261, 418
Pedro Ximénez, 373
Sherry vinegar, 357
Zesty Pork with Honey and Sherry Vinegar Sauce, 360
shichimi togarashi
Napa Pickles, 250
shiraz, 16, 118, 295, 395
shrimp
Asian Shrimp Cocktail, 98
Coconut Curry Shrimp, 382
Fritto Misto with Italian Tartar Sauce, 412–13
Grapefruit Salad Saigon Style, 350
Shrimp Catalan, 179
Sidecar, 351
Silky Tofu Soup, 166
Simple Plum Cardamom Cake, 337
Six-Minute Eggs on Fresh Field Greens, 138
skills and techniques
to braise meat, 208
to brine meats or poultry, 267
to brown butter, 176
to cook pasta al dente, 258
to cut and use lemongrass, 379
to dry apples or pears, 342
to flame orange peel, 351
to French green beans, 421
to make risotto, 131
to mix martinis, 328
to peel asparagus, 148
to reduce apple cider, 320
to shave vegetables, 371
to smoke meats in a barbecue, 99
Slow-Baked Arctic Char with Crisp Potatoes, 61
Smoked Caesar, 43, 122
Smoky Corn and Tomato Salsa, 110
Smoky Dark Chocolate Bars, 103
smoky flavours, 93–5
to smoke meat, 99
Snow Peas, Frenched Green Beans and, 421
Soave, 132, 258, 322, 413
recioto di Soave, 260
Sopaipillas, 75
sorrel, 24
Sorrel Soup with Chive Oil, 24
soups
Apple and Avocado Soup, 70
Bourride from Marseille, 156
Carrot, Ginger and Coriander Soup, 292
Chicken Soup with Vegetables and Parmesan Dumplings, 418
Cream of Lentil Soup with Horseradish, 224
Fennel and Turnip Soup, 130
Kale and Bean Soup, 53
Quick Umami Miso Soup, 431
Senegalese Soup, 386
Silky Tofu Soup, 166
Sorrel Soup with Chive Oil, 24
Spicy Chilled Pea Soup with Crisp Mint, 402
Sweet Potato Mulligatawny Soup, 369
Thai Clam Chowder, 378
Watermelon Gazpacho, 78
South African Bobotie, 394
sparkling wines
with brunch dishes, 311, 322
with cabernet franc icewine, 304
for Champagne Cocktail, 191, 415
with limoncello, 383
sparkling icewines, 152
sparkling rosés, 304
See also specific types (Cava, Champagne, Crémant d'Alsace, prosecco)
Speedy Spanish Halibut, 43
spices and spicy flavours, 363–5
in bitters, 390–1
curries and curry pastes, 248, 368
in Global Store Cupboard, 5–6
vs herbs, 63
rub for spareribs, 115
sweet varieties, 288, 295

Spicy Chilled Pea Soup with Crisp Mint, 402
Spicy Fish Cakes with Zesty Citrus Sauce, 380–1
Spicy Green Herb Mayonnaise, 88
Spicy Mango Slaw, 281
spinach
Chicken Adobo, 358
Chicken Soup with Vegetables and Parmesan Dumplings, 418
Coconut Curry Shrimp, 382
Creamy Spinach, 186
Double-Baked Soufflés with English Cheddar, 310–11
Japanese Chicken Curry, 247–8
Korean Beef Noodle Stir-Fry, 168
Marmalade of Greens, 49
Quick Umami Miso Soup, 431
Quinoa Spinach Risotto, 80
squash
Grilled Bread and Vegetable Salad, 106
Shaved Root Vegetable Salad, 34
squid
Fritto Misto with Italian Tartar Sauce, 412–13
star anise
Apple Amaretti Parfait, 231
Chicken Liver Pâté in a Foie Gras Style, 303
Court Bouillon, 88
Fruit in Spiced Syrup, 383
Pear, Apple and Cornmeal Crunch, 221
St-Germain, 251
Sticky Toffee Bacon, 314
stout. *See under* beers
Stout Cake, 37
strawberries
Fruit Ice Cubes, 311
Fruit in Spiced Syrup, 383
supertasters, 31
sweet flavours, 285–7, 288
sweet potatoes
Chicken Yassa, 387
Sweet Potato and Black Bean Empanadas, 202–3
Sweet Potato Mulligatawny Soup, 369
Sweet-Spicy Garlic Chicken, 294

T

Tagliatelle with Anchovies, Olive Oil, Ripe Tomatoes, Garlic and Parmesan, 410
tannins, 145, 269
tapas, 42, 173–9
tarragon, fresh French, 280
Brûléed Rice Pudding with Icewine-Soaked Raisins, 306
Frenched Green Beans and Snow Peas, 421
Lobster Rolls, 278
Six-Minute Eggs on Fresh Field Greens, 138
Tarragon Dressing, 60
Unbreakable Béarnaise, 323
tart flavours, 325–7
tea
green, 251
hibiscus, 386
Red and Green, 101, 198
Tea-smoked Salmon, 101
tequila, 275, 391
Clammy Sammy, 138, 275
Thai basil, 83
Coconut Curry Shrimp, 382
Grapefruit Salad Saigon Style, 350
Thai Clam Chowder, 378
Thai curry pastes, 368
Asian Shrimp Cocktail, 98
Coconut Curry Shrimp, 382
Spicy Chilled Pea Soup with Crisp Mint, 402
Spicy Fish Cakes with Zesty Citrus Sauce, 380–1
Spicy Green Herb Mayonnaise, 88
Thai Clam Chowder, 378
thyme, fresh, 81, 91
Argentinian Short Ribs, 204
Bourride from Marseille, 156
Grilled Hanger Steak with Smoky Corn and Tomato Salsa, 108
Herbalicious Rack of Lamb, 79
Lemon Dijon Vinaigrette, 106
Savoury Apple and Thyme Tart, 90
See also lemon thyme
tofu
Quick Umami Miso Soup, 431
Silky Tofu Soup, 166
tokaji, 211, 386
tomatoes
Anchovy and Tomato Tapas, 42
Argentinian Short Ribs, 204
Bourride from Marseille, 156
Buffalo Mozzarella and Pickled Fennel, 257
Chicken from Fez with Preserved Lemon and Olives, 334–5
Coconut Curry Shrimp, 382
Grilled Bread and Vegetable Salad, 106
Grilled Hanger Steak with Smoky Corn and Tomato Salsa, 108
Kale and White Anchovy Salad, 177
Mediterranean Relish, 426
Roasted Eggplant Salad, 336
Shrimp Catalan, 179
Speedy Spanish Halibut, 43
Tagliatelle with Anchovies, Olive Oil, Ripe Tomatoes, Garlic and Parmesan, 410
Thai Clam Chowder, 378
Tomato Ketchup, 219
Ultimate Umami Paste, 430
Veal Scaloppine with Tomato Caper Sauce, 259

Vegetarian Charcuterie, 60
torrontes, 203, 379
Triple Ginger Cake, 251
trockenbeerenauslese, 152
truffled Pecorino, 404
truffle oil, 230
Barley Pilaf, 230
truffle salt, 230
Tuna Ceviche with Endive Watermelon Salad, 332
turmeric, 395
Yellow Rice, 395
turnips
Fennel and Turnip Soup, 130
Shaved Root Vegetable Salad, 34
20-Hour Lamb Shoulder Roast, 232

U

Ultimate Umami Paste, 430
Umami Apple Pie, 423
umami flavours, 397–9
Unbreakable Béarnaise, 323

V

Valencia wines, 108
Valpolicella, 413
veal
Porcini-Dusted Veal Chops, 403
Veal Scaloppine with Tomato Caper Sauce, 259
vegetables, to shave, 371
vegetable side dishes
Anchovy-Roasted Fingerlings, 404
Belgian Baked Fries, 280
Bok Choy Stir-Fry, 102
Braised Escarole, 45
Braised Winter Greens, 268
Creamy Spinach, 186
Crisp Potatoes, 61
Dandelion Pesto on Naan, 27
Frenched Green Beans and Snow Peas, 421
Green Beans with Red Onions, 64
Jerusalem Artichoke and Potato Purée, 207
Perfect Roast Potatoes, 420
Quinoa Spinach Risotto, 80
Roasted Eggplant Salad, 336
Shallot and Brussels Sprout Compote, 229
Shaved Cauliflower and Swiss Chard Curry, 371
Spicy Mango Slaw, 281
vegetarian dishes
Caramelized Onion and Cheese Fondue, 192
Chestnut-Stuffed Portobello Mushrooms, 226–7
Mushroom Ragu with Polenta, 140–1
Six-Minute Eggs on Fresh Field Greens, 138
Vegetarian Charcuterie, 60
A Vegetarian Holiday Dinner, 223–31
verdicchio, 27, 410
verduzzo friulano, 260
vermouth, 9
in Manhattan, 375, 424
for martinis, 328
vernaccia di San Gimignano, 106, 410
vidal, late-harvest, 282, 306, 307
Vietnamese Fried Chicken, 353–4
vinaigrettes. *See* salad dressings
vinegars, 6, 356–7
vinho verde, 106, 174
Vin Santo, 189, 306, 415
Viognier, 371
vodka, 9, 283
martinis, 328, 329
Vouvray, 216, 321, 379

W

walnuts
Caramelized Walnuts, 144
Walnut and Endive Salad, 315
Warm Chocolate Caramel Cakes, 271–2
Warm Lemon Poppy Seed Cakes, 345–7
wasabi powder
Triple Ginger Cake, 251
watercress
Grapefruit Salad Saigon Style, 350
Tuna Ceviche with Endive Watermelon Salad, 332
West Indian curries, 368
whisk(e)y
bourbon, 9, 14, 375
Canadian, 9, 375
Irish, 167
rye, 9, 14, 375, 391
Scotch, 9, 14, 117
whisk(e)y-based cocktails
Bacon-Washed Bourbon, 424
Manhattan, 375, 424
Red and Green, 101, 198
Sazerac, 390
Smoked Caesar, 43, 122
white chocolate
Orange Almond Tart with White Chocolate Cream, 170–1
whiting
Spicy Fish Cakes with Zesty Citrus Sauce, 380–1
Wild Salmon with Balsamic Glaze and Fennel Confit, 359
wines
aromatic blends, 386
bare-bones pantry, 10
bargain bottles, 16
creaminess, 127
garrigué, 57, 83
glassware for, 12–13
herbal flavours, 57, 410
kosher, 292, 295, 297

wines (*cont.*)
mineraliy of, 212
to serve with anchovies, 174
to serve with cheese, 143, 145
to serve with desserts, 211
to serve with tapas, 174
tannins, 145, 269
terroir, 83
wine vinegars, 357
Homemade Ricotta with Rhubarb Compote and Grilled Bread, 154–5
Pebre, 74
Red Rice Salad with Red Wine Vinegar, 361
Tomato Ketchup, 219

Y

Yellow Rice, 395
yogurt
Rum Mango Lassi, 393
Watermelon Gazpacho, 78
Yogurt Cheese, 158
yogurt, frozen
Jewel in the Crown Ice Cream Cake, 373

Z

Zesty Pork with Honey and Sherry Vinegar Sauce, 360
zinfandel, 116, 118, 150, 168, 218
zucchini
to shave, 371
Cucumber Pickles, 249
Grilled Bread and Vegetable Salad, 106
Silky Tofu Soup, 166
Speedy Spanish Halibut, 43